JAPANESE ENCOUNTERS WITH POSTMODERNITY

Japanese Studies
General Editor: Yoshio Sugimoto

JAPANESE ENCOUNTERS WITH POSTMODERNITY

jointly edited by

Johann P. Arnason
and
Yoshio Sugimoto

KEGAN PAUL INTERNATIONAL
London and New York

First published in 1995 by
Kegan Paul International Limited
UK: P.O. Box 256, London WC1B 3SW, England
Tel: (0171) 5805511 Fax: (0171) 436 0899
USA: 562 West 113th Street, New York, NY 10025, USA
Tel: (212) 666 1000 Fax: (212) 316 3100

Distributed by
John Wiley & Sons Ltd
Southern Cross Trading Estate
1 Oldlands Way, Bognor Regis,
West Sussex, PO22 9SA, England
Tel: (01243) 819121 Fax: (01243) 820250

Columbia University Press
562 West 113th Street
New York, NY 10025, USA
Tel: (212) 666 1000 Fax: (212) 316 3100

© Johann P. Arnason and Yoshio Sugimoto 1995

Phototypeset in 10/12 Times Roman by Intype, London

Printed in Great Britain by TJ Press, Padstow, Cornwall
ISBN 0–7103–0513–3

British Library Cataloguing in Publication Data

Japanese Encounters with Postmodernity. –
(Japanese Studies)
I. Arnason, Johann Pall II. Sugimoto, Yoshio III. Series
952.04

ISBN 0–7103–0513–3

US Library of Congress Cataloging in Publication Data

Japanese encounters with postmodernity / jointly edited by Johann P.
  Arnason and Yoshio Sugimoto.
    310pp. 22cm. — (Japanese studies)
    Includes bibliographical references and index.
    ISBN 0–7103–0513–3
    1. Japan—Civilization—1945– I. Arnason, Jōhann Pāll, 1940–
II. Sugimoto, Yoshio, 1940–   . III. Series.
DS822.5.J44   1995
952.04—dc20   95–11916
                                                                   CIP

Contents

Contents

Plates

Figures

Tables

It is a Japanese convention that in written references to names, the family name is placed before the given name. In most English-language publications, the Japanese name order is made consistent with the English practice where the given name is followed by the family name. The editors of this volume allowed each contributor to use his or her own preference. When in doubt, readers are requested to refer to the bibliography and the index.

Contributors

Joint Editors
Johann Arnason and Yoshio Sugimoto, Professors of Sociology, School of Sociology and Anthropology, La Trobe University, Melbourne.

Contributors
John Clark,
School of Asian Studies,
University of Sydney.

Toshiko Ellis,
College of Arts and Sciences,
University of Tokyo.

Paul Harrison,
Queensland University of Technology,
Zillmere.

Tetsuro Kato,
Faculty of Social Sciences,
Hitotsubashi University,
Tokyo.

Kenji Kosaka,
School of Sociology,
Kwansei Gakuin University,
Nishinomiya.

Vera Mackie,
Department of History,
University of Melbourne.

Tessa Morris-Suzuki,
Research School of Pacific Studies,
Australian National University,
Canberra.

Contributors

Ross Mouer,
Department of Japanese Studies,
Monash University,
Melbourne.

J. V. Neustupný,
Faculty of Letters,
Osaka University.

Rob Steven,
School of Political Science,
University of New South Wales,
Sydney.

Most papers of this volume were initially submitted to the Seventh Biennial Conference of the Japanese Studies Association of Australia held at the Australian National University in July 1991. The joint editors are grateful for generous financial assistance, provided in support of publication, by the Japanese Studies Association of Australia Inc., the Faculty of Social Sciences and the School of Sociology and Anthropology at La Trobe University.

1 INTRODUCTION

Johann P. Arnason and Yoshio Sugimoto

Approaches to the Debate

This volume comprises eleven essays which all address the post-modernity debate in the context of Japanese society and culture. They collectively represent the first attempt in the English language to explore the idea of postmodernity in the Japanese situation from both sociological and cultural perspectives.[1] The areas under investigation cover a wide range of fields, including work, industrial relations, gender, science, literature, fine arts, communication, social stratification, politics and Japanese studies.

The notion of postmodernity is notoriously vague, and is adaptable to the most diverse lines of argument. Diagnosis of a postmodern condition depends, most importantly, on underlying images of modernity: whether and how we can envisage an overcoming or exhaustion of the modern paradigm is determined by our prior definitions of it, and those who try to analyse the transition to postmodernity often find it difficult to do so without falling back on developmental models drawn from modern history. The most elementary conceptual demarcations are thus fraught with problems, and rival theories in the field tend to neglect the task of clarifying their common background. As a result, the debate falls short of the 'structured disagreement'[2] which has prevailed in more developed areas of social theory.

We can, nevertheless, identify some more or less well-established positions and describe them in terms of their ways of defending, questioning or rejecting the idea of postmodernity. The papers included in this collection represent four such positions.

The first is based on the assumption that a postmodern pattern of social or cultural life can be clearly distinguished from the core structures of modernity, and that recent developments can be analysed in the light of this dichotomy. Theories of postmodernity or postmodernisation are thus put to an empirical test, and contemporary trends are brought into a theoretical perspective. As the arguments developed here show, this approach may involve important distinctions between Western and Japanese versions of the break with modernity.

Ross Mouer raises the question of changes to industrial relations and the organisation of work; he accepts that a major shift in this domain, especially with regard to the interrelationship of work and play, might be significant enough to show that modern arrangements are giving way to postmodern ones, but his conclusions with regard to the Japanese experience are sceptical. Both general considerations and the comparative results of fieldwork in Japan and the United States cast doubt on the notion of Japan as a pioneer of 'postmodernisation'. If the latter term refers to a weakening of work-related constraints and an increase in playfulness, Japanese developments in this direction are, at best, uneven and inconclusive. The dominant trend is, rather, 'a continuation of the modernist thrust for economic rationality'; the juxtaposition of different types of work practices has more to do with strategies of control and exploitation than with playfulness.

J. V. Neustupný defines the concept of postmodernity in much more comprehensive terms and regards it as more relevant to contemporary Japan. As he sees it, modernity and postmodernity form developmental types, made up of determinants, maxims and strategies (these three categories represent descending levels of generality). Intuitive descriptions of postmodern attitudes – such as acceptance of conflict and variation and attention to processes rather than structures – can be integrated into this framework. It is also, as Neustupný argues, congruent with an emergent paradigm in Japanese studies, and the two lines of argument lead to the conclusion that Japan is in the process of transition to postmodernity. More specific illustrations of this trend have to do with the domains of language and communication: indications of postmodernity can be seen in such changes as the more positive view of dialects, the lifting of restrictions on official language use, and a more flexible attitude to borrowed words. But the process has yet to be adequately reflected on the metalinguistic level, that is, in the theoretical analysis and practical planning of language.

Kenji Kosaka's paper differs from the two others in that it does not presuppose a definite concept of postmodernity. Rather, he reconstructs the differences of opinion (and the implicit debate) between two prominent Japanese sociologists with regard to their position on this issue. Imada and Tominaga can, in a very general sense, be said to agree on an interpretation of contemporary Japanese society as a mixture of premodern, modern and post-modern elements, but their respective views on the pattern of combination are so different that they lead to fundamentally divergent conclusions (this situation is, as Kosaka shows, reminiscent of earlier controversies within Japanese Marxism). Kosaka's main thesis is that the concept of postmodernity is still too underdeveloped for the debate to be conducted in a productive fashion, and for the phenomena invoked by postmodernist commentators (such as the new concern with issues of social justice and the quality of life that go beyond traditional class politics) to be put in an adequate perspective. The question of Japan's transition to postmodernity has yet to be posed in precise and testable terms, but this could, in principle, be achieved through further clarification of the underlying concepts.

A second approach, diametrically opposed to the first one, rejects the very notion of postmodernity as misleading and suggests that the issues in question should be reformulated within the framework of a theory of modernity. It is only because of a specific theoretical and ideological background – the predominance of oversimplified images of modernity – that recent developments are perceived as marking the beginning of a new epoch; for analytical purposes, it is more useful to locate them in the context of a multidimensional and conflictual modernity.

Tessa Morris-Suzuki discusses various Japanese versions of a 'new paradigm' for scientific and social development, more or less explicitly identified with notions of postmodernity. In this context, the postmodernist turn is closely linked with a rehabilitation of Japanese tradition and a reaction against the two dominant discourses of the postwar era: those of Marxism and modernisation theory. These two discourses had converged in a highly critical perspective on contemporary Japan. By contrast, Japanese postmodernists are attracted to the idea of affinities between new science and traditional Japanese culture. This obviously ideological twist raises questions about the idea of postmodernity as such: it seems too adaptable to political conjunctures to be of much use as an analytical tool. Moreover, the most questionable assumptions of modernisation theory are left intact or put to new use without further reflection: the notion of a new science relies on modernist conceptions of the autonomy of scientific development, and the reified notion of tradition as a closed and static world is merely given a more positive content. As Morris-Suzuki argues, an intellectual break with modernisation theory would be more fruitful than the imaginary break with modernity: we should learn to think in terms of 'postmodernis-ation', that is, the new problematic which emerges after the failure of classical modernisation theory, rather than 'postmodern-isation' in the sense of a transition from modernity to postmod-ernity.

Johann P. Arnason also argues against the concept of postmod-ernity and attempts to show that it is, at best, a misnomer for unresolved problems in the theory of modernity. His thesis is that the concept of modernity can be reconstructed as a self-interpret-ive but also self-relativising product of Western history: it refers to the particular self-transcending and self-transformative capacity that Western civilisation came to exemplify. However, further progress towards a balanced theory of modernity depends on comparison with other civilisations, and although the Japanese experience is of particular interest in this respect, it has generally been neglected by major Western analysts of modernity. Arnason lists some particularly salient aspects of the Japanese road to modernity – from the sixteenth-century transformation to the postwar economic miracle – and outlines some theoretical impli-cations. He then argues that the issues singled out by Japanese postmodernists – and Western postmodernists writing on Japan – can be located within the framework of comparative analyses of modernity. This applies to the recent transformations of Japanese society and its position in the international arena, as well as to some enduring aspects of Japanese tradition.

It is possible to argue for a middle road between the first two approaches, and to accept a definition of postmodernity which does not validate the most radical claims of the postmodernists, but allows for a change – or a set of changes – which constitute more than just another episode of the modern era. From this third perspective, postmodernity is not a new historical phase, different from and comparable with modernity; it is a reorien-tation of modernity, and the prefix 'post' has a double-edged meaning in that it refers to the break with a preceding constel-lation as well as the re-appearance of interrupted and forgotten themes of modern culture.

This minimalist position is most explicitly defended by Paul Harrison. His view is that the term 'postmodernity' is best understood in the light of changes in the political system and the political universe of discourse; its broader implications have to do with reflections of and reactions to these key developments. In the West, the end of the period of long-term growth and the broad social consensus which accompanied it led to a comprehensive redefinition of the political agenda. Within the 'newly-created field of disputation', new or reactivated themes – difference, civil society, market and globalisation – have come to the fore; the conflict between liberalism and socialism is no longer what it was, and older countercurrents – such as those of the romantic tradition – have re-emerged in various guises. Harrison argues that developments in Japan are similar in some respects but very different in others. Both the legacy of the developmental state and the cultural background of Japanese particularism make for a much less liberal version of postmodernity than the Western one. The general conclusion suggested by this analysis is that patterns of postmodernity reflect the prior variants of modernity. Neither Japan nor the West has moved or is moving from modernity to postmodernity, but both are – in different ways – going through changes of such magnitude that a conceptual focus on discontinuity seems useful.

Two other papers can – with some qualifications – be read as examples of the same line of argument. John Clark views postmodernism in art 'as an inversion on itself of the self-critical logic of modernism', that is, as a movement internal to modernity but too radical to be reducible to one experiment among others. His main concern is with the technical, institutional and interpretive conditions for the maturing of this movement. The postmodern situation of art cannot be defined on the basis of purely aesthetic properties; rather, the contextualisation of the aesthetic – in relation to the systems of patronage, diffusion and discursive appreciation – is at the same time a way of clarifying the relationship between modernism and postmodernism.

Toshiko Ellis discusses some of the problems and paradoxes that have arisen out of the transfer of postmodernist ideas from Western to Japanese contexts. If 'postmodernism as a theory was developed in certain countries of the West to challenge existing perceptions of their own culture', and particularly in opposition to earlier idealisations of Western power and predominance, it can be seen as a continuation of critical trends in modern culture, but also as a conscious attempt to give them a more radical turn.

When postmodernist themes are taken up in a Japanese context, this ambiguity is compounded by a paradox. On the one hand, the Japanese response to this new product of Western culture follows a pattern that has been characteristic of the Japanese modernising process as a whole: postmodernism is transmitted from the centre to the periphery in the same way as the earlier ideas which it proposes to challenge. On the other hand, the postmodernist critique of modernity can reinforce the Japanese tradition of particularist reaction against Western universalism (the idea of 'overcoming modernity' was a philosophical echo of Japanese nationalism in its most militant phase). As Ellis shows, the result has so far been an exacerbation, rather than an overcoming, of the contradictions built into Japanese modernity. From this point of view, the notion of postmodernity can certainly not be taken at face value, that is, as referring to a new era that comes after or goes beyond modernity; but it can be used to underline a particularly intriguing aspect of the broader problematic of modernity.

Finally, there is a fourth school of thought which bypasses the explicit debate on postmodernity but takes up some of its substantive issues from a more traditional angle. The most convenient framework for such attempts is a more-or-less revised and amplified version of Marxist theory; ideas from this tradition can also be combined with more recent currents of radical thought.

Tetsuro Kato and Rob Steven deal with the problematic of industrial relations in Japan and criticise Western attempts to present the Japanese enterprise as a model of post-Fordism. As they argue, the very dichotomy of Fordism and post-Fordism is deceptive: both concepts serve to lump together various aspects of industrial organisation that can, in fact, vary independently of each other, and when their unity is taken for granted, this can – as it has done in the case of Japan – serve as an excuse for neglecting the empirical study of each feature. A critical examination of key themes suggests that the transformations of work in Japan have more to do with the essential strategy of capital – 'dividing and ruling through organised competition' – than with any evolutionary progress beyond Fordism. According to Kato and Steven, the distinctive characteristics of Japanese management are the result of the defeat of Japanese trade unions during the postwar phase of transition, and if we are looking for parallels between Japan and the West in this area, the current shift towards a 'more exploitative system of class domination' in Western countries is more relevant than any utopian constructions.

Vera Mackie relates her argument directly to the debate on postmodernity: the 'conjunction of feminism and postmodernism in the Japanese context' is her starting-point for a discussion of substantive issues of identity and equality. Notwithstanding the problematic position of Japan in narratives of modernity and postmodernity, it is, if anything, more true there than in the West that feminist theory and politics have profited from the contact with postmodernist currents. But this conjunctural link should not overshadow the more structural link with the 'modernist narratives' of liberalism and socialism. Mackie's analysis suggests that the most important developments in Japanese feminist politics are best understood as the outcome of interaction with these two other modern currents, rather than as reflections of an overall shift to postmodernity. Feminism is part of a more complex modern configuration, and the critical relationship with both liberal and socialist strategies is a permanent aspect of its identity. This is exemplified by feminist involvement in the discourses of equality and protection. Inasmuch as the emphasis is on the internal logic of feminism and its modern roots, the paper has more in common with the bypassing approach than with the others.

Finally, the concluding paper by Ross Mouer and Yoshio Sugimoto may be read as another variant of the fourth strategy. While their main concern in the past has been with rival paradigms in Japanese studies, more particularly with the 'conflict-variation' model and the 'consensus-homogeneity' model for understanding Japanese society, their attention is directed at attempts to provide a 'definitive definition of the Japanese'. Their argument makes use of postmodernist themes without subscribing to the claims often associated with them. The postmodern questioning of established boundaries and identities warns against overintegrated and monoculturalist images of Japan. The multiculturalist alternative proposed by Mouer and Sugimoto would highlight the diversity of groups and traditions as well as the ongoing processes of differentiation. Although postmodernist misgivings about universality are taken seriously, they are translated into a more flexible formulation of the problem rather than a debunking of the very idea of universality. A multicultural Japan is also a 'Japan with significant universal components', but the universals are contextual: they reflect the globalising process and its many-sided impact on Japanese society. The transnational culture of technoprofessional elites differs from the less established international subcultures of environmentalist or feminist groups, but both are significant sources of diversity within Japan. It is argued that the 'conflict-variation' paradigm is more receptive to this problematic than its rivals. While some 153 Japanese books published during the five-year period from 1986 to 1990 had the term 'postmodern' in their titles[3], there is little indication that such interest has seriously affected the debate on *nihonjinron* within Japan. In this context, the Mouer-Sugimoto argument provides a fresh postmodernist perspective in the genre of meta-*nihonjinron*.

Directions of Inquiry

The papers were all written before the political crisis which began with the downfall of the LDP government in 1993 and which seems likely to end with the restoration of conservative hegemony in a more flexible form. It may therefore be useful to consider the implications of this turning point for the questions and positions discussed above.

The rapid succession of unstable coalition governments is only the most visible part of a more complex transformation. We can distinguish four main aspects of the change that Japanese politics, economics and society are now undergoing.

There is, first, the flagging performance of a developmental model, exceptionally effective in the past but now in obvious need of readjustment. Both the 'bubble economy' of the late 1980s and the subsequent recession have highlighted problems in this area; and while predictions of an imminent collapse are no more convincing than the description of Japan as a place 'where communism works',[4] it seems clear that the institutions of Japanese capitalism (especially the relationship between economic forces and the developmental state) are going through a critical phase.

At the same time, epoch-making changes in the global constellation have made it necessary to redefine Japan's international concerns and strategies. The end of the Cold War and the emergence of the United States as the sole superpower have affected all aspects of Japanese-American relations; the demise of the

Soviet Union and the uncertainties of post-communism have created new problems as well as opportunities for Japanese foreign policy. Last but not least, development in the East Asian region – both the growth of Chinese power and the prospect of Korean unification – are confronting the Japanese state with a new geopolitical situation.

The third transformation may be seen as a response to the first two: it is a more demanding domestic and foreign environment that has exacerbated weaknesses of the postwar political system and prompted the search for alternatives. And as the misfortunes of the Social Democratic Party have shown, it is not only the ruling party, but a whole political regime – including a permanent opposition – that has been thrown into crisis.

Finally, the changing cultural orientations that accompany these structural shifts are less clearly defined, but the widely proclaimed commitment to 'internationalisation' and the various signs of resurgent nationalism may be seen as opposite – not necessarily incompatible – aspects of a mutation in progress. Both trends are controversial, and the outcome of their interaction will depend on the strategies which prevail in practice.

These interconnected changes are not irrelevant to the theoretical issues discussed above. If there are good reasons to believe that a combination of internal and external factors is transforming the Japanese pattern of development, it seems equally obvious that the new constellation does not represent a radical break with the recent past, and therefore does not fit into the global vision of a transition to postmodernity. Rather, the four transformations signalise a major shift within a framework which has shaped the course of Japanese modernisation and set it apart from other cases. Japan's history since 1868 has been marked by a close connection between the imperatives of interstate competition and those of capitalist development, as well as by a notable capacity to redefine the relationship between them in response to changing conditions (most conspicuously after 1945). The present agenda of reform – determined by new demands made on state and economy by a changing global and domestic environment – reflects the search for a new variant of this pattern. As for the cultural reorientation, it has to do with the two themes that have been central to the self-understanding of Japanese civilisation not only in its modern phase, but also at critical junctures in earlier history: the maintenance of collective identity structured around an exceptionally resilient particularistic core, and the management of changes induced by contact with the outside world. It is the need for corrections to this peculiar combination of closure and opening that sustains the debate on nationalism and internationalisation.

It may thus be suggested that the postmodernist approach is not proving particularly well-suited to dealing with the most recent phase of the Japanese trajectory. On the other hand, the papers in this collection seem to share a substantive focus which is perhaps more important than disagreement on theoretical labels. Irrespective of their diverse conceptual frameworks, they are – more or less explicitly – engaged in contextualising ideas drawn from Western sources but seen as relevant to the Japanese case. Even when strong claims are made about parallels between Western and Japanese developments, the authors are aware that contextual differences must be taken into account; both the modernists and the postmodernists are thus committed to a line of inquiry which recognises the originality and specificity of the Japanese experience (this attitude was not characteristic of classical modernisation theory, and is by no means self-evident for mainstream postmodernism). Their analyses can, in other words, be read as contributions to a research program which is still very far from having exhausted its potential. There is further work to be done on the interplay of identity and difference in the modern destinies of Japan and the West. The reconstruction of common patterns must be balanced by insight into the sources of diversity: situations, strategies and traditions. But a properly balanced version of this project would have to combine the view from the West more systematically with a Japan-centred perspective. Although the former can be sensitised to other experiences and should therefore not be equated with Eurocentrism, that does not bring the specific gains to be expected from the latter. Notions and constellations that have been central to the Japanese side of the story could be used as starting-points for a comparative analysis of Western counterparts (an obvious but neglected case in point is Masao Maruyama's account of ultra-nationalism). That approach is hardly represented in our collection, but it would be a logical and desirable complement to the main themes explored by the authors.

Notes

1. Though a volume edited by Miyoshi and Harootunian (1989) deals with a similar theme, it analyses postmodernism issues primarily from the vantage point of literary and cultural studies. The present volume attempts to address the area mainly from the sociological point of view, while incorporating studies of literature and fine arts as well.
2. Alexander, 1982: 9.
3. Nichigai Associates. Data files on books published during this period.
4. Kenrick, 1991.

2 THEORY
Modernity, Postmodernity and the Japanese Experience

Johann P. Arnason

The Idea of Modernity

It can hardly be denied that comparative analysis has been one of the weaker points of Western theories of modernity and modernisation. An understandably one-sided focus on the emergence, expansion and hegemony of the West has led to the direct translation of a historical trajectory into a general theory. This trend is now being reversed by those who argue that we should discard superfluous concepts and rest content with the notion of Westernisation as a worldwide process.[1] By way of contrast, the following reflections are based on the assumption that both these ways of absolutising the West should be avoided, and that the relationship between Westernisation and modernisation should, therefore, be defined in a way that allows us to keep open the question of the relative weight of the former within the latter. The case for a distinction between the two concepts can be briefly stated in general terms: if we describe the rise of the West as the first breakthrough to modernity, this is because of the particular self-transcending and self-transformative capacity that Western civilisation came to exemplify. The dynamic that was thus set in motion draws on many sources (which cannot be discussed here) and manifests itself in many forms. At one end of the spectrum it leads to the unlimited maximisation of wealth and power and the ongoing adaptation of social institutions to this goal; at the other end, it opens the way to an unconstrained problematisation of cultural meanings and their social embodiments. In relation to the non-Western world the uniqueness of the West does not – as Lévi-Strauss has suggested – consist only in its unequalled destructive capacity. It also involves an unprecedented effort to understand other civilisations and to confront Western assumptions and achievements with their experience. It may be objected that the latter aspect has had much less impact on the course of history than the former, but this is not a valid reason for ignoring it or denying its significance as a component of Western culture.

From the present point of view, then, modernity is not simply another label for the ascendant West. Nor is it a universal cultural paradigm which, for contingent reasons, happened to emerge in the West earlier than in other places. Rather, we define the idea of modernity in hermeneutical terms: as an essential part of the self-articulation of the West, but a part which has the specific function of opening up a horizon beyond the existing social order of things. The self-transcendence which is thus made possible is, as suggested above, open to conflicting interpretations; it can appear as accumulation or critique, self-maximisation or self-problematisation. In more concrete patterns of modernity, this horizon of indeterminacy is circumscribed by social and cultural forms which enhance certain possibilities at the expense of others.

On the basis of this idea of modernity, we can understand the double-edged impact of the West on the rest of the world: it represented a model that could spread beyond its original borders, and at the same time opened up a cultural space that could be mapped out in more ways than one. Westernisation and modernisation are complementary aspects of the historical process which is thus set in motion. On the one hand, the enforced or imitative adaptation to Western models is a worldwide phenomenon, although its significance varies from epoch to epoch and region to region. On the other hand, more autonomous responses to the Western challenge vary in terms of scope and efficacy. At the most elementary level, the search for functional equivalents to Western techniques and institutions has been characteristic of many latecomers; the substitution of state intervention for private and collective initiatives is perhaps the most familiar example. More ambitious and more problematic were the attempts to borrow the rules of technical rationality from the West whilst conserving the core elements of non-Western cultural traditions (including the conceptions of power that were built into them). A classic but short-lived example was the strategy of 'self-strengthening' in late imperial China, based on the assumption that a Confucian sociocultural order could adopt Western technology for its own purposes. If the modernisation of Japan had never gone beyond the idea of *wakon yōsai*, it would belong in this category. The same can be said about the more recent phenomenon of Islamic fundamentalism: it strives to combine a 'return to the sources' with the mastery of modern sources of power. The obviously self-contradictory character of such projects – some critics have diagnosed them as cases of cultural schizophrenia – does not mean that they can have no impact on history. A third and much more significant type of response gives rise to more complex and coherent structures that might be described as counterparadigms of modernity, that is, configurations of economic, political and cultural patterns which differ significantly from those that had developed in the West. The history of the twentieth century was dominated by the rise, expansion, decline and demise of the most important among these configurations: the Soviet model. Its fate makes the very different course and character of the Japanese counterparadigm seem all the more relevant.

The Japanese Experience

The theory of modernity is thus faced with a question which it is badly equipped to answer. In fact, the neglect of comparative analysis – at least on the level of general theory – has been particularly pronounced in relation to Japan, where it ought to have been most obviously necessary. Max Weber's brief and dismissive treatment of Japan contrasts with his much more extensive analyses of India and China. As for the mainstream version of postwar modernisation theory, it had something to say on the Japanese experience, but took no notice of its most original aspects. The Japanese version of modernity was, to put it briefly, seen as imitative, unbalanced and incomplete. Its main patterns are, in this view, mere reproductions of Western models (the more detailed comparisons have mostly focused on the eastern part of the West, with particular reference to Germany, Russia and Turkey). The imbalance between the rapid modernisation of economy and administration and a more backward legal and political culture seemed to pose a threat to the whole system. A society characterised by such flaws could not be described as fully modern; its transformation was incomplete in a more radical sense than the unfinished project of modernity in the West. Parsons' discussion of Japan in *The System of Modern Societies* is perhaps the most representative example of this approach. But post-Parsonian theories of modernity have not made much progress in this area. The attempts to construct more flexible and

14

more genuinely multidimensional conceptual frameworks have not drawn on the Japanese experience; rather, the interest in this 'delight and despair of comparative history'[2] seems to have declined. This applies in almost equal measure to the two most influential post-Parsonians, Jürgen Habermas and Anthony Giddens. Alain Touraine seems to have taken more interest in Japan, but it can hardly be said that he has integrated it into his theory.

This retreat of Western social theory from the Japanese question is happening at a time when the importance of coming to grips with it is more obvious than ever. Before going on to discuss the idea of postmodernity in this context, it may be useful to summarise some reasons for taking Japanese modernity seriously.

It seems appropriate to begin with the rise of Japan as an economic superpower. The significance of this development is clearer when we discuss it in its global context. On the one hand, there can be no doubt that it has something to do with the crisis and collapse of the Soviet model. The grand strategy of the Soviet leadership in the post-Stalin era centred on economic competition with the other superpower; it was only when the idea of 'overtaking and surpassing' the American economy had proved illusory that a more traditional (and, as we now know, self-defeating) strategy of imperial expansion was adopted as a substitute. In the meantime, the Soviet Union was overtaken and surpassed by Japan, which thus became the world's second strongest economy. In other words: Japan did to the Soviet Union what the Soviet Union had proposed to do to America. This challenge must have been a much more critical factor and a much stronger incentive to experiment with reform than either the notorious SDI program or the dissatisfaction of the Soviet élite with its lifestyle.[3] In view of the outcome, it seems clear that there is a close connection between the resurgence of Japanese power and the most significant restructuring of the global balance of power since the end of World War II. On the other hand, it is now increasingly recognised that the rivalry between Japan and the United States is not simply a matter of competition between the two strongest capitalist economies; over and above this, it represents a conflict between two particularly divergent patterns of capitalist development. They may not be the only viable ones, as some observers now seem to believe, but the contrast between them is a useful starting point for the analysis and location of more mixed or transitional forms. The reference to Japan is thus essential for a typology of modern capitalism and an adequate understanding of the variety which is no longer overshadowed by a 'really existing' but essentially illusory alternative. And if institutions are, as Chalmers Johnson has convincingly argued, 'the critical variable in explaining Japan's modern economic success',[4] the study of Japanese capitalism – the most formidable economic machine the world has ever seen – and its sociocultural context should be a particularly attractive testing-ground for the institutional approach to economic structures. This perspective, opened up by the classics of the sociological tradition but insufficiently developed by their successors, is the only one that can still make sense of the idea of a critique of political economy.

The postwar economic success was preceded by a cultural, political and military disaster. The continuity between pre- and post-1945 Japan has often been emphasised, mainly with regard to the bureaucratic core of the state and the imaginary core of the *tennōsei* ideology, but these valid points should not lead us to forget that 1945 was both an end and a beginning. Together with a new international strategy and a far-reaching de-militarisation of the state, the changes in social structure, political regime and cultural climate were radical enough to set the contemporary version of Japanese modernity clearly apart from the one which self-destructed in the Pacific War. This discontinuity is important for comparative analysis. The abrupt and complete collapse of a paradigm of modernity is a rare but not unique phenomenon; the two other examples that come to mind are the defeat of Nazi Germany and the terminal crisis of the Soviet model, and the Japanese experience might seem much more reminiscent of the former case than of the latter. A closer look at both cases suggests that a less one-sided comparison might be useful. The general conclusion that can be drawn from historical research is that the continuity between late Meiji Japan and the ultranationalist regime of the 1930s was more pronounced than between imperial and Nazi Germany, and that the episode of Taishō democracy was correspondingly less important than the Weimar Republic (this is, admittedly, a controversial area, and I cannot go further into it here). The Nazi regime had, as the more insightful analyses have shown, its own image of modernity, but it was too short-lived and its destructive dynamic too extreme to be put on a par with the others. On the other hand, it is true that Japan fought and lost a global war, whereas the Soviet regime collapsed under its own weight without becoming involved in a major internal or external conflict. A self-destructive imperial dynamic was, however, at work in both cases, and the fallout from the Soviet disaster might yet spark a whole series of local wars. It would, in other words, be premature to stress the contrast between a violent and a peaceful demise. And although the post-Soviet world is – in contrast to post-1945 Japan – being transformed without foreign occupation, the influence of the most simplistic visions of the West is so strong that, in some cases, it does not seem too far-fetched to talk about an ideological occupation.

One of the most popular explanations for the rise of Japan, the so-called 'latecomer thesis', has now been thoroughly discredited. According to this line of argument, the otherwise different societies that embark upon modernisation in order to catch up with more advanced ones are likely to follow a common pattern of development; both the constraints and the opportunities inherent in this situation impose certain strategic choices. But as the number of examples has multiplied, such claims have become less plausible. There have been several generations of latecomers, but no second Japan. The differences between late developers are, on the whole, more visible than the affinities. In more theoretical terms, it now seems clear that all assumptions about the situational logic of latecomers are subject to four major qualifications. Firstly, the original formulations of the thesis in question were based on a narrow and economistic conception of development. The 'advantages of backwardness' had to do with the availability of advanced technology and the ability to skip or shorten intermediary phases. For the more complex theories of modernisation, that is, those more sensitive to cultural and political components, the impact of economic imperatives on the pattern of modernity is less clear-cut. Secondly, the global context of modernisation – whether we want to call it a capitalist world-economy or a 'nationally hierarchised world-system'[5] – is subject to historical change, and the concrete situation of latecomers depends on the general characteristics of the epoch. In the era of microelectronics and an emergent multipolar world, the implications of a late beginning are not the same as in the age of colonial expansion and the second industrial revolution. Another part of the background is the concrete historical situation in which the entry into the global arena of modernisation takes place. The orientations, initiatives and strategies of social actors involved in the process, as well as the conflicts between them, can be of major importance for later stages of development. In the case of Japan, this applies most obviously to the mid-nineteenth century constellation and the Meiji revolution. Last but not least, the resources and traditions of the states, societies and civilisations that are drawn into the global modernising process can be more or less conducive to autonomous development and more or less capable of codetermining the resultant version of modernity. It is a commonplace that the Japanese trajectory has been a particularly prominent example of this interpenetration of tradition and modernity.

But if it is true that no recent latecomer has matched the performance of modern Japan, a comparison with some states in the region is nevertheless more relevant than with any other examples. The 'little tigers', especially Taiwan and South Korea, have undergone a transformation that sets them apart from other developing countries, even if it is not on the same scale as the Japanese phenomenon. Their relationship to Japan can be analysed on two levels. On the one hand, there is no doubt that their political and economic power élites have drawn some lessons from the Japanese experience, and it may be possible to explain their economic systems as variations of the same underlying principle. There are contrasts and similarities with regard to the role of the state in economic development, as well as to the structure of the private sector. As for the latter question, the most interesting idea that has grown out of recent debates is that East Asian capitalism differs from its Western counterpart in that it relies less on markets and more on networks, and that variations within the East Asian region are mainly due to the fact that the dominant types of networks differ from country to country.[6] On the other hand, these recent developments throw new light on the common civilisational heritage of the region. Of the two major cultural traditions involved, Buddhism and Confucianism, it is the latter that most analysts have taken to be more important: it represents an older civilisational layer, it is more exclusively typical of the region, and it was more actively involved in the later phases of its history. The widespread interest in this connection has already given rise to the notion of 'Confucian capitalism'. The contrast with Weber's well-known analysis of Confucianism is striking: for Weber, this was the antimodern culture *par excel-*

lence, as opposed to rational calculation as it was to activistic values.[7] But although there are, undoubtedly, good reasons to question Weber's understanding of the Far East, no balanced account of Confucianism can ignore the more conservative aspect of its role in traditional China. There is something to be said for the view that it was the imperial order and its selective combination of traditions, not Confucianism *per se*, that blocked China's road to modernity and paralysed its response to the Western challenge, and that the transformative potential of Confucianism becomes more relevant when it is no longer controlled by an imperial centre. Another suggestion is that the Confucian tradition is made up of heterogeneous elements, and that the group- or family-centred attitudes of popular Confucianism are much more attuned to a modern economy than was the state-centred ideology of the Confucian scholars.[8] In any case, the comparative analysis of Confucian cultures, their internal patterns and their contextual determinants, as well as their changing relationship to modernity, is still faced with a long list of open questions.

Most Western and Japanese historians now seem to agree that the three centuries between the unification and the reopening of Japan can be described as an 'early modern' phase (this is the accepted translation of *kinsei*). But this insight – based on extensive research and debate – has yet to be assimilated by social theory. If it can be shown that Japan's road to modernity began long before it was drawn into permanent contact with the West (the sixteenth-century encounter was too brief to have more than a limited impact on the changes that were already underway inside Japan), the implications for comparative analysis are obvious. There is no other country with a similar sequence of parallel development, rapid response and effective counterchallenge to the West. The early and endogenous modernity that laid the groundwork for later progress has now been thoroughly documented by historians of the Tokugawa era. The two-tiered process of state formation, institutionalised in the *bakuhan* system, and the bureaucratisation of the ruling military élite paved the way for a more radical remodelling of Japanese institutions after 1868. There was a flourishing market economy and a complex urban culture which, in many ways, bears comparison with the early modern West, even if its legacy to Meiji Japan was less important than that of the samurai and their statecraft. The reinterpretation of cultural traditions contributed to the development of Japanese nationalism, although both the scope and the direction of rationalising processes in this area is more controversial than in the political or economic dimension. But if we want to use the notion of modernity in the strong sense indicated at the beginning of this paper, it is not enough to identify historical equivalents or parallels with the West. There is a more difficult question that must be raised: to what extent did the transformative dynamic of early modern Japanese society open up a broader context of possible alternatives? A detailed discussion of the problem is beyond the scope of the present paper, but the evidence seems strong enough to justify at least a tentative answer: the opening was more limited and more easily controllable than in the West, but real enough to constitute a more interesting counterpoint to it than any other non-Western experience prior to the onset of global Westernisation. In this respect, the sixteenth-century background of the Tokugawa regime is more revealing than developments during the *sakoku* epoch. The conflicts which preceded unification changed the social balance of power; the new warlords who had emerged during the late fifteenth and early sixteenth century had to overcome the resistance of a rival 'historical bloc' that included the Buddhist establishment as well as local warriors and peasants. The losers of this struggle were probably too weak and their coalition too fragile to develop into a viable alternative (if there was a societal project, its theocratic elements were stronger than the plebeian ones), but they did at least represent other patterns of social organisation. And even after the definitive victory of the warlords, the Tokugawa option was not a foregone conclusion. The strategy of the first two unifiers, Nobunaga and Hideyoshi, might – if taken further – have given rise to a more rationalised, secular and outward-looking regime than the one which took shape under Ieyasu's leadership, and their imperial ambitions stand out in contrast with the calculated minimisation of foreign contacts after 1600. From this point of view, the policies of the Tokugawa regime can perhaps be described as a re-traditionalisation of Japanese society, but not in the sense of a simple return to traditional patterns. The concept of a 'pseudo-archaic society' has been used to single out institutional arrangements where 'the so-called archaic features have been transformed or invented in accordance with a rational goal';[9] in this sense, it is tempting to interpret Tokugawa Japan as a pseudo-traditional society – if we bear in mind that the traditional ingredient in a pseudo-traditional mix is real and essential.

One more point should be added to this provisional list. Encounters with and insights into non-Western traditions have, from the outset, played an important role in the self-articulation of the West, and in this respect as in others, each case has its specific characteristics. The fashionable caricature of 'Orientalism' obscures the differences and reduces the whole constellation to its most superficial aspects. If we compare Japan with other examples of such interpretive appropriations, the changes which its Western image has undergone seem particularly striking. For the nineteenth-century writers and artists who launched the fashion known as 'japonisme', Japan was the aesthetic culture (more particularly: the culture of the image) *par excellence*. This perspective was, of course, open to further variations: in some cases, the Japanese connection was simply a metaphor for an escapist and absolutist conception of the aesthetic sphere, but a more authentic 'fusion of horizons' could establish a cross-cultural contact between processes of aesthetic rationalisation.[10] By contrast, current perceptions of Japan tend to focus on its unique performance in the economic sphere. This theme is inherently ambiguous: Japan can be portrayed as the paradise of economic rationality (and different conceptions of economic rationality give rise to correspondingly different interpretations of Japan) or as the antiutopia of a society swallowed by its economy. If Western interpretations of other civilisations are, as suggested above, an integral part of the process through which the West transforms and transcends itself, it seems clear that Japan – the last major non-Western civilisation to be discovered by the West – has in this context been reinterpreted more radically than any of the others. In comparison, there is a much stronger affinity between eighteenth-century idealisations of China and the Maoist aberrations of the declining Western Left.

The Debate on Postmodernity

As we have seen, the Japanese experience raises a whole series of questions that are – or ought to be – central to the problematic of modernity. The failure of the most representative theorists to confront this challenge is all the more striking if we contrast it with the frequent references to Japan in the context of postmodernist arguments. The meaning of postmodernity is, of course, as elusive on this level as on all others, but there is no doubt that its relevance to Japan is widely accepted. A brief glance at the historical background may help to explain this belief.

For our present purposes, we can treat official Marxism and mainstream functionalism as rival versions of modernisation theory; both schools of thought (and their common premises) were increasingly called into question during the 1960s. In response to the crisis of modernisation theory, various attempts have been made to revise and retheorise the underlying conceptions of modernity, but none of these projects (which mostly took shape during the 1970s) has established itself as a dominant paradigm or matched the ideological potential of Marxist and Parsonian theories. As far as the broader intellectual public is concerned, they have – especially during the 1980s – clearly been overshadowed by another response to the crisis of modernisation theory: the idea of a postmodern epoch or condition and the attempts to define its contours and characteristics in more precise ways. In view of the resonance of this theme, postmodernism (or the postmodern syndrome, if we prefer a more clinical term) must be taken seriously as a cultural phenomenon, but this does not mean that 'postmodernity' should be taken at face value as a theoretical concept. There are some obvious reasons to doubt its validity.

To begin with, the very notion of postmodernity is – as Castoriadis has pointed out – fatally flawed: it suggests a negation of, demarcation from or movement beyond an earlier epoch, but that epoch – modernity – was already defining itself in terms of a departure from precedents, rather than any distinctive features. The term 'modern' was first used in opposition to the models and traditions derived from classical antiquity; its later role in social theory rests on the contrast with tradition in general; and, as suggested above, it is now best defined in a way that relativises all established patterns and confronts them with an open historical horizon. If this procedure – definition by negation – is then used again to indicate a movement or situation beyond modernity, the result can only be a self-referential repetition without any positive content. Some basic concepts of social theory have been described as 'essentially contested'; it is tempting to call 'postmodernity' an essentially incoherent concept, and to suggest that, as such, it belongs in the company of conceptual freaks like people's capitalism or the dictatorship of the proletariat.

The emptiness of the concept makes it adaptable to the most diverse ideological positions. At one end of the spectrum, radicals disillusioned with their traditional frames of reference now expect postmodernism 'to remedy the modernist error of Western, male, bourgeois domination';[11] at the other extreme, postmodernist language has also – especially in Germany – been used to defend a Christian-Aristotelian world-view against the modern and supposedly defunct ideas of progress and emancipation. There is no need to survey the whole field in between; it seems obvious that an ideologically ultraflexible notion cannot be a reliable theoretical tool.

But although it is easy to dismiss the concept of postmodernity, the matter cannot rest there. We will have to consider some of the more specific meanings and messages that have been associated with this exceptionally infectious vogue, and to judge them on their own merits. Broadly speaking, the notion of postmodernity migrated from aesthetics into the more general debate on contemporary culture and from there into social theory. In the latter field, which is our main concern, it has – apart from overtly ideological functions – served a double purpose. On the one hand, it has been turned against some entrenched philosophical presuppositions and the cultural orientations in which they are grounded. On this level, postmodernism is equated with the rejection of such apparent axioms of modernity as a sovereign subject, a universal reason and an overall direction of history. On the other hand, mainstream conceptions of the social order have come under criticism, and some new characteristics of social life have been read as symptoms of a postmodern condition. In particular, the institutionalisation of pluralism and indeterminacy seems – on this view – to have progressed far beyond the limits of modern theory and practice.[12]

Both lines of argument are open to the same objections: the turn towards pluralism and relativity, as cultural themes or as social forms, is neither as definitive nor as new as the postmodernists would have us believe. The most decisive unifying and globalising mechanisms of the modern world continue to function, and their cultural sources have by no means been exhausted. This applies most obviously to the capitalist world economy. The rejuvenation of *homo oeconomicus* during the 1980s (the connections with postmodernism would be worth exploring in detail, but cannot be discussed here) has brought back some of the most levelling modern versions of rationality and subjectivity; the ideology that has been refashioned on this basis tends to emphasise competitivity rather than progress or development, but the core content is the same: a rationalising process geared to the accumulation of wealth and power. At the same time, the nation-state, with its mechanisms of control and constructions of identity – the historical reality behind modern ideas of society and social system – is clearly getting a new lease of life in some parts of the world and seems capable of adjusting to other trends elsewhere. The unifying and homogenising forces have, of course, always met with resistance, and postmodernism – in both its radical and conservative versions – has obvious affinities with this aspect of the modernising process. In particular, it owes much to the romantic tradition.

From this point of view, the postmodern epoch is merely another episode within the unfolding and open-ended constellation of modernity, and the critique which is now directed at some manifestations of modernity exaggerates their role in the past while underestimating their present and prospective significance. Postmodernism is then best described as a temporary self-misunderstanding of modernity, facilitated by its earlier self-idealisations, or – at its best – as a detour towards a better understanding of some previously neglected or forgotten dimensions of the modern world. If there is a lesson to be learnt from the debate, it concerns the need for a more complex theory of modernity – one that would do more justice to its diverse and interconnected, but often artificially polarised aspects.

It remains to relate this suggestion to the Japanese experience. The following remarks will deal with some of the attempts to interpret it from a postmodernist angle; they can, as I will try to show, be reinterpreted as partial insights into the problematic of Japanese modernity, coupled with optical illusions that the comparison with the West may help to dispel, and as pointers towards a more general framework for comparative analysis.[13]

Some authors have tried to describe and analyse recent changes in Japanese society in terms of a transition to postmodernity. It goes without saying that this paper will not attempt an exhaustive coverage of the area, but the main trends in question are easily identifiable and have been widely discussed. They include, in particular, a decline of the work ethic and a new emphasis on consumption as well as on the quality of life; the growing role of information technology in all areas of economic and social life; a shift towards more flexible forms of control, and a levelling of the social structure, a rapid growth of the middle class, and a de-polarisation of politics.[14] On the empirical level, all these claims – or at least their broader implications – are controversial, and the debate seems likely to go on for some time. But even if we accept that significant changes have taken place along all the above-mentioned lines, it would still be unclear whether they add up to a unified pattern of postmodernity. The first and the last of the four processes involve phenomena which, in the West, have normally been regarded as long-term consequences or accompani-ments of modernity, whereas the second and the third come closer to the concerns of Western postmodernists. This discrepancy would seem to confirm the above observation on the derivative and conjunctural character of the notion of postmodernity. As a result of the difference in developmental patterns, some trans-formations of modern society took place in Japan at roughly the same time as in the West, whereas others were delayed and therefore came to be associated with phenomena which in the West signalised a later phase. In both cases, the notion of post-modernity is used to pinpoint a whole set of landmarks in the overall modernising process, but the two usages coincide only in part, and the differences are best explained in terms of the respective patterns of modernity.

Another line of argument has to do with a general interpre-tation of postwar Japan and its exceptional – at first marginal but later perhaps pioneering – position within the capitalist world. The developmental model which prevailed after 1945 has, at first sight, some points of contact with Western visions of postmod-ernity. For those who would like to analyse the postmodern con-dition in terms of a de-differentiation of institutions or subsystems (and thus a shift towards more flexible patterns of plurality), the well-known Japanese interpenetration of economics and politics is a suggestive example. The managerial character of Japanese capitalism, its reliance on networks, and its diffuse patterns of authority have been contrasted with Western economies and their dependence on the modern principles of individualism and entre-preneurial initiative. On the political side, the informal power exercised by the bureaucracy, together with the transformation of the imperial institution and the demilitarisation of the state, has led some observers to describe Japan as a polity without a strong and visible centre. In brief, the de-differentiating, de-centring and de-subjectivising logic of a society which has nevertheless in some respects outstripped the West suggests at least one possible version of postmodernity in action. But this idea should be handled with care. To begin with the most elementary point: the postmodernists tend to focus on the most visible aspects of the cultural representation of power (its *'mise en scène'*, to quote Claude Lefort) and to neglect the more complex mechanisms of its social distribution. One of the most pronounced divisions in the field of Japanese studies is the disagreement between those who treat cultural traditions as an autonomous and decisive factor and those who claim that Japanese history was and is mostly about 'power disguised as culture' (Karel van Wolferen). The question of Japanese postmodernity should not be isolated from this debate. Furthermore, a brief glance at the historical background is enough to raise doubts about the epoch-making character of the changes. The postwar pattern of political and economic life reflects a new strategy of interstate competition, developed in response to foreign occupation and as a joint result of American attempts to reconstruct Japan and Japanese efforts to contain the American impact; the most decisive innovation was a shift from imperial expansion to a long-term project of economic development. The restructuring of Japanese society is thus inseparable from a new response to an environment which is still dominated by the modern – and mutually constitutive – forces of a world market and a global state system. On the other hand, it is at least arguable that the collapse of the imperial project brought some older undercurrents to the surface and enabled them to take part in the formation of the new order. It has even been suggested that the real result is 'the archaic constellation of a closed harmony which takes on the appearance of postmodernity'.[15] In more empirical terms, the question of the influence of the peasant tradition on the economic and political culture which took shape in the post-1945 vacuum is at least worth exploring.[16]

The idea of a convergence between archaism and postmodernity – or of postmodernity as merely a mask for a resurgent archaism – brings us to the last and most interesting variation on this theme. The search for Japanese postmodernity has sometimes led to the conclusion that its main sources are to be found in the indigenous tradition, rather than in any global trends or Japanese responses to them: 'And indeed it could be argued that in some sense Japan has always been a "postmodern" society – one in which the "metanarratives" have never been important, a true culture of feeling in which capitalist consumption is itself turned into an art form, in which aesthetics is central and in which emphasis on context creates the very relativism so characteristic of postmodernity.'[17] The emphasis is, in other words, on some lasting and salient characteristics of Japanese civilisation and their affinities with the aspirations which Western thought is now projecting into the idea of postmodernity. But a similar connection can be made in a much more critical vein and with reference to the most problematic aspects of the Japanese experience: 'What stubbornly resisted the "modernisation" of Japanese thought and literature in the twentieth century was not simply a premodern sensibility but a mode of thought which in some senses had already transcended the modern. This naturally took the form of a citation of the anti-Western elements of Western thought. Its grand finale was the wartime ideology of "overcoming the modern" '.[18]

Most analysts would agree that the absence of institutionalised orthodoxy, the prominence – or even as some would see it, the primacy – of aesthetics and the emphasis on contextuality at all levels of meaning are some of the most distinctive features of the Japanese tradition. If we follow Katō Shūichi's argument, the fact that 'in Japan literature took over the role of philosophy' is obviously not unrelated to the 'general cultural tendency for values not to transcend a particular situation' and to de-emphasise the 'universal validity of written statements'.[19] The plurality of cultural traditions, capable of mutual adaptation and open to partial fusions but never absorbed by an overall synthesis, is another part of the same pattern. But if it can be shown that this cultural constellation prefigured the postmodern condition (or at least some versions of it), that would seem to be an argument against the very idea of postmodernity: the road through and beyond modernity is no longer seen as an essential precondition of the phenomena in question. In line with the above suggestions, it could perhaps be argued that the postmodernist attempt to annex Japan is one of the symptoms of a new interest in comparative cultural hermeneutics, stimulated by one of the recurrent self-reflexive turns of Western modernity. If this search for anchorages in other epochs and civilisations were to open up new comparative perspectives on Japan, the postmodernist detour would at least be leading somewhere. But a new language would be needed to make sense of its results. To conclude, I will briefly suggest a way of relating the problematic of the Japanese tradition – and, in particular, those of its aspects that seem to have become more visible from a postmodernist angle – to the above discussion of Japanese modernity.

If it is easy to agree that the Japanese experience is character-ised by a particularly close and complex relationship between tradition and modernity, it is much more difficult to translate this intuition into adequate theoretical terms, and cultural critics on opposite sides have often been tempted to look for extreme solutions to the problem. One of them was the idea of 'over-coming modernity', that is (at least according to some of its proponents), of reactivating the Japanese tradition in opposition to the cultural levelling which accompanied Western dominance of the world. At the other end of the spectrum, Maruyama Masao's well-known essay on 'Thought in Japan' pleaded for a radical critique of the Japanese tradition as a precondition for the overdue self-critique of Japanese modernity.[20] As Maruyama saw it, the dominant feature of the Japanese tradition was the 'absence of structure'; it was, in other words, equally incapable of sustaining a long-term growth of knowledge and a genuine confrontation between rival schools of thought. A similarly dif-fuse pattern had then shaped the course of modernisation and led to an indiscriminate juxtaposition of archaic, modern and super-modern elements. Maruyama later changed his view of the Japanese tradition, but not his critical stance towards it; as he now saw it, its failure to measure up to Western paradigms of tradition did not mean that it did not have a structure *sui generis*, made up of core themes that had endured as the *basso ostinato* of Japanese cultural history, and which had succeeded in contain-ing rather than overcoming modernity.

The shift in Maruyama's approach and the idea of postmod-ernity *avant la lettre* point to the same problem: the difficulty of understanding patterns of traditionalisation that diverge substan-tially from those of the West. A closer examination would have to start with the most elementary issues. If it can be said that the Japanese polity has, in various ways during various phases of its history, combined some characteristics of a centralised state with some attributes of a state system (the latter aspect was of crucial importance during the *sengoku* era and played an important but more subordinate role during the Tokugawa epoch), Japanese culture has similarly combined – and oscillated between – the pattern of a unified tradition and that of a plurality of traditions. It is not so much the presence of both aspects as the peculiar relationship between them that seems to set Japanese civilisation apart from others. To mention only the most obvious contrasts: the Japanese version of unity differs not only from the successive syntheses into which Western civilisation integrated its multiple sources, but also from the Chinese imperial tradition and its cosmological framework. In the Japanese case, the unity is less articulated but more directly linked to images of collective identity and their primordial foundations; the plurality is correspondingly less organised and less polarised.

The questions raised above in connection with Japanese modernity and its metamorphoses are more or less directly related to one central problem: the specific characteristics of a civilisation which obviously combines a highly developed transformative capacity with a no less pronounced ability to contain its dynamics within limited horizons. The latter point applies to the geopolitical context (the *sakoku* policy was only the most extreme episode in a long history of autonomous development) as well as to the historical continuity embedded in symbols and institutions. This duality could be taken as a guideline for the interpretation of Japanese civilisation and its road to modernity. One of the main tasks would then be to show how the above-mentioned characteristics – the interplay of unifying and pluralising factors within the patterns of culture and power, and the interaction of those two dimensions – is related to the dialectic of dynamism and containment. This is, obviously, a program to be pursued elsewhere; but we might end with the suggestion that if postmodernism has helped to sensitise social theory to some questions in this area, its role is rather like that of the proverbial ladder which should be climbed and then kicked away.[21]

Notes

1. von Laue, 1987; Latouche, 1989.
2. The source of this description is worth quoting at greater length: 'Japan is the comparative historian's delight and despair because

29

all the elements which shaped what we loosely call Western history – feudalism, faith, religion, the forces of the organized market, and the existence of groups interested in the workings of nature – were present *together* with the factors which formed what we loosely call Far Eastern history – rice monoculture, sophisticated village and clan structures, literati bureaucracies, and an ideographic script' (Steenstrup, 1976: 2). Something similar might be said about modern Japan: it is both the most striking example of modernisation going beyond Westernisation and the most conspicuous example of the reactivation of premodern traditions. That this mixture has already proved explosive – and might do so again – is not a reason for not taking it seriously.

3. Most commentators on *glasnost* and *perestroika* have neglected this Japanese connection. If I am not mistaken, the first to draw attention to it was the French geographer Lacoste (Lacoste, 1989).

4. Johnson, 1988: 3.

5. Beaud, 1990.

6. For a particularly clear formulation of this thesis, cf. Hamilton, 1989.

7. It should be noted that Weber's analysis of Confucianism has always been controversial; some of his earliest critics took the view that Confucian teachings were conducive to economic rationalisation, but that this path had been blocked by other forces in Chinese society.

8. Cf. Murakami, 1990: 16–19.

9. Murray (Murray and Price, 1990: 10) applies the concept to ancient Sparta, but quotes Lévi-Strauss as its original source.

10. For a very interesting discussion of this cultural phenomenon, cf. Arzeni, 1987. As Arzeni shows, 'The Japanese tradition had, mainly through processes of simplification and symbolization, anticipated some trends that rose to prominence in Western culture during the nineteenth century' (p. 28); in her view, 'Japanism' thus made a genuine contribution to the new vision of the relationship between man and nature that was most forcefully expressed in impressionist painting.

11. Miyoshi and Harootunian, 1987: VIII 'Introduction'.

12. Cf. Bauman, 1991: 33–46. This is perhaps the most interesting attempt to theorise the notion of postmodernity, but in the last instance Bauman's argument seems to point to the conclusion that postmodernity is an episode within modernity, rather than an epoch which comes after it.

13. This paper is primarily concerned with Western uses of the concept of postmodernity in relation to Japan, as well as with some Japanese echoes of them. Japanese visions of Western postmodernity are

another matter, and to the best of my knowledge, there is no extensive account of them in any Western language. But an early and interesting example is worth mentioning. The historian Naitō Konan (1866–1934), whose pioneering work on Chinese history influenced later Western scholars, argued that China had reached the stage of 'early modernity' under the Song dynasty (960–1279). This interpretation raised new questions about the subsequent divergence of developmental patterns in China and the West; one of Naitō's disciples took the following view: 'China had both a renaissance and a reformation, though it had neither a French revolution nor an industrial revolution. The latter are characteristic of post-modern (*saikinsei*) rather than of modern Europe' (Miyakawa, 1954–5: 546). In this case, the concept of postmodernity is applied to the very events which its present advocates regard as the main landmarks of modernity.

14. Cf. Sugimoto, 1990: 48–59. Cf. also Kosaka's paper in the present volume.

15. Asada's (1985: 101) position is ambiguous: he sets out to analyse the phenomenon of postmodern capitalism, but arrives at conclusions which seem to undermine this idea.

16. I am indebted to Professor Kobayashi Yasuo, Tokyo University, for this suggestion.

17. Clammer, 1991: 66.

18. Karatani, 1987: 271.

19. Kato, 1979: 4, 8.

20. Somewhat surprisingly, there seems to be no English translation of this seminal text. I have used the German one (Maruyama, 1988b). The above interpretation of Maruyama's later work draws on a discussion with Professor Watanabe Hiroshi, Tokyo University, to whom I am also indebted for comments on an earlier version of this paper. On the notion of '*basso ostinato*', cf. also Maruyama, 1988a.

21. For an argument which emphasises the relevance of Japan to the Western search for postmodernity, rather than of post-modernism to Japan, cf. Berque, 1992. Berque argues for a 'non-Saidian' approach (in the sense that Western interpretations of Japan cannot be subsumed under the stereotype of Orientalism) and outlines a 'Nipponese paradigm' (based, among other things, on a low degree of centrality of the subject and a strong emphasis on the present) which he sees as a prefiguration of an 'anti-modern Western paradigm'.

3 Work
Postmodernism or Ultramodernism: The Japanese Dilemma at Work

Ross Mouer

Japan as Model: The Postmodern Problematique

In the early 1970s, Dore[1] pointed to the possibility of a reverse convergence in industrial relations by suggesting that Japan had gone beyond the industrial relations of class conflict and work segmentation commonly associated with industrialisation in the West (especially the United Kingdom). While he did not refer to Japan as being 'postmodern' or 'postindustrial', he clearly implied that Japan's industrial relations were qualitatively more advanced than those in the West. He labelled the Japanese approach 'corporate welfarism'. Since then numerous observers have written about the just-in-time system, noting that it too is qualitatively more advanced than the just-in-case systems developed in the West in terms of enforcing new levels of quality control and efficiency on the economy.[2]

Nearly a decade after Dore, Johnson[3] sought to explain Japan's economic structures and strategies in terms of the 'developmental state'. Both scholars found a point of departure in late development theory; both accepted that Japan had somehow leapfrogged from pre-industrialism to postindustrialism without many of the traumas associated with early developers; both saw Japan as 'out in front' in some way. However, the two reached very different conclusions about the meaning of the Japanese experience.

Dore and many others who have sought to push for the adoption of Japanese strategies in industrial relations tended to look favourably on the Japanese approach, seeing in it the seed for a qualitatively different type of industrial relations – an approach which was at the same time more humane and more productive. For Dore, certain Japanese styles might be emulated. Johnson tended to see in the Japanese experience the extension of certain universal themes common to the processes of state-led development which, in his view, had yielded an excessive emphasis on industrial competition and the mobilisation of societies to achieve

the 'goals of development' (that is, superior international economic competitiveness).

For Johnson, there was a warning that the Japanese-style developmental state (which was also emerging elsewhere in East Asia)
might result in the sacrifice of certain democratic principles for
the sake of enhanced competitiveness in narrow terms of international trade. In his warning, we see a further articulation of a
position taken up by numerous others including Nakayama[4] and
Woronoff.[5]

With the push to learn from Japan in the late 1970s and early
1980s, we can see a certain overlap or reinforcement of Dore's
view, a kind of codification of a cultural theory of Japanese
industrial relations and an idealisation of Japanese-style management which is juxtaposed against what is perceived to be a Western style of management. At the same time, in the criticisms of
nihonjinron[6], and in the work of the revisionists (who have sometimes been dismissed simply as 'the Japan bashers'), we find a
deeper questioning as to the extent to which the Japanese experience is unique in a cultural sense, and as to whether Japan's
economic achievements have been born out of a qualitatively
different or desirable state of affairs.

In the area of industrial relations, these two views have been
summarised as the 'post-Fordist view' and the 'ultra-Fordist
view'.[7] For those interested in the future of the modern state and
industrialised societies, the burning question is: Will a system like
that found in Japan take us beyond what we know as advanced
capitalism or beyond the modern arrangements which characterise the industrial state? Or will they serve only to exacerbate
the contradictions which have emerged in many industrialised
societies, though apparently not in Japan? How do just-in-time
systems and other features of Japanese-style management compare with Fordism, just-in-case systems, and other features associated with management in other industrialised societies – not so
much in terms of producing economic efficiencies, but more in
terms of the social arrangements they foster?

The task of sorting through this comparison is not easy or
straightforward. As many writers have noted, we still do not have
a very precise definition of postmodernity. The 'post-ness' of
postmodernity invites us to think in linear terms and to look for
a qualitative and quantitative jump further out into development.
However, as Miyoshi and Harootunian[8] comment, many of the

difficulties involved in assessing the nature of postmodernity in Japan appeared earlier in the assessment of its modernity. They even warn about the dangers of confusing Japan's nonmodernity with the West's postmodernity. This warning has a particular relevance when discussing Japan's industrial relations because so much of it is attributed to tradition, a tradition which was once dismissed as premodern and feudalistic but which also clearly contained modernising and postmodernising elements.

Although the debate about the merits of Japanese-style industrial relations has continued for more than a decade, we still have little more than the shift to postindustrial production (that is, the emergence of the tertiary and high-tech sectors and the re-allocation of the labour force accompanying that shift) as concrete evidence of qualitative change. There are significant differences among the systems developed by Toyota, Fujitsu, Sony and a few other firms in Japan's exporting industries, and certainly great differences between the practices of firms in those industries as a whole and the practices found in firms in Japan's many non-competitive industries. Can the advanced experiences of a few firms be extrapolated and used to characterise as 'advanced' or 'postmodern' relationships in Japanese society as a whole? Or is it the tremendous variation in practice, the very willingness of Japanese firms to experiment in different ways in a truly *ad hoc* manner, that represents the playfulness associated with postmodernity?

Unfortunately, as Bauman writes, the literature on postmodernism seldom goes 'beyond the boundary of the spiritual, into the changing social figuration which the artistic, cultural and cognitive developments, bracketed as postmodern, may reflect'.[9] To be sure, in the case of Japan's industrial relations, we are still at the stage of trying to assess the spiritual and the cultural at work.

Bauman's solution[10] is to accept postmodernism both as an extension of modernity and as a distinctly new problematic. However, while accepting an historical link, for the postmodern is born out of the modern, it is in the distinguishing features that we have the rationale for a new label. One strategy, then, is to examine the extent to which we have old wine in new skins. To what extent have the values of modernity simply been taken to, or even beyond, their logical conclusions? The other strategy is to search for qualitatively new departures – that which is new, that which cuts across the push for modernity, and that which takes society neither forward nor backwards in terms of modernity but rather in altogether different directions.

Changes in the relationship of the household to the firm and in the divisions of labour which separate housework from paid work connect to both these lines of inquiry. There is a general acceptance that the emergence of the wage labour market was accompanied by the siphoning-off of workers (especially males) from economic activity within the household to production within the firm. A major consequence has been the separation of male and female economic domains, and the emergence of a new ethic to legitimate this division of labour. Another has been the tendency to attach value to work outside the home and not to recognise the economic value of work inside the home. In the discourse of economics and modernisation, cottage industry has always been associated with backwardness and feudalistic human relationships. Along with this has gone the tendency for work outside the home to be seen as a more rational means to accomplish goals within the home. One comes to work for a living, and the connection between work and that living becomes more problematic – a source of higher productivity in narrow monetary terms of comparative advantage but also a source of alienation as specialisation deepens and the nexus between the ends and the means becomes increasingly intangible.

The sense of alienation is at least twofold. One aspect concerns playfulness. As the importance of the family declines as an economic unit, the locus of formal discipline necessary for higher levels of interdependent specialisation is shifted outside the home; one must work seriously at work and can play or relax only at home. The delineation between the domains of work and leisure becomes clearer. The second sense of alienation is in terms of greater skill specification, the increasing assignment of individuals to specific and monotonous functions. Individuals come to be seen as being interchangeable, and as being of less importance in terms of any critical contribution to a final product.

Both the commonly perceived experience in Japan and the second industrial revolution seem to challenge the viability of these industrial relations, although, to be sure, we have had theories of embourgeoisement in the West. As for the Japanese experience, since the 1950s a growing emphasis has been placed on the ability of paternalistic management to subsume the Japanese family – partly by replicating functions of the family and enhancing the sense of the employee's belonging through corporate welfarism as described by Dore, partly through the maintenance of an age-based social order parallelling that of the family, and partly by integrating households *per se* into the production system through an elaborate system of subcontracting, which may be said to have culminated in the just-in-time system. On the other hand, given a strong commitment to the firm, the development of broad skills or multiskilling is seen as having been one reason for lower levels of alienation at work. The image of the well-adjusted Japanese worker doing callisthenics, singing the company song and taking pride in his company's products and his small contribution to their success in the marketplace is often contrasted with the alienated American worker dependent on drugs and somewhat oblivious to his organic link to the wellbeing of his firm or to any final product it might produce. While the early American experiments with humanistic management and the later Swedish attempts to involve workers in the total production process seemed to address such issues, they were focused on arrangements at work and never really incorporated the family the way Japanese management has allegedly done.

Quite apart from the Japanese experience, observers have, over some decades, noted more universal effects flowing from the global revolution in technology. In particular, the high tech industries and the concomitant growth of the service industries has highlighted the move to different arrangements at work. The drop in unionisation common both to Japan and the other capitalist economies has been attributed to the shift of the labour force away from traditional manufacturing to the high-tech and service industries. Not only has there been a demand for more highly educated or more sophisticated workers with more flexible sets of skills; the need of these new industries to respond to a greater variety of tastes or niche markets has also put a premium on a greater interconnectedness with the product market (for example, with the worker's family as consumers). The appearance of taste and touch cultures has underlined the importance of feedback through interpersonal communication. The ability of Japanese firms to respond to changes internationally has been attributed to a peculiarly Japanese pattern of multiskilling and to the firm's ability to remain in touch with ordinary households.[11]

It is in the context of the search for the more universal characteristics which might depict postmodernism that we become aware

also of a certain alienation in Japan. In the past the union movement has, in the modernist mode, simply pushed for higher wages
– incomes on par with those in Europe and North America.
Having achieved those incomes and the fullest array of consumer
durables, however, many Japanese continue to feel a certain emptiness, and there seems to be a realisation that high incomes do
not necessarily transform into a high standard of living. Two
operative phrases in Japanese are *'yutaka na seikatsu'* and *'yutori
no aru seikatsu'* (both referring to a certain margin or quality
allowing ordinary folk to have a sense of being magnanimous in
their everyday lives).

In shifting its emphasis from wages on par with those in Europe
to attaining a standard of living on par with that in Europe, the
union movement has come to attach more importance to increasing leisure time and to having a sense of humanity restored to
work. This sense of humanity is quite ambiguous, but refers to a
decrease of invidious forms of competition among workmates
and some kind of fuller integration of the individual's life at work
with his or her life at home. How to achieve these two goals is
not clear. As numerous scholars have argued, increased leisure
is not meaningful without the infrastructure and income guarantees necessary for workers to utilise such time fully. A major
characteristic of leisure in Japan is that it is used passively.
Further, there has been a strong separation of work from family
life, although many Japanese have felt the need to enrich themselves for work by reading volumes on self-improvement and
specific work skills during their leisure time. Finally, the *ie*
(traditional Japanese concept of the household) as a producing
economic unit probably remains implanted in the minds of many
Japanese; employment outside the home and strict constraints on
the household as an economic unit (for example, high taxes
on inheritance, or crowded housing conditions and the shortage
of land) have undermined the ability of the family to function as
the *ie*.

My feeling from talking to several union officials over recent
years and from reading some of the literature coming out of the
union movement is that the unions are groping for a way ahead,
but are still locked into the modernist mode, ultimately unable
to view the standard of living as separate from higher monetary
income and, therefore, from a further commitment to the present
arrangements for raising productivity. Rather than having a defi-

nite plan to raise the standard of living, they are left simply hoping for an increase in absolute size of their share of the pie. In that, there is nothing new. This is not to say that Japanese unions have not been effective in their strategy to raise incomes. It is, however, to say that we have yet to see a departure radically different enough to be labelled 'postmodern'.

The interrelationships between increased leisure and the restoration of humanity are not clear. However, without clarifying such relationships, it will be difficult to evaluate shifts in the organisation of work in Japan in terms of a concept like postmodernity. This paper reports on some research designed to clarify the interrelationship between the leisure and work domains. For this research, the key concept in terms of postmodernity is 'playfulness'. The key questions then are: How much play is there in work? How much work is there in play? What are the overlaps between work and play? How specialised are the domains of work and leisure, and what are the possibilities that the two can be juxtaposed or intertwined in an integrated manner? Is the relationship between work and leisure such that synergies are created which lift the standard of living of the ordinary employee's family beyond what is achieved purely by increases in monetary income? Is there a changed perception that further specialisation may be irrational? Is there in the lives of workers (as opposed to attitude surveys) any sign that new attitudes towards work and leisure are emerging?

To answer those sorts of questions, four areas at work were examined in a Japanese and an American bakery. First, how did skills at work relate to skills at home? Second, to what extent was the final product at work utilised at home? Third, to what extent were social relationships at work integrated with those at home? Fourth, to what extent were the physical means of production (tools, machinery etc.) utilised at home? Before reporting on the findings, however, the two case studies need to be introduced.

The Case Studies

To examine the connections between life at work and life at home, the experiences of production workers in an American bakery were compared with those in a Japanese bakery. Fieldwork was carried out for three weeks in the United States in December 1990 and for two weeks in Japan in January 1991. The fieldwork began with interviews with the plant managers and production submanagers or supervisors. A day was spent 'mapping out' the physical setup and memorising the worker's names as they

Table 3.1 The two bakeries

	Japan	US
Number of employees at bakery	100	100
Number of employees involved in production	60–70	60–70
Batch size	small	medium–large
Union situation	no union	3 unions (firm) 2 unions (in production)
Location	satellite city servicing area with 10–12 million persons	satellite city servicing area with 3–5 million persons
Age of factory	10 years	5 years
Production process	standard sponge packaging	standard sponge packaging
Divisions at the factory	mechanised baking hand-made baking	mechanised baking maintenance sanitation
Labour force composition	ethnically homogenous several employment statuses drawn from peripheral labour force	ethnically mixed homogeneous in terms of employment status drawn from mainstream labour force

appeared on factory lists and were noted during a tour of the premises on the first day. The remaining time was spent freely roaming the factory floor and discussing various matters with the workers, both on the job and in the canteens during breaks. I was able to take photographs freely in the Japanese bakery but was not permitted to do so in the American plant. The bakeries were chosen for having similar production processes, for not being involved in exporting or in competing with exports, and for not having foreign investment/management inputs.

Table 3.1 provides information on the main parameters for each case study. Each bakery employed about 100 persons, with around 60–70 being involved in production. In neither factory was the factory manager involved in production, although in both factories the production supervisor or sub-manager frequently moved around the factory and filled in where necessary after the production plan for the day had been put in motion. The American manager had worked his way up through sales, whereas the Japanese factory manager had been invited in after a successful career in a large flour company which had supplied confectionery goods to the bakery. Both managers were married. The American was in his forties and had school-aged children; his counterpart was in his late fifties, with children who had already become independent. Both managers were in the process of familiarising themselves with production matters and left all baking decisions to the production supervisor. The American manager made a point of working several jobs on each shift to get a feel for the work and processes. He dressed casually and frequently walked around the factory or came into the canteens and seemed to have a very good first name rapport with the employees. The Japanese manager always wore a suit and was less likely to be seen on the floor; he seemed to have a somewhat more formal and distant relationship with his employees.

At both bakeries the production submanagers were single males in their thirties. Each had, or had had, a steady relationship with one of the females under their supervision.

Owing to differences in organisation and in the product mix, it is difficult to draw meaningful comparisons of worker productivity. The same tonnage of dough can be stretched and used in many ways. Pieces of output come in many shapes and sizes, sometimes with fillings and sometimes without. However, the basic processes were the same, and included each of the steps shown in Figure 3.1. Nevertheless, the two factories differed significantly in four ways.

Marketing strategy

The first difference lay in marketing strategy. The American bakery produced about 250 product lines. However, the lines were basically variations of the same dough mix, from which rolls of different sizes and shapes were formed.

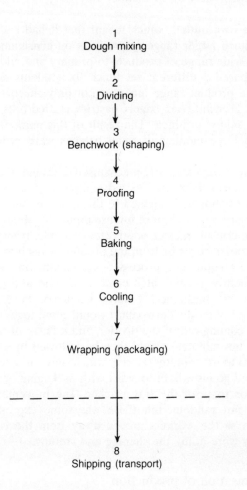

Figure 3.1 The production process

Although the bread was marketed in retail stores, and production requirements varied considerably from week to week as the seasons changed, reaching peaks on certain holiday weekends, in the summer and at the end of the year, important to the bakery's marketing strategy were its accounts with a large number of restaurants for large batches of a smaller range of items on any given day.

The Japanese bakery produced a similar number of products,

but had its own outlets, which meant that it had consistently to supply a much larger range of products on consignment. It also supplied a wide range of products to primary and middle schools which prepared a different set lunch for students across many grades. The product range included not only sliced white bread loaves, but French bread, bagels, pastries, stuffed rolls, curry buns and other 'fiddly' products. The result of this marketing strategy was that a large number of small batches were produced each day.

Both plants were similarly mechanised, although the American plant had newer, more automated equipment that could handle much larger volumes. It seemed to this observer that the American machinery required more intense inputs of labour at a steady pace at the crucial transfer points (for example, from the divider into the proofer boxes or from the proofer boxes into the ovens). The Japanese equipment processed less volume and was stopped more frequently as one batch came to an end and another was started, or as mechanical failures occurred. Several workers (including an older dividerwoman) would come together to shape the dough coming out of the divider, and a flurry of activity (say, for five to ten minutes) would then be followed by a brief down period (two to ten minutes) during which time the workers would disperse and go elsewhere to assist with packaging or to do some sweeping or to reset the tray stacker. The movement to other work was not random, but there was some expression of re-orientation as the workers moved away from the conveyor on which they were doing the shaping and stuffing.

The organisation of production

The second difference lay in production organisation. The American bakery was run by three organisationally distinct groups of employees over three shifts. In addition to the 50 bakers and packers directly on the production line, there were about ten sanitors and ten maintenance workers. These groups strongly affected the way the plant was organised and skill was conceived. Those in the first two groups were members of the Bakers' Union and could move back and forth through bidding as described below. The engineers had their own union. However, rather than hardening lines of work demarcation, this clear division of labour tended to facilitate labour exchange. It also meant that the factory was always immaculately clean, and that machinery seldom broke down. The three shifts meant that there was a shift consciousness, an identity with members of the same shift which seemed to cut across the lines of work demarcation. Workers used the same two canteens for meals and breaks, and this also served to bridge cleavages resulting from demarcation.

The Japanese bakery was run by one group of workers over an extended single shift. The bakers were all responsible for maintenance and sanitation. The result, however, was not multi-skilling. Rather, maintenance and sanitation were left in limbo; the factory was filthy and minor breakdowns (including tray jams) were frequent. The major organisational division was between the production of handmade bread and pastries in small batches on the second floor and the production line approach for loaves and larger batches of standardised items on the first floor. The analysis presented here focuses largely on the workers on the first floor.

Composition of the labour force

The third difference lay in labour force composition. The Japanese bakery drew on an ethnically homogenous labour force. The seventy workers in the American bakery consisted of fifteen Vietnamese-Americans, five Cambodian-Americans, fifteen Mexican-Americans, five black Americans and perhaps thirty 'white Americans' (although some of these had identities as Polish- or Italian-Americans). The foremen were drawn from each of these groups, an arrangement which seemed to minimise communication problems, although each ethnic group seemed to be spread across the three shifts. The production submanager was white; his assistant, black. The engineers were all male and all 'white'. The Asians and women seemed to be concentrated more in packaging, though not completely so. One foreman was a woman. Racial tensions seemed to be absent and drugs did not appear to be in use.

Two divisions were pronounced at the Japanese bakery. One was the use of older women on a part-time basis to do the packaging. These women arrived late in the morning and worked until about 5–6 p.m. Most were grandmothers; they had a robust sense of comradery and were the most jovial group in the factory (despite being the least well remunerated). The second division was among workers on each of the two floors. Those on the second were the more skilled, and unlike those on the first floor, usually engaged in the whole range of tasks from dough mixing to baking and rack cooling. While some women performed this kind of work, they seemed to be called upon to do the packaging. I did not witness any movement of workers between the two floors.

Overall, the feeling one received on the Japanese shop floor was that the workers on this level represented the 'down-and-out' of the Japanese labour force. In appearance, many of the employees had physical characteristics which somehow symbolised their work status – an oddly shaped nose, buck teeth or conspicuously filled teeth, awkward mannerisms, inarticulate speech, and unsightly scars and untreated growths which would set them apart from the mainstream. Compared with their American counterparts, the Japanese employees seemed to be less responsive not only to my presence but also to that of their workmates. In their interactions with workmates, they tended to keep their eyes on their work. Although management mentioned the high turnover rate, one had the distinct feeling that few of these workers would do any better elsewhere in the workforce. The ambience of the American factory provided a sharp contrast. Not only were there a good number of attractive men and women in each ethnic group; they exhibited in their carriage an optimism absent in the Japanese factory.

Workers in both factories were aware of the big bakeries with more than 1,000 employees. Workers in both factories knew that workers in the larger bakeries had better wages (perhaps 30–50 per cent more in Japan and 10–20 per cent more in the US). Both sets of workers saw those better wages as being accompanied by more regulated work practices. In Japan, however, the large bakeries were also seen as offering a clean work environment, neat uniforms and a secure economic future. Movement to the larger factory was, however, not a matter of choice for the Japanese workers. They saw the larger firm as being closed off from their world. They seemed resigned to their situation, free to move to work elsewhere but with little opportunity or strategy for upward mobility. The American workers seemed much more optimistic about their chances for mobility. There was a feeling that their factory had the best maintenance team around, a view which enhanced their sense of professionalism 'in being able to get the job done' and which served to legitimate the somewhat (20–30 per cent) higher wages which the engineers received. In each factory there was one university graduate; however, 10–15 of the American workers had some tertiary education or were doing part-time study, and this was not the case in Japan. Most had plans for the future which meant that some would stay where they were and some would eventually move on. In summary, those in the Japanese bakery were clearly part of an understratum, at the periphery of the Japanese labour force. Their American counterparts were in a more intermediate position, with access to positions much in the mainstream of the American work experience. In appearance, they would not have stood out from others in the workforce.

The union

The last of the four major differences lay in the domain of the union. As explained above, the American workers belonged to one of two unions. While the production submanager was not a union member, the factory manager had worked his way up through sales and was a member of yet a third union, the Teamsters (which had organised sales representatives and those in the transportation division). There was no union at the Japanese firm.

Without further comparative research, it is difficult to assess the impact of the union in only the one culture. However, its presence seemed significant on two counts. First, by implementing a strict seniority system, it imposed order on the labour force and served to minimise the intrusion of arbitrary or discriminatory treatment. However, seniority did not come through in terms of wages as it did in Japan. The engineers aside (at about $18 per hour), the hourly wages earned by the bakers varied only slightly, from about $12 for those in packaging to $13 for those in mixing, with only an extra dollar per hour for foremen. Seniority was very important, not only in terms of job security but even more importantly in terms of job and shift bidding. The choice of one's shift and the right to a shift position on explicit and objective grounds was critical in the workers' high levels of motivation. Although management was not so constrained in appointing foremen, rapport with other workers was a key qualification. To some extent, older workers seemed happy for younger workers to fill that demanding position and to be paid extra for the trouble.

The union functioned in a second manner to reinforce discipline. Although the union would describe this set of functions in terms of its machinery for handling grievances, and would emphasise the eradication of the boss's unfair directives or harassment of workers, the system worked because of the no-nonsense approach to discipline. The rules were clear, and safeguards were in place to protect the employee. However, they were not there to protect bludgers; the union had a drug program, but it was one which required a worker to get his or her own house in order. I was unaware of drugs being used on the premises. I observed and was impressed by the commitment of workers to 'getting the job done'.

One other peculiarity stood out. Although the union representative did not visit while I was doing my fieldwork, I was able to accompany him on several trips to bakeries. He was on a first-name basis with most of the workers (not just the shop stewards), and in making his rounds was constantly asking about family members and other personal matters. He had been in the industry for over thirty years; his father too had been a baker. With older members he served as a news medium, for example relaying news about the recovery from a heart attack of an older worker in one bakery to an older worker in another bakery. The news was carried not only from one bakery to another, but also from one region to another. The shop stewards where I did my fieldwork spoke highly of the union representative. These stewards were quite conscientous, and were more likely to attend training sessions, held once or twice a year at the union's offices on a Saturday.

It was evident from my talks with both the union representative and the factory manager that there was a good deal of mutual respect and a businesslike working arrangement between the two. For both, time was money, and neither had time for employees or unionists who sought to disrupt the ability of management or workers 'to get the job done'. This is not to say that either was unfamiliar with the frailties of human nature and would not bend over backwards to assist a specific employee through a hardship. However, there seemed to be a firm capacity to step back and draw a line at some point.

Although this aspect of the union's presence was not investigated further, it did seem that the presence of this union representative would have contributed to a sense of family both at the place of work and in the industry (or that part of it that was unionised).

The Findings on the Overlap of the Work and Leisure Domains

The initial findings are summarised in Table 3.2. Although they seem to be fairly straightforward, a few comments might be added.

Table 3.2 The linkages between the work and home domains

	Japan	US
Use of final products	very little, from discount store	some purchases from the floor making custom-designed loaves
Use of tools	none	extensive use among engineers limited use by sanitors some on-site baking by bakers
Use of work skills	none	extensive use among engineers limited use by sanitors little by bakers
Interpersonal relationships	some outside socialising with workmates but very limited almost no overlap with home domain	extensive socialising with workmates outside of work considerable overlap with the home domain

Use of the final product

Both bakeries had a discount store stocked with their products. A few of the Japanese employees would purchase goods there for lunch or to take home. The Americans consistently brought their own lunches, although they could occasionally be seen eating bread off the production line. The day's products could be bought

directly from the production supervisor at a nominal price. Overall, the feedback I received was that neither group of workers
took bread home as a staple for their family. At both bakeries
employees mentioned that their wives preferred to buy other
brands largely because of convenience (that is, their own bread
was not available in the local store). I had the feeling from talks
with both managements that they would be pleased if workers
took more of an interest in the final product, and that arrangements would be made to encourage any worker with an interest
in learning more about the factory's products. Management at
both firms lamented the fact that most of the employees were
not really able to discern good bread from inferior bread apart
from seeing that a piece might be soiled or misshaped in one
way or another. Management in both bakeries would like to
have thought the families of their employees identified with their
product, but neither management was under any illusion in that
regard.

Two practices, however, were peculiar to the American
workers. One was the practice of some workers occasionally to
purchase sizeable amounts of bread off the floor to take home
for a party or to give to neighbours or relatives. The second was
the occasional use of the facilities (usually on the graveyard shift)
to make specially designed bread. The idea of doing so no doubt
came from the fact that restaurants sometimes ordered such
bread. One worker mentioned having made a 20-foot-long dinner
roll for a party to celebrate the end of the season for his son's
Little League Team. Others mentioned making bread in the shape
of a lobster or some animal for a birthday party or other celebration. It was clear that there was a stronger identification with the
product in America which extended into one's family domain.[12]

Use of tools

Here the organisational structure could be said to have made a
significant difference. In the bakery processes themselves, there
are no real tools to be used and little equipment that can easily
be transported home. One can think of some pans, moulds and
trays. There are many of each of these types of items around,
but I had the feeling that both managements would be wary of
opening the way for the borrowing of these things, perhaps
because such a policy would be difficult to police.

However, there was considerable leeway for the engineers, and to a lesser extent the sanitors, to use tools and equipment from the American bakery. Officially, their management took a dim view of such borrowings and would doubtless have turned down any direct request for permission to do so. However, the factory manager was aware that borrowings did occur, but seemed willing to leave it as an informal practice, as long as the division sub-managers took full responsibility and there was no loss and no disruption to production. There had previously been a vehicle division which looked after the company's delivery trucks. Rumour was that persons in that division had used the facilities to work on their own private vehicles and that things had gotten out of hand. However, the engineers frequently borrowed tools and equipment to work on their cars or other jobs *at home*, and seemed to be very disciplined in the matter of returning the tools. A small group, they were fairly tightly knit and had a strong *espirit de corps*. The sanitation division did not have many tools, and most of the equipment was run off a central compressor system. Nevertheless, the sanitors did use various kinds of insecticides and cleaning agents, and some had a special state license or were studying for such to be able to use certain chemicals. The rumour was that their homes were usually freer from cockroaches and similar vermin than were their neighbours' homes.

Use of work skills

As would be apparent from the preceding discussion, engineers and sanitors had opportunities to use their work skills at home. In the case of the engineers, one would have to say that the flow of skills was two-way. Much of their work involved general repair (for example, to electrical wiring and switches, to mechanical devices, as well as fabricating new items and performing plumbing) or the adjustment of settings. Their skills had been learned over the years from actually solving specific problems. Accordingly, it is not surprising that in solving problems with personal projects at home, they came across more general solutions for problems that might arise at work, and thus a work skill was acquired.

With regard to the transfer of skills, it might also be mentioned that sanitors were responsible for disassembling equipment in order to clean it thoroughly, and this added not only to their machine literacy in the factory, but also to their latent pool of 'home repair skills'. They were also well positioned at times to look over the shoulder of one of the engineers when equipment was being repaired. This allowed them to further acquire some of the more obvious skills simply by watching. Among the engineers there was one who had specialised knowledge of electrical matters, one who was a metal fabricator, one who was a carpenter, one who was a refrigeration mechanic, and one who was a machine specialist. Although each engineer had a specific machine for which they were responsible, at the same time each was able to draw on the expertise of the team's specialist when his 'baby' required specialist treatment. This arrangement allowed the engineers to acquire a broad range of skills on the job. Several times one of the youngest and least skilled engineers commented on how great it was to be working with such a capable set of engineers who were always willing to share their skills.

A common topic of discussion among the engineers was the repair of a vehicle at home. It was a common assumption that each would work on their own cars and do all home repairs. In their workshop, discussion commonly revolved around problems that would arise because of the peculiarities of the specific model of car, lawn mower, refrigerator or television for which a part could not be obtained, or around the procedures for some kind of fabrication.

The extension of interpersonal relations

Although my examination of this area was inadequate in the Japanese bakery, my feeling was that there was very little interaction either among workmates away from the factory or between workmates and their families. Much of the information I obtained in this regard in the American bakery was picked up in the canteens during the meal and coffee breaks. In the canteens, workers talked at great length among themselves about their outings together or about family matters. The movement in and out of the canteens was constant, with some there for the 30-minute meal break and others for the short breaks. I was able simply to overhear and then at times follow up conversations when others returned to work leaving only one employee behind.

In Japan, however, I found that many workers only took their lunch breaks and that many of the male workers did not come to the canteen. I was told that they went to their cars, ate by themselves, and listened to music while quietly resting during their break. In the factory canteen, most interaction occurred among the older women. They were quick to initiate conversation among themselves and with me about their social activities and the doings of their family members. In some cases, the younger women (recent graduates from secondary school) were brought into their conversations, and sometimes the younger women would talk about news events and such, but in a more reserved manner. When the men did talk, they would comment mainly on an aspect of work, on the weather, or on sports or a popular entertainer as their attention was drawn to something on the television.

On the job as well, the older women were much more talkative. Their animated exchanges could be said to have had a play-like quality. Among the male workers and the younger women, play-like activity was conspicuously absent. One had much the sense that the bakery was a dungeon for hard physical work, not a plaza for social exchange. This atmosphere was accentuated by the general accumulation of dark gunge on the floor and equipment (owing to there being no sanitors) and to the dim lighting.

The ambience of the American bakery was quite different. Clean, brightly lit and cheerful, there was a constant flow of conversation, often about leisure-time activities, friends and family, but the workers could shift into information-relay mode should a hitch occur in the rhythm of the work. Management seemed to tolerate that kind of interaction, but for safety and productivity reasons held a fairly tight reign over horseplay in the production area.

However, there was a striking difference in the extent to which the Americans socialised outside of work. Some played cards together each week. Several went off and played darts regularly. Still others had formed a basketball team and competed in a league of factory teams. Some went less frequently on extended excursions together (for example, driving some two to four hours) to sports or entertainment events. One or two fellows even took workmates in different years on fishing or hunting trips utilising the full two weeks of annual leave, trips which were done on a family basis or at least with married couples. As far as I could tell, these were fairly spontaneous activities; aside from the card players, there was little compulsion to participate and the activities were not ethnically-based.

At the Japanese bakery, this kind of socialising did not seem to occur. One person mentioned the fact that they worked six days a week (compared with five in the American situation), and that there were long commuting times between work and home and between the homes of different workmates. There did not seem to be a particular aversion to socialising; it was just not convenient, and the practice of having workmates over to one's home for socialising was less common. Nor were there the *tsukiai* relationships described by Atsumi[13] in her study of salaried office workers, or found amongst the more skilled printers studied by Leung.[14]

While I was doing fieldwork at the Japanese bakery, the annual New Year's party was held at the best local hotel. I was shown a video of the previous party. Families were not invited and the affair tended to be rather formal, with the directors and managers wearing dark suits and sitting together, and 'responsible' persons making speeches. One of the older women (who was somewhat accomplished at dancing) performed and a few groups of younger workers sang songs. A fairly typical Japanese company party, a gathering where people could not really interact or extend relationships developed at work into their home domain. Indeed, during the week leading up to the party, several workers confided that they did not really want to go, that they did not enjoy such occasions, and that they felt they would nevertheless have to go to 'show the flag'. The Japanese bakery also organised a cherry blossom party at a nearby park in the spring. It was a more spontaneous, less formal occasion and seemed to be a more welcome event. Again, families did not join in.

Accounts of the New Year's party in Japan contrasted with accounts of the Fourth of July party held at the American bakery. Families gathered at the American factory in the late afternoon for a picnic which the company paid for. Workers and their families were able to sit on the factory roof and watch fireworks at a nearby fairground. According to the workers I spoke with, the party was remembered as a time when families got together. In the lead-up to Christmas there was a Christmas lunch. The company supplied a turkey and each worker brought a contribution from home. The result was a mixture of ethnic food. This was during a working day, and the families were not involved.

It was held in the engineers' workshop, which the engineers had appropriately decorated with the names of all employees on trees or stockings. Workers wandered in during their breaks and carried on with the ordinary conversation from the canteens, save for the frequent query as to how one employee's family or another would be spending the holidays.

In neither factory did the bakers cook at home. Some indicated that they had had enough of ovens at work; others implied that it was their wife's domain. However, the American bakers were still different, in that they did many of the kinds of jobs around the home which have been mentioned above with regard to the engineers. In particular, they did a good bit of work on their own cars (though of a much simpler, straightforward nature), and many mentioned tools they had around the house for home repairs. They obviously did not have the skills of the engineers or sanitors, but this seemed to be compensated to some extent by a fairly extensive network involving labour exchange. Those who were especially friendly sometimes asked engineers for advice or even invited them over for direct assistance. In so offering their assistance, there may have been a slight sense of *noblesse oblige* on the part of the engineers, but this kind of assistance would have been seen by some as a kind of obligation legitimating their somewhat higher pay and status within the factory. For their labour they might receive a product of the baker's household (some freshly baked cookies) or a ticket to a game, although the guidelines for such exchange were not strict and such an expression of appreciation may not be expected for a one-off visit. I had the feeling that the exchanges among the engineers and perhaps among the sanitors occurred with a bit more calculation of the values involved. Sometimes the bakers themselves would assist each other with yard work or some such activity. An important aspect of these exchanges was that they brought the one worker directly into the house (or yard) of the other, and thereby facilitated a more than passing acquaintance with family.

Postmodernity and Work

In assessing work practices in Japan, one is immediately impressed by the commitment to work – not in the Protestant ethic, value-orientation sense, but in the pervasiveness of work-related pressures on the ordinary family. This can be seen in the high labour force participation rate, the long hours of work, the reluctance to exhaust all of one's accrued annual leave, and in the generally low level of absenteeism and tardiness. Over time, the percentage of working Japanese who are employees has increased, from slightly over 50 per cent in 1960 to nearly 80 per cent by 1990. Although monthly hours of work declined from 203 hours in 1960 to 172 hours in 1975, they have remained rather steady since, even rising slightly to 176 hours in the late 1980s. While the average number of days of annual leave accrued rose from 14.4 days in 1980 to 15.1 days in 1990, the rate of consumption dropped from 61 per cent to 50 per cent over that decade, meaning a drop over the decade in annual leave actually taken from 8.8 days to 7.6 days. Internationally, the Japanese are seen to have exceptionally long work years, with an annual average of around 2,100 hours as compared with 1,600–1,700 hours in many Western European countries (in the US it is about 1,900 hours). Comparatively, this means that Japanese are working the equivalent of 14–15 Western European or American months per year.

Cultural explanations of this phenomenon abound. They are not, however, very satisfactory, because we find that hours of work vary considerably with the workers in the better-paid industries and large firms working the shortest hours, a pattern which would conform to a backward-bending labour supply curve. Moreover, Japanese workaholics abound in the same careers that workaholics do in other countries. Four other kinds of explanation seem more useful. One is the high cost of living. Workers are motivated across the board to seek overtime in order to pay for housing and for various consumer durables (for example, a car, a video player or a stereo), and to save for contingencies generally covered by social welfare schemes in many other countries. Given that this may be the case, a second explanation is that the strong desire of families to achieve a target income and a standard of living in keeping with the norm results in lower income earners doing overtime to catch up. This explanation is also consistent with the inverse relationship commonly observed between the income of the household head (as the primary income earner) and the labour force participation rate of other household members (as secondary income earners). Yet another explanation may be found in the generally low investment in the infrastructure necessary for workers to enjoy their leisure time – public tennis courts and other sports facilities, parkland, better housing. Workers often find their offices air conditioned and attractive, while their homes are not.

A fourth explanation turns attention to the absence of strong unions interested in pursuing minimum standards with regard to social welfare and the above-mentioned types of infrastructure, or, even more importantly, in regulating hours of work. This facet of unionism is particularly important in a country like Australia, where four weeks of paid annual leave and the eight-hour day have a long tradition. A full appreciation of the union situation in Japan requires a long explanation about the 30-year struggle between industrial unions concerned with notions of across-the-board social minimums and the enterprise unions concerned with firm-based productivity improvements.[15] As the latter wins out, we come to see the change in the role of the union from being a defender of minimum conditions to being an administrator facilitating microeconomic reform and the implementation of schemes to maintain hours of work, even extending overtime so that productivity goals can be achieved.

The consequences of the long hours of work in Japan are several. First, many Japanese live a highly monetised lifestyle, with high incomes and high living costs. Japanese eat out a lot, and many other household services are purchased rather than being performed by the worker. Second, male Japanese lack household skills, and housework and similar tasks are almost exclusively left to women, although this might be changing. If we use the term 'housework', this would also be true of many of the male American workers interviewed. However, if we used the term 'work around the house', I suspect that a rather different response would have been forthcoming from the American sample.[16]

It is common for Japanese businessmen to complain about the work ethic in countries like Australia and America. Absenteeism is seen as being high and 'dole bludgers' are thought to wander about aimlessly in great numbers. Workers may put in a fair day's work, but are seen as being uninterested in overtime and lacking in commitment to give that extra bit. Seeing these workers as always being anxious to leave at the end of their shift, the Japanese businessmen seem to assume that in these contries employees are more oriented toward enjoying their leisure in some self-satisfying manner, spending rather than producing and thereby undermining their national economies.

I remember mentioning these perceptions to one of my classes after an article appeared in a local paper with the title, 'Large, Lucky and Lazy!'[17] Immediately, a mature-aged student stood up and exclaimed, 'What do the Japanese mean by "lazy"? I have just spent the weekend changing the oil in my car, mowing two acres of lawn and cleaning my swimming pool!' Other students soon joined in with tales of painting, plumbing, gardening, repairing cars, and building furniture, fences and even house extensions.

Most economic analyses of labour force behaviour utilise some form of indifference curve analysis and tend to divide time into work and leisure. However, my students and the American workers in this research have indicated that there may be yet another category which needs careful consideration in any dissection of their work ethic. For them, one use of leisure is purely for personal enjoyment and involves no serious accounting. Time, in this category, is used for rest, recreation and rehabilitation. However, they clearly conceived of another type of leisure which is used for working around the home and engaging in activities which have a clear economic return: painting, gardening, auto repairs and servicing, and various building projects. The pursuit of many hobbies could also fit into this category.

Conspicuous in the literature on the uses of leisure in Japan are the frequent references to the large amount of time which is used in a passive fashion – watching, reading, listening, or just lying down. Even when we add in the more active uses of leisure (for example, playing tennis, skiing or overseas travel), we are still dealing exclusively with the first type of leisure (hereafter, 'Leisure Type I'). This use of time contrasts not only with work for income at one's place of employment (Work Type I), but also with economically meaningful activity without pay, which also has an element of relaxation and relief from the strict, productivity-oriented supervision associated with Work Type I (hereafter, 'Work/Leisure Type II').

Following this line of reasoning, it might be hypothesised that worker motivation in countries like Australia and the United States must be conceived in terms of this broader meaning of work, which includes both (i) employment in an economic organisation outside the home and (ii) Work/Leisure Type II, which provides considerable economic return within the home. Workers at the American bakery were appreciative of the good wages they received, but also judged their working conditions in terms of how much time and flexibility was provided for engaging in Work/Leisure Type II.

The Japanese workers   The American workers

Work Type I   Work Type I
(12 hours)   (8 hours)

Work/Leisure Type II
(4 hours)

Leisure Type I   Leisure Type I
(12 hours)   (12 hours)

Figure 3.2 The daily use of time by workers in the American and Japanese bakeries

The fieldwork carried out thus far in Japan and the United States generally supports the hypothesis. The uses of time might be along the lines shown for a typical 24–hour period in Figure 3.2. The workers in the Japanese factory did not engage in Work/Leisure Type II, whereas the American workers did. Preliminary interviews in Australia lead me to suspect the same would be true of workers in an Australian bakery. Consistent with this conclusion is the presence of a number of factors at work and in the worker's living environment which allow this to be the case for workers at the American bakery. Those factors were largely missing from the work and home environments of their Japanese counterparts.

Table 3.3 Comparison of Japanese and American factors shaping the utilisation of Leisure/Work Type II

Item		Japan	US
I.	Engagement in Work/Leisure Type II	none or very little	considerable
II.	Factors supporting Work/ Leisure Type II	absent	present
(A)	Work organisation	not supportive	supportive
	(1) use of work skills at home	none	some
	(2) use of work tools at home	none	some
	(3) use of work products at home	very little	some
	(4) labour exchange with work mates	none	considerable
	(5) wage system	productivity based	egalitarian
	(a) seniority	in wages	in shift times
	(b) ability/skill	some in job assgmt	some in job assgmt
		effect on wages	no effect on wages
	(c) performance	effect on bonus	little: job assgmt
(B)	Private life environment		
	(1) possibility of using Work/Leisure Type II	low	high
	(a) Work Type II skills	no	yes
	(b) home ownership	low	high
	(c) chance to learn skills	not available	available
	(d) space	lacking	available
	(2) hours of work	48 (plus commutation)	40 (w/o much commuting)
	(3) security	low	high
	(a) union	nil	strong
	(b) location in labour force	marginal	core-like
	(c) opportunity for mobility	segmented market	open market
	i. upward	nil	some
	ii. sideways	some	considerable
	iii. downwards	already at the bottom	some/nil

Conclusions

Now, what do we make of all this in terms of the debate on modernity and postmodernity? First, much of what is written about the new welfare corporatism is about life in the large firms that collectively employ something like 10–15 per cent of Japan's employees in the private sector. Nearly 80 per cent of Japan's employees are in firms with less than 100 employees and without union representation. The question of the small-scale sector in Japan needs to be understood in terms of the many-tiered system of subcontracting which characterises many industries in Japan, and without which the just-in-time system could not operate. There is little evidence to suggest a major change in the way this system segments the labour force in Japan and allows for an understratum to accumulate in small firms like the Japanese bakery examined in this research.

Second, Japanese society is being restratified. While the new strata vary from the old, there is nothing new about the new order. Indeed, it is now well-enough established to reproduce itself, and in that we see the common features of any system of structured social inequality. If the process of postmodernisation is going ahead in Japan, it is doing so in an uneven manner. The appearance of taste cultures is in no small measure a reflection of strata-linked market segmentation.

Third, the monetisation of life in Japan over the past four decades has tended to result in a lifestyle with sizable cash flows (high incomes and high expenditures) and in the reinforcement of a modernist outlook rather than a postmodernist outlook. The view continues to be that work is primarily a means to an end, without end-product properties (for example, friendship, final products for home use, fun activities as in Work/Leisure Type II) being built into the act of work itself.

In this regard, the mid-1970s seemed to be a turning point. Until then economic growth brought very visible and very tangible improvements to a broad cross-section of the Japanese population. That was the period during which most Japanese households acquired a succession of basic consumer durables and many families moved into more acceptable housing. After that time the more advanced consumer durables have been diffused to only a selected portion of the populace (Figure 3.3).

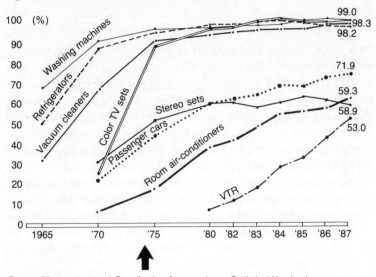

Source: Management and Coordination Agency, *Japan Statistical Yearbook*.
Note: The surveyed units were ordinary households and unmarried laborers by 1981. Since 1982 it is 6,000 ordinary households with two or more persons excluded foreign households.

Figure 3.3 The diffusion rate of durable goods

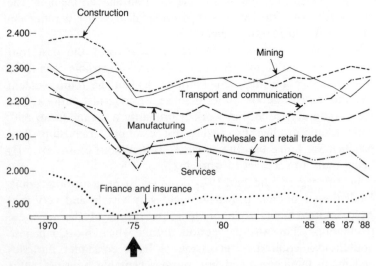

Source: Ministry of Labor, *Monthly Labor Survey*.

Figure 3.4 Trends in total hours of work by industry

60

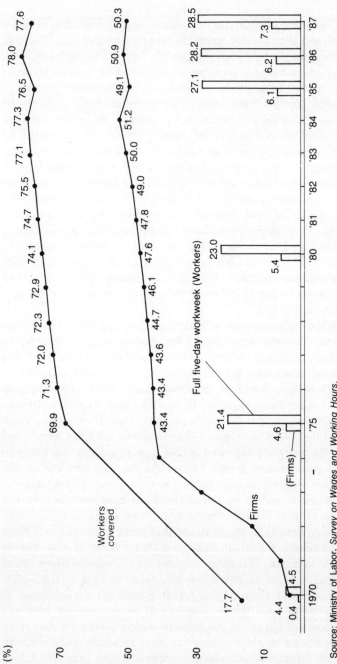

Source: Ministry of Labor, *Survey on Wages and Working Hours.*

Note: Firms with 30 employees or more were surveyed.

Figure 3.5 The spread of the five-day workweek

This bifurcation of lifestyles can also be seen in variation in hours of work and the two-day weekend (Figures 3.4 and 3.5). There is, then, a widening of the gap between the 'haves' and the 'have nots', a division which is seen by many as a cause of the various forms of alienation which seem to be so widespread in the school system.

Related to this, one must also mention Japan's industrial relations in terms of the changing balance of power between unions and management. The turning point here can also be located in the early 1970s. Most theorists writing about Japanese-style management emphasise how its dynamism arose from a delicate balance within the firm between the forces for democracy (humanistic management) and those for efficiency (cf. Table 3.4). While presenting that balance as a uniquely Japanese trait fostered by certain Japanese cultural sensitivities, what most of those theorists failed to show is that the delicate balance ultimately depended on a balance of power between the strong industrial unions and management. With the continuing shift of power to management in the 1970s and 1980s,[18] any semblance of balance was completely lost.

With the union movement undermined or neutralised by 'enterprisation', the way was opened for management to contrive to place high demands on the labour force. One such demand has been long hours of work. In terms of the worker's standard of living, their high degree of mobilisation into Work Type I activity prevents them from engaging in Work/Leisure Type II activities. While the returns for increases in Work Type I were quite large up until the 1970s in terms of the consumer durables mentioned above, the marginal returns for that type of activity are likely to be less pronounced in the future. As the appreciation of the American workers in this study for their good wages suggests, the solution is not to be found simply in home production, but in some kind of balance between the two types of work. High population density in Japan means that many of the opportunities which Americans have to engage in Work Type II may not be available in Japan. This raises another set of considerations about the future of work in Japan, but also takes us back to the advice of Miyoshi and Harootunian[19] that postmodernity in Japan is unlikely to fit exactly the patterns of postmodernity in many other societies. However, the pastiche which is work for American and Australian employees suggests ways in which postmodernity might be differentiated from modernity. For the American worker, the patterns of consumption and work seem to be more varied. Just as postmodernity in architecture may be seen as a juxtaposition of the modern and the premodern, so too in the realm of work might the postmodern be a juxtaposing of work in different domains, one paid in wages and the other in kind, one requiring of the individual a repetitive demonstration of a limited number of specialised skills, and the other the

Table 3.4 Four formulations of the basic components of Japanese-style management

Japanese author	Need for economic efficiency	Need for participation	End product
Nakayama	Efficiency (*nōritsu*)	Fairness (*kōsei*) and Democratisation (*minshuka*)	True Efficiency (*honrai no nōritsu*)
Tsuda	Rationality (*gōrisei*) and Efficiency (*nooritsusei*)	Persuasion (*nattokusei*) and Consent (*gōi*)	Cooperative Life Community (*kyōdō seikatsutai*)
Hazama	Profit-making (*eiri no tsuikyū*)	Continuity of the Company (*kaisha no eizoku*)	Group-Oriented Labour-Management Relations (*shūdanteki rōshi kankei*)
Iwata	Needs of the Organisation (*soshiki no yōkū*)	Individual Needs (*kojin no yōkyū*)	The Formative Principles of Japanese Management (*nihonteki keiei no hensei genri*)

application of a much broader range of skills often in loosely conceived exchanges of labour. To the extent that Japanese firms continue to demand long hours of their workers, work will continue to be dominated by the modernist push for economic rationality as measured in monetary terms and the surplus in the annual balance of payments.

Notes

1. Dore, 1974.
2. For example, Ford, 1991.
3. Johnson, 1982.
4. Nakayama, 1975.
5. Woronoff, 1980.
6. Cf. Sugimoto and Mouer, 1989.
7. Cf. Kato and Steven, 1991.
8. Miyoshi and Harootunian, 1989.
9. Bauman, 1989: 37–63.
10. Bauman, 1991: 33–46.
11. To a considerable degree, that which has been perceived as useful or convenient by Japanese households has been so perceived abroad, and that input has been important in Japanese product design. Of course, the spread of products which can satisfy some universal postmodern taste is not a one-way movement, as the consumption of Coca-Cola and Kentucky Fried Chicken in Japan attest.
12. Here it should be noted that bread has a different status in the diet of Japanese and Americans. However, the Asian-Americans tended to bring rice dishes to work but still found a place for the company product as indicated above. Moreover, bread is a common complement with school lunches and many Japanese have bread or toast at breakfast. Also, the Japanese bakery produced a range of products such as rolls filled with sweet *azuki* bean paste – a common product in most food stores and corner shops. More basic than national differences in diet, I had the feeling that the Japanese bakery's products were not particularly outstanding and did not have a niche in the market as prestige items, as tended to be the case with the American products.
13. Atsumi, 1979: 63–70.
14. Leung, 1991.
15. Cf. Kawanishi, 1992.
16. Mouer, 1987a.
17. Ormonde, 1990: 1 and 6.
18. Cf. Kawanishi, 1992: Chapters 4–7.
19. Miyoshi and Harootunian, 1989.

4 INDUSTRIAL RELATIONS
Is Japanese Capitalism Post-Fordist?

Tetsuro Kato and Rob Steven

Introduction

If present-day Japanese imperialism has a dangerous ideological dimension, then it lies in the myth that Japanese management is, from the worker's point of view, an advance on Western management. It is extraordinary how many people with little direct contact with Japanese workers have become strong advocates of 'Japanese industrial relations'. Although it is not surprising to find such advocates among academics, who endlessly and abstractly 'debate' the issue, it is disturbing to find left-wing circles outside Japan presenting that country's industrial relations system as a progressive alternative. In the United States, Kenney and Florida[1] vigorously argue that what they call *Fujitsuism* is a new progressive stage in the development of capitalism. In Britain, Murray[2] is more ambiguous, but still sees the essentials of the Japanese system as at least containing the seeds of a progressive alternative. In New Zealand, just as ambiguously, the Socialist Unity Party is split over the issue and has members on both sides of a long and bitter dispute over the 'Nissan Way'.

We have decided to contribute to this debate, not by repeating arguments already made, for example by Dohse and others,[3] but by focusing on why the Japanese system is able to present itself as benevolent. Why is one of the cruellest and most oppressive systems of capitalist domination over labour commonly perceived as being one of the most enlightened? The debate today appears in a strange guise and context. A number of left-wing journals in various parts of the world are running articles which suggest that a change to a qualitatively new industrial era, from Fordism to post-Fordism, is taking place in Europe, America and even New Zealand. Historicist assumptions have led certain superficial similarities between the Japanese social formation and the anticipated new era to be taken as evidence that the Japanese system is not backwardly 'superexploitative' after all. Rather, Japan is being

65

seen as nurturing the most advanced form of capitalism, a higher and better stage for workers as well as for everyone else.

In this paper, we concentrate on the debate in the left-wing forums, particularly as presented by Kenney and Florida,[4] Murray[5] and a group of sociologists at Massey University in New Zealand.[6] Of these, only Kenney and Florida claim any expert knowledge of Japan.

The Distortion of Japanese History

Since the debate about the move from Fordism to post-Fordism is about industrial eras or epochs, the Japanese context must be understood in terms of the great moments in Japanese history. Kenney and Florida see the postwar trade union struggles as heralding such a moment, initiating a shift all the way from the tyranny of the prewar regime right into the early stages of post-Fordism. However, with very little historical argument to support their case, they end up grossly exaggerating the gains made by workers in the postwar struggles, arguing that 'many of the characteristics of the Japanese system now interpreted as indicating capital's control of labour were initially worker demands'.[7] Elsewhere they are more explicit:

> Of fundamental importance were the tremendous social
> upheavals and labor militance of the immediate postwar era,
> which helped give rise to the Japanese system of industrial
> relations anchored by enterprise unionism, long-term
> employment tenure, and high degrees of capital-labor
> accommodation.[8]

Although they accept that workers were ultimately defeated in these struggles and that 'an important management weapon was the creation of conservative "enterprise" unions',[9] they do not recognise the full extent of the reverse course. Their implicit conclusion is that Japanese workers won vastly more at that time than their Western counterparts, enough power to initiate a move to a new epoch: 'neither the state nor powerful industrial sectors were able to impose Fordist solutions on postwar Japan'.[10] We know of few Japanese historians bold enough to make such a claim. There is certainly very little evidence for it.

Certain tendencies in the 'regulation theory' they use might account to some extent for what Kenney and Florida have read into working class struggles in postwar Japan. Among these is an historicist assumption that ignores the open-endedness of class struggles, an unconscious assumption that the new 'mode of regulation' must have represented a higher stage of development than the old one. Such a claim might have some plausibility if its implications were confined to Japan. Postwar methods of social control in that country, although regressive from the point of view of Western practice at the time, were nonetheless not as oppressive as what Japanese workers had to endure in the prewar period.

The problem arises when this conclusion is stretched. The postwar industrial unions were ultimately very roundly defeated, and it was in firms where the defeat was most thorough, such as Nissan, that the 'new' managerial practices and company unions were introduced. Nissan was able to bring in a similar package in Britain only after the defeat of militant unionism among British autoworkers.[11] In New Zealand, when the company tried to do so without smashing the relevant unions, it was largely unsuccessful. Class struggles always open the possibility of something new, but there is no necessary reason why history should not on occasion move backwards rather than forwards. Workers can, after all, be defeated.

Kenney and Florida thus greatly exaggerate the newness of the Japanese system which emerged in the 1950s after the defeat of the militant unionism. Many of its features, such as payment by length of service and sizeable bonuses for regular (male) workers in large private firms, with very little of anything for workers in small subcontracted firms, had become widespread in the prewar period.[12] The system was, if anything, pre-Fordist rather than post-Fordist. In fact, one could argue that the defeats sustained by militant unions in the late 1940s and early 1950s resulted in the gains won just after the war being lost and in workers having to accept many features of an older and more reactionary order. True, the system that emerged in the 1950s might not have been the full-blown prewar one, but it was certainly closer to the latter than it was to what workers had hoped for and briefly won after the war, or to what Western workers had won by that time.

Problems in the Debate

The confusion of non-Fordist with post-Fordist

It is not uncommon for Western scholars to draw unwarranted conclusions about Japan from features of Japanese society which they do not find in either Europe or the US. In this case, along with many other regulation theorists, Kenney and Florida[13] tend to call what is apparently non-Fordist, or even pre-Fordist, in Japan (such as the just-in-time system), 'post-Fordist'.[14] The connotation of 'post-Fordism' is that it represents an advance from the worker's point of view:

> The social organisation of production in Japan replaces the fundamental characteristics of Fordism – functional specialisation, task fragmentation, and assembly-line production – with overlapping work roles, job rotation, team-based work units, and relatively flexible production lines.[15]
> ... Japanese corporations actively experimented with new forms of work organisation and production to move beyond the extreme functional specialisation and deskilling of Fordist corporations. The social organisation of Japanese labor is not simply a better or more advanced version of Fordism, it is a distinct alternative to it.[16]
> Postfordist production grew out of an era of intense class conflict and is premised on the particular balance of class power that emerged in postwar Japan.[17]

In Britain, Murray is less sure about how progressive the post-Fordist system actually is:

> it cuts the labour force in two, and leaves large numbers without any work at all.... Post-Fordist capital is restructuring working time for its own convenience: with new shifts, rostering, weekend working, and the regulation of labour, through part-time and casual contracts.[18]

But he then argues that there is a left-wing (socialist) alternative to 'capitalist' post-Fordism:

> Some [of the tendencies of our times] are rooted in the

popular opposition to Fordism. They represent an alternative
version of post-Fordism, which flowered after 1968 in the
community movements and the new craft trade unionism of
alternative plans. Their organisational forms – networks,
workplace democracy, co-operatives, the dissolving of the
platform speaker into meetings in the round – have echoes
in the new textbooks of management, indeed capital has
been quick to take up progressive innovations for its own
purposes. . . . Underlying this split is the post-Fordist bargain
which offers security in return for flexibility. Because of its
cost Japanese capital restricts this bargain to the core; in the
peripheral workforce flexibility is achieved through
insecurity.[19]

Murray is really quite mistaken in putting side by side the flexibility which the new grassroots movements gain through more
democratic organisation and the flexibility which Japanese management imposes on workers in order to shunt them around the
company.

In adhering to the 'British line', Maharey[20] follows the tendency
of both the left and the right in New Zealand. However, he adds
little if anything about Japan. Neither does he seem to recognise
that technologically advanced capitalist societies are very remote
from ones that supply raw materials and food:

At the heart of these changes [in New Zealand] is a more
pluralist, more diverse post-Fordist society where the
individual is taking centre stage. The New Right have
responded to these changes by seeking to reprivatise society. . . .
The alternative response is to develop a democratic
individualism which offers an expansion of rights.[21]

Sources

One final preliminary point needs to be made before we look
more carefully at what Fordism and post-Fordism are meant to
be, and that concerns the sources used by Kenney and Florida.
While we do not wish to argue that any unorthodoxy, such as
their version of regulation theory, might account for their misunderstandings of the Japanese system, their heavy reliance on right-
wing sources written in English is a serious problem. For example,

they seem to accept approvingly Aoki's characterisation of Japanese factories as 'information systems' rather than 'production systems',[22] quite unaware that this is a common move in debates with the left in Japan and also quite unaware of left-wing replies. Although the scarcity of good left-wing literature on Japan in English is well known, one would think that writers who claim to be in the Marxist tradition would make a special effort to locate what is available. Their attempt to be exhaustive as far as right-wing sources are concerned contrasts embarrassingly with their almost total failure to locate quite well-known left-wing sources.

The Essential Elements

Fordism

There is no agreement among regulation theorists on exactly what Fordism is, partly because there is still a lot of debate about what requires regulation. Nevertheless, for the purposes of this paper, we loosely bring together seven features of what is supposed to characterise Fordism:

(1) Products, parts and jobs are highly *standardised*.
(2) Mass-production plants mechanise these standard tasks, so that workers become *unskilled*.
(3) Remaining tasks are subjected to Taylorism; they are scientifically broken down and then assigned to workers by a *hierarchical* management.
(4) Payment is for the *job* rather than for the person doing it, and jobs are clearly demarcated; monotonous ones are rewarded with high wages.
(5) Since mass production requires *mass consumption*, national markets are protected by a Keynesian state.
(6) Monotonous jobs and high labour turnover produce shopfloor *resistance* and strikes.
(7) Rising workplace resistance chokes off the rate of productivity increase and eventually leads to *crisis* and the possibility of a new order, post-Fordism.

Post-Fordism

Although neither Fordism nor post-Fordism exists anywhere in any sort of completeness, regulation theorists tend to see the latter as an emerging tendency in opposition to the existing Fordist order. They identify some of its features in embryonic form in Europe and the US, and in a more advanced form in Japan. The following seven characteristics of post-Fordism have been pieced together by us from a variety of sources:

(1) Products, parts and tasks are *varied*; products aim at different sections of the market (age, gender, income group etc.) and their life becomes much shorter.

(2) Part of the new, more flexible production is achieved by new technology: 'Flexible automation uses general-purpose machines to produce a variety of products'.[23] Workers thus need to have *many skills*.

(3) Management becomes less hierarchical, as multiskilled workers win more *control* over the labour process and take on more of the 'intellectual' tasks previously in the hands of management.

(4) The end of job demarcation means payment is for the *person* rather than the job. Labour can thus be used more flexibly.

(5) The problem of managing the demand for a wide variety of parts and products is met by ordering supplies which coincide more exactly with immediate demand (*just-in-time*).

(6) Security of tenure puts an *end to much resistance and strike* activity, so that workers are more willing to allow use of new technology.

(7) New technology and flexible uses of labour raise productivity and *end the crisis*.

It is beyond the scope of this paper to offer a theoretical critique of the notion of post-Fordism or to look at its so-called embryonic manifestations outside Japan. The Japanese political economy is examined in relation to the above seven characteristics of post-Fordism, in particular to the claims made by Kenney and Florida, and to a lesser extent Murray and Maharey.

The Case of Japan

Standardisation or variety

Astonishingly, none of the writers on post-Fordism in Japan has actually addressed the question of how far Japanese companies have moved away from the mass production of standardised consumer goods. Throughout the boom until 1974, and then again during the years of slower growth, Japanese capital's dominant strategy, at home and abroad, has been to capture the maximum market share for mass-produced consumer goods rather than to aim at high profit rates on shorter runs. It has relied heavily on imports, not just of technology from the US and Europe, but also for the variety of specialised (luxury) goods which are supposed to signify Japan's advance towards post-Fordism somewhat ahead of the countries from which the imports have been coming.

While very recently there has been a lot of talk in Japan about the need for CAD (computer-aided design) and CAM (computer-aided manufacturing) systems to produce a greater variety of goods, this has been mainly a response to the sudden increase in purchasing power among the asset-rich middle and upper classes since the rise of the yen.[24] It is also a consequence of the current internationalisation of Japanese capital, which is locating much of its mass production in low-wage Asian countries so that it can concentrate on newer high-tech lines. However, it has little to do with any so-called change from one industrial era to another. The claim that Japan is in the forefront of a move from mass to specialised production is not borne out by the facts.

Unskilled or multiskilled

According to Murray, who does recognise Toyota's role in breaking industrial unions in Japan, the company then:

> developed a core of multi-skilled workers, whose tasks include
> ... the improvement of the products and processes under
> their control ... tasks customarily reserved for management
> in Fordism.[25]

Murray claims that the experience workers accumulate during their lifelong contracts makes them multiskilled and not easily interchangeable with new workers. Ken Douglas, the President of the New Zealand Council of Trade Unions, argues along the same lines:

> One alternative to Taylorism is to organise production by work groups. Under this form of work organisation a group of workers have a range of work to perform and they determine how it is done. Part of the process is the concept of up-skilling under which workers learn a range of skills because they learn to perform a range of different tasks.[26]

For their part, Kenney and Florida see the Japanese system as being characterised by 'work teams, job rotation, learning by doing, flexible production, and integrated production complexes'.[27] They argue as follows:

> Learning by doing contrasts sharply with traditional Fordist corporate organisation characterised by extreme traditional specialisation and highly compartmentalised information flows.[28]
>
> Japanese production lines are more flexible than traditional assembly lines. . . . Workers thus perform a number of tasks on different machines simultaneously while individual machines 'mind' themselves. . . . Rotation within teams allows workers to familiarise themselves with various aspects of the work process. This creates a powerful learning dynamic and enhances the problem-solving capabilities of both individual workers and teams.[29]
>
> Multi-skilling is absolutely essential for this strategy to be successful. . . . Information sharing is also encouraged by a policy of more open access to information practiced in many Japanese corporations.[30]

However, since the overwhelming strategy is still to win market shares for mass produced consumer goods, we should pause to think about what Japanese workers actually learn to do in their companies.

The essential difference between Western and Japanese workers is not *what* they learn to do, but *for whom* they do it. Western workers who change jobs many times during their lives learn a multiplicity of skills, as do Japanese workers who get moved round the same company during their working lives. However, the appearance at any one point in time is very different. The job the Western worker is doing at that particular time is all that he or she appears skilled enough to do. However, the Japanese worker, who may also at that time be performing only a limited range of relatively simple tasks, can point to other skills possessed because they had previously been learnt and performed in the same workplace. In both cases, when people start new jobs they are told what to do and they learn the job's finer points by actually doing the work. The commonly drawn contrast between so-called Taylorist management in the West, in which the last detail of the simplest of tasks is spelt out by management, and a Japanese system, in which highly versatile workers fathom for themselves what needs to be done, has little basis in fact.

More relevant are the debates about deskilling and reskilling that have always accompanied capitalist development, crisis and restructuring. There have always been unevennesses, short-term contractions and variations by industry, although for the working class as a whole there appears both in Japan and in the West to be a gradual long-term process of deskilling. The reskilling needed for the new industries always tends to apply to a smaller range of workers than were affected by the deskilling process. It is thus difficult to see why Kenney and Florida would select certain skills required in the late 1980s by a limited range of workers in a company like Fujitsu, let alone those found in Fanuc (which makes factory automation equipment), and then to hold them out as the skills needed in a new industrial era. It is impossible to build a case that Japan is different from the West in this regard.

Another of the myths which props up the image of the 'multi-skilled' Japanese worker is the amount of formal education people go through in that country. The 'more educated' Japanese workforce is supposed to be more suited to the skill requirements of the new era's corporations. However, anyone with any knowledge of the Japanese education system knows that it produces graduates with fewer capacities, and certainly with a reduced capacity for innovative thinking, than do the education systems in most Western countries. Its overwhelming emphasis on passing tests to secure access to 'famous' universities actually functions to sort people, not into skilled and unskilled categories, but into students with stoic self-discipline and endless self-sacrifice and students without those qualities. Giving up in the *juku sensō* (war of cram schools) indicates a less than total capacity for self-sacrifice, which is what the recruiting companies really want to acquire. That is why they hire new recruits, not on the basis of their academic results, but on the name of the university whose entrance exam they managed to pass. To pass the exams of the 'top' universities requires little originality, but a capacity to reproduce information which can be memorised only by spending years in one cram school after another.[31] It is absurd to see the Japanese education system as contributing to the creation of a 'multi-skilled' workforce.

Hierarchical management or worker control

According to Kenney and Florida:

> The management structure of Japanese companies is more flexible than that of Fordism. Managers are usually not specialists in accounting, finance, or marketing but generalists who rotate among posts. Management rotation results in flexibility and learning by doing similar to that experienced on the shopfloor. This blurs distinctions between departments, between line and staff managers, and between management and workers.[32]

The argument is related to the question of skill: being multi-skilled rather than having a specific skill, or performing many tasks rather than only one, is supposed to be a source of power. The assumption is that management's control over labour lies in the limitation of workers' skills to one or two simple tasks. However, in practice the opposite has been the case: workers' power to resist the authority of management has always depended on their (collective) capacity to protect their particular jobs. Job rotation undermines workers' power and prepares them for total submission to do whatever tasks management assigns. By constantly being moved from one simple task to another, workers are left with nothing except their status as employees, which is all that management is really interested in, because employees can be used for *any task* whatsoever.

The myth of lifelong job security in Japan is fundamental to the myth of worker control. First, as we have argued elsewhere,[33] lifelong job security applies at most to only about one-third of the Japanese working class (we discuss below what happens to the rest). Second, when it does occur it is accompanied by a system of payment by length of service. That results in some very nasty fishhooks being attached to it. For example, since starting wages for anyone are rarely living wages in Japan – workers only get those after some ten years of loyal service – it is essentially a system of *withheld wages*. In other words, one *has to* stay on in the same company if ever one is to get living wages, and the benefits really only begin to accrue in middle age. Ever since the bubble burst in the mid-1970s, Japanese capital has found its ageing workforce to be a growing burden, and it has been trying to get rid of its older workers well before they reach the legal retirement age of around 60. Lump sum payments are increasingly being offered to middle-aged workers in return for early retirement, a strange thing to do if the multiplicity of skills which workers are supposed to accumulate during their working lives are so valuable to management in the era of post-Fordism.

Japanese management has always and still does prefer younger workers to older workers. For this reason it is happy to employ women who can be induced to retire before they receive their withheld wages. However, Japanese management has had at least to promise higher pay after an extended period of loyal service. A minimal commitment to keep this promise has thus been necessary, and about a third of the workforce – a proportion no higher than the proportion of secure jobs under Western Fordism – has had some sort of security of tenure. On all indicators, apart from the government's official (and somewhat distorted) measures of unemployment, real joblessness in Japan today is higher than it is in the United States.[34]

The third questionable aspect of lifelong employment, to the limited extent that it does exist in Japan, offers workers, not job security – no Japanese worker has that, shunted as they are from one task to another – but the promise of a secure, though not necessarily adequate, livelihood. Since, in an era of mounting worldwide unemployment, such a promise might look more attractive than luxuries such as worker control, it is small wonder that the Japanese system appears attractive and that progressive people are being taken in by it.

In practice, a multiplicity of simple skills acquired over their lifetime offers workers less protection from layoffs than does the power that comes with being needed for a particular job. The real meaning of being multiskilled is being willing to be pushed about for the entirety of one's working life. That is the real qualification which is so 'highly prized' in the Japanese system, and which is now increasingly being sought by envious employers in the West. In a crunch, Japanese workers have been laid off with as cavalier a concern for their wellbeing as Western workers, but they have been *less able* to defend themselves. There are numerous examples which illustrate this basic fact. The most spectacular examples in recent years have been in the steel, aluminium and shipbuilding industries.[35] Separating workers from specific jobs, far from giving them power, has thus been one of the sources of their powerlessness. It has been one of the conditions which make Japanese management more authoritarian than Fordist management.

Along with the so-called lifelong employment system, the quality control circle (QCC) also serves to enhance the control of management over the worker. However, this mechanism too is now seen as a positive way in which workers win control over matters previously in the hands of management. According to Kenney and Florida:

> Work organisation is based on self-managing teams. ... Team organisation and increased worker input not only increase productivity but also reduce certain aspects of worker alienation that result in high rates of sabotage and absenteeism under Fordism.[36]

While this may be the appearance, in reality QC circles are not institutions of worker solidarity and control. Workers are forced into competitive struggles with one another to see who can become management's most faithful employee. Within the group, relationships are competitive. One by one each member is isolated and pressured into finding some way to raise productivity or to eliminate waste. Often, all a member can come up with is a suggestion that everyone should work faster or longer. Groups are also organised into competitive struggles and given accolades for being management's favourite team.

While Kenney and Florida recognise that workers who do not contribute suggestions at Toyota 'may receive smaller bonuses',[37] their overall assessment of Japanese management remains unambiguously favourable. In that regard they are not unlike the many scholars who present management's view in the English language sources that they rely on. Indeed, the following claim almost implies that class itself has disappeared from Japanese capitalism:

> Consensus decision making provides an environment in which ideas can surface, ensures thorough dissemination of information, and mitigates problems associated with the lack of commitment to new decisions.[38]

It seems that Kenney and Florida have never heard of the ways 'consensus' is achieved in Japan by means of manipulation and intimidation. Sugimoto,[39] for example, mentions some of these.

The reality behind the agreements made by QC circles is that workers lack the power to resist managerial control over *what* they do. Even without receiving explicit instructions from individual managers, they feel pressured in the circles to police one another in a never-ending quest for less and less control over their jobs. The QC circle is a process whereby the workers lose power to defend their interests while becoming more preoccupied with management's objectives. The QC circle converts workers, not into managers, but into servants of managers, and it rewards them, not with managerial pay and conditions, but with the pay and conditions of servants. Unlike managers, who themselves escape productive work by loading it onto others, Japanese workers in the QC circle relieve management of even their basic administrative work by taking it on themselves. The QC circle is an ingenious device for ensuring that, when workers come together, the agenda is how to further management's interests rather than their own. The dynamic is competition rather than cooperation. Organising workers into competitive struggles with one another is not the mark of a new or more progressive order, but a very old trick used by capital to impose its will on labour.

Although Japanese workers have long since lost control over the labour process, the QC circle brings workers together in a way which maintains the status quo. In the area of wages, one of the few remaining areas where unions still attempt to defend the *interests of employees* (rather than management's interests), albeit at the expense of the much larger number of nonunion employees, workers are isolated from one another. Herein lies the power of the QC circle. Workers come together in the QC circles to ensure that the collective power of labour is marshalled in favour of capital. However, when the needs of that labour are at stake, each worker is an individual on his or her own.

Payment for person rather than job: flexibility for whom?

Kenney and Florida compare 'the job-specific, productivity-based system of US Fordism' unfavourably with the Japanese:

> ... tripartite wage composed of seniority, base, and merit
> components. . . . The seniority component provides
> significant incentives for workers to remain with the company;
> semiannual bonuses hinge individual remuneration to
> corporate performance and create increased incentives for
> greater work effort, and the merit-based component spurs
> individual effort.[40]

We have seen that the seniority component is in reality a system of withheld wages used to eliminate worker control over the labour process and to convert them into simple employees, available for anything at all. The twice-yearly bonus, which can be equal to quite a few months' pay, is also a form of withheld wages. Bonuses are withheld so that they can be easily cut and thereby bolster management against any drop in profitability. Overtime is paid at only 1.25 times the monthly rate, which is calculated from the monthly salary, rather than the annual salary that includes bonuses. This means that overtime, which is in practice compulsory, is paid at a *lower* rate than regular time. Finally, the merit-based component, the only factor supposedly within workers' power to influence, varies from one individual to the next according to management's measures of merit: loyalty, performance in QC circles, willingness to work overtime, and willingness to forego sick leave and annual holidays.[41]

Payment for the person rather than the job is pivotal to management's strategy of dividing persons so that they cannot protect their jobs. But the wage system is more than the three elements mentioned so far. Attention must also be given to the income differentials between regular and nonregular employees, between men and women, and between workers in large firms and those in small firms (see Figure 4.1).

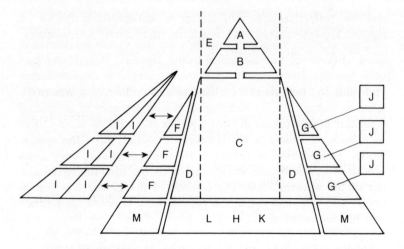

A Top managers
B Middle managers (partly union members)
C Male regular workers in large companies (union members)
D Female regular workers in large companies (union members)
E Previously retired workers
F Subcontracted workers
G Leased workers
H Part-time workers (married women)
I Workers in small companies
J Labour leasing companies
K Seasonal workers (mainly farmers)
L Part-time workers (students)
M Foreign workers

Source: Kumazawa 1988:30.

Figure 4.1 The structure of labour in contemporary Japan

At times Kenney and Florida come close to recognising these divisions: 'guaranteed employment for male workers in core firms became a fundamental feature of postwar Japan, with dismissal falling largely outside routine management prerogative'.[42] Unfortunately, there is not a word about the insecurity of women workers, the temporaries (of which there are a large variety), or those in small firms which are not unionised.[43] Neither is there any mention of the growing corruption of Japanese trade unions after they were divided from this insecure mass of the working class.

Temporary and part-time workers are generally excluded from the company unions, their wage rates can be as little as a quarter of those of regular workers, and they are first in line for dismissal. Such workers are not incidental to the Japanese system, but part of a broader arrangement whose very essence is discrimination and division maintained by a careful distribution of minor privileges to individuals. To focus on only one category of individual – regular male workers in core companies – without seeing them *in relation to others* is to misrepresent totally how the system works. The position of regular male workers in core companies is both protected by and threatened by the position of the remainder of the working class. The essence of the Japanese system is divide and rule, and organised competition. It is not, as Kenney and Florida claim, a:

> balance of class power, or 'class accord', characterised by enterprise unionism, long-term employment tenure, and a distinct style of class accommodation.[44]

To the extent that they do notice the relationship among the different fractions of the working class, their argument becomes contradictory:

> Small firm–large firm relations and gender segmentation constitute a unique set of supports for the core of the Japanese economy and, in doing so, help create the topography on which a new post-Fordist organisation of production can rest.[45]

The argument is flawed because Kenney and Florida do not, in fact, explore the implications of either division, or the division between regular and irregular workers. The almost unique degree to which capitalist and patriarchal relations overlap in Japan has been noted by Steven[46] but is totally glossed over by Kenney and Florida.

One example of that oversight can be seen in the treatment of the tripartite wage system as a concession to workers' demands for a need-based system.[47] However, one must distinguish between male and female workers. Men's patriarchal need to receive wages sufficient to 'keep' women is hardly accompanied by women's 'need' to receive such low wages that they have to be kept by men. Japan has been unique among advanced capitalist societies in preserving an earnings differential between men and women of two-to-one throughout the postwar period. It is inappropriate to interpret this central feature of the Japanese wage system as part of the post-Fordist 'accord' which should be emulated as an advance on Fordism. Women workers, who are pressured by patriarchal relations into retirement to parent their children before they ever receive their withheld wages, have no interest whatsoever in the system of payment by length of service. Insofar as that system expresses needs other than those of capital, they are needs which belong to men.

Kenney and Florida assume throughout a harmony of interests among all workers, ignoring Japanese capital's essential strategy, of dividing and ruling through organised competition. They take the 'highest uncommon' denominator, the conditions conceded to the most favoured individuals, as a sign of a victory for the class, instead of the conditions of the great mass as evidence of its defeat. This is a bit like seeing the conditions conceded to a few Blacks who collaborated with the forces of apartheid as a victory for all Black people in South Africa.

Managing demand: The *Kanban* (just-in-time) system

One also needs to understand the conditions of workers in the *kanban* system *in relation* to the rest of the working class. The system of tiered subcontracting prevalent in many Japanese industries does not provide equally for employees in the large firms and those in the small firms that do work under contract. The view of this tiered structure which is presented by Kenney and Florida is also one-sided:

> The result was that small, flexible companies came to be an integral component of Japan's industrial structure ... [and] large firms eventually became dependent on the flexibility and specialised skills possessed by small firms. Over time, a hybrid system of industrial organisation emerged as a distinct alternative to Fordism.[48]
>
> The *kanban* system replaces Fordist top-down coordination with mutual adjustment among contiguous work groups. ... Constant communication reduces planning and supervision

costs and creates another location of shared knowledge and work-based learning.[49]

The objective of the JIT system is to increase productivity not through super-exploitation of labor but rather through increased technological efficiency, heightened utilisation of equipment, minimal scrappage or rework, decreased inventory, and higher quality. It thus increases the 'value' extracted in production, decreases materials consumed per unit output, and minimises circulation time, making the actual production process much more efficient.[50]

Kenney and Florida do not attempt to disentangle appearance from reality. For example, they approve of Japan's system of having subcontractors located 'in close proximity to final assembly facilities' and contrast this with 'Fordism in which different elements of the production process are dispersed throughout the world'.[51] Maharey is just as ignorant of the Japanese reality, which he compares with New Zealand supermarkets:

> Retailers began to develop information and supply systems which allow them to order goods to coincide with demand. The result is the 'just-in-time' delivery system which allows supermarkets to restock overnight according to the shifting tastes of the consumer.
>
> Manufacturers have made similar changes. Toyota is today one of the pioneers of the new era. . . . The company has adopted methods of labour control and production which enable it to provide multiple variations of each model and serve specialised markets; so putting it at the leading edge of post-Fordism. Toyota television advertisements stress the company's ability to provide the model, shape, and colour of vehicle to match the customer's needs.[52]

The essence of the *kanban* system is not the geographical proximity of the 'child' to the 'parent' companies, although this is a feature of the Toyota and Mazda networks. The basis of the *kanban* system is the capacity of the parent companies to shift burdens onto the smaller companies and their workers. Nissan has long done this very effectively, not simply by using subcontractors all over Japan, but through a worldwide network of vulnerable suppliers. Close proximity and other 'communications systems' simply aid, but are not essential to, control. And control ensures the ability to transfer costs.

Kenney and Florida are also fully taken in by the appearance of paternalism: 'Parent or core companies take an active hand in assisting suppliers to cope with problems and typically dispatch personnel to help solve them'.[53] Even if there is a modicum of benevolence among capitalists in small and large firms, the implication that workers in the latter are adequately cared for is totally without foundation.

Kenney and Florida again show their willingness to take employer propaganda at face value when they claim that 'employees may even be transferred among companies in the JIT complex, a process that typically occurs late in an employee's career cycle as retiring executives of corporate parents are absorbed by smaller subsidiaries'.[54] The reality, once again, is very different. Most of the transfers are of older workers whose wages have become too high for the parent firm's profit calculations. In the past most of them might have been able to remain in the core companies, albeit as lower paid temporaries. Now that joblessness has become so much more widespread, a second best, from the workers' point of view, is secondment into subcontracted companies. The worst alternative, of course, is unemployment following mandatory retirement, a situation affecting over a quarter of such retired workers in the 1980s.[55]

It never occurs to Kenney and Florida that the *kanban* system might have costs. They do not appear to consider those who might have to pay such costs. For example, 'eliminating the need for inventory stockpiling'[56] is really transferring the need to the subcontractors. Sometimes they almost recognise this: 'Since workers in subsidiaries generally receive lower wages than those in core firms, the overall costs of production are reduced'.[57] In fact, this is a means of cutting general wage costs by singling out non-unionised workers who are divided from one another by the institutional separation of workers in parent and child companies. It is essentially pre-Fordist or ultra-Fordist,[58] a leftover from the old putting-out system, rather than post-Fordist. Its essence is that, by keeping workers scattered and divided from one another, it functions as a superexploitative system.

With no evidence of their own, and even in the face of evidence to the contrary,[59] Kenney and Florida claim that 'the use of subcontractors to absorb business cycle downturns does not appear to be as widespread as [it was] previously'.[60] To support this claim, we are referred to Aoki, and to Patrick and Rohlen, but are given no hard evidence. Our research, however, reveals a continued and perhaps even increased reliance on subcontractors. No evidence is cited for the claim that 'risk sharing between core companies and the primary subcontractors has become the norm',[61] and nothing is said about the distribution of risk among the remaining subcontractors situated further down the tier. Citing simply the opinions of right-wing scholars, they provide no concrete evidence. They simply state that the accord is now being extended to the mass of Japanese workers:

> However, recent research indicates that wage and salary differentials between workers in large and small firms have narrowed and that employment guarantees are being extended to male permanent employees in small companies.[62]

This is simply not true.[63] It seems to us that some of the remaining claims made by Kenney and Florida also stem as much from ignorance about Japan as from their reliance on conservative sources:

> The Japanese consumption bundle is increasingly oriented to information and electronics-based goods, design-lifestyle products, and consumer services as opposed to high levels of housing and consumer durable consumption of U.S. Fordism.[64]

In a world where there are no classes, or to those unable to identify classes, upper and middle class consumption power is confused with universal 'taste'.[65] Kenney and Florida show little sympathy for the struggles of the great mass of Japanese to make ends meet. They make no mention of the astronomical cost of housing, social security, education and transport. To illustrate this reality, we cite a letter by a Japanese woman, Tokiko Iwamoto-Sakurai, to *Time*:

> In our country, few families can afford a modern house with a clothes dryer and a dishwasher. We don't have to line up for food, but the prices are terribly high. Most wives spend

hours trying to find cheaper food or take low-paying part-time jobs to be able to buy more groceries. Can ordinary Westerners imagine paying $2 for three small tomatoes or $8 for a pound of the cheapest meat? Japanese husbands are usually too busy to help their wives. Because they cannot get houses or apartments near their offices, men leave home at 6 or 7 in the morning and return at 9 or 10 at night. For most Japanese, the dream of having a bigger house or an apartment with one room for each family member will never come true.[66]

Murray at least seems to recognise some of the dangers of the *kanban* system:

The costs of employing lifetime workers, means an incentive to sub-contract all jobs not essential to the core. The other side of the Japanese jobs for life is a majority of low-paid, fragmented peripheral workers, facing an underfunded and inadequate welfare state. The duality in the labour market, and in the welfare economy, could be taken as a description of Thatcherism.[67]

In some sectors where the manufacturers are little more than subcontractors to the retailers, their flexibility has been achieved at the expense of labour. In others, capital itself has suffered.[68]

The puzzling thing, however, is how both Murray and Maharey implicitly see Thatcherism as a sort of progressive alternative to Fordism. Murray regards Toyota as the pioneer in the manufacturing industry, the first to apply the just-in-time system to component suppliers.[69] A key question here is whether 'the elimination of waste' achieved by Toyota is at the expense of workers in the subcontracted firms, or whether, as Murray seems to imply, it simply and without any apparent costs cuts capital's turnover time, better utilising capital that would otherwise lie idle and be wasted. Murray does not see that the extra flexibility and faster turnover time achieved by Toyota means that subsidiary firms turn their capital over at a slower rate, thus squeezing their profits. The burden is shifted to labour in the subsidiary firms.

Substituting the Thatcherite state and the *kanban* system for the Keynesian state as a mechanism of demand management is hardly the beginning of a progressive alternative. Thatcherism is pre-Fordist, or ultra-Fordist, rather than post-Fordist. Holloway[70] correctly contrasts it with Keynesianism, which he equates with Fordism and which he sees as a system of class domination in which trade union power is substantial. He argues that the breakdown of the Keynesian system of domination (which is what a capitalist crisis is) and the struggles that ended with the destruction of trade union power have set the stage for the emergence of a 'new' system of domination. But what has actually emerged is a return to an older order with no unions. Thatcherism is about the destruction of the trade union power which was consolidated under Fordism. It is really absurd to call the rolling back of that power post-Fordist, particularly if that term is made to connote an advance on Fordism.

Flexibility

The fundamental claim of the post-Fordists is that the 'accord' (that is, the guarantee of tenure) reduced workers' resistance to automation and resulted in them being more receptive to the introduction of new technology. Kenney and Florida see in this flexibility the essence of post-Fordism. They call the 'new' arrangements which promote such receptivity '*Fujitsuism*'. Fujitsuism has two very different facets. One is the tendency towards 'information-based companies'. This is arguably occurring in *certain industries*. The second is that capital is increasingly able to introduce and control technology. The second type of change may also be occurring; however, it cannot be seen as either a progressive or an inevitable development. The greater success of Japanese capital compared with Western capital in introducing new technology, may only reflect the fact that Japanese capital has more fully broken the power of workers to resist the resulting destruction of their jobs.

Why should workers see this as a progressive development? Because the more profitable their employers the more secure their jobs and livelihood? Whilst this has always been the logic capitalism forces on workers, progressive politics has always tried to alter the system responsible for that logic. The goal of progressives has been an arrangement whereby workers do not have to choose between accepting wage cuts, being made redundant by new technology, and losing their jobs because their employers went bankrupt due to the workers' failure to accept wage cuts or new technology. Often workers have to submit to such Hobsonian choices. However, when they start *buying into* the logic of capital, or singling out other workers for the chop in order to protect themselves, submission becomes collaboration. The notion of 'an alternative post-Fordist or "Fujitsuist" set of social relationships'[71] is thus quite absurd, at best. At worst, it is collaborationist.

The end of the crisis and the new order

Kenney and Florida fully reproduce the current line being put forward by Japanese capital in its conflicts with both labour and American and European capital:

> Tight integration of production and innovation is a primary reason why Japan has become one of the world's most innovative political economies. ... [T]he most recent statistics on U.S.-Japan trade in high technology show the United States running a $16 billion across-the-board deficit.[72]

Once again, this is not true. Japanese capital continues to import more technology from the West than it exports, and this continues to fuel its conflict with US capital.[73]

The crisis in Japan is very far from being solved. For most workers, namely women, irregulars and the mass in small firms, even the boom years were ones of uninterrupted crisis. But since the mid-1970s, there has been a growing division even among members of the core labour force. A 'new rich class' has unquestionably emerged. Some have become rich because of skyrocketing land and share prices, while others have done well because of their positions in the giant corporations. However, growing numbers of previously secure workers are joining the ranks of the 'new' (old) poor, and new technology is deepening rather than solving the crisis for them. Their jobs are also being destroyed by the 'hollowing out' (*kūdōka*) of Japan's core productive industries as Japanese capital relocates abroad.[74] When an all-out effort was made by Japanese capital to solve the 'high yen crisis' in 1987 and 1988, workers were the chief victims.

Transplanting Japanese Management

Kenney and Florida are on their weakest ground when they attempt to push the virtues of Japanese management on the basis of its record outside Japan, since English-speaking workers' own experience powerfully contradicts the propaganda. Despite the important evidence from workers themselves, which they even cite from Junkerman,[75] Kenney and Florida greatly exaggerate the benefits which flow to workers from Japanese-owned firms. For example, they claim that interviews of American suppliers of Japanese companies confirm that the JIT system was successfully transplanted. But they did not interview the workers themselves to ascertain the cost of this success. Nissan workers at Smyrna have complained bitterly about a number of common practices used by Japanese management. Junkerman's research suggests that the situation at Smyrna is as follows:

(a) Two thousand workers were selected from a pool of 130,000 applicants after endless interviews and tests; and workers are constantly told that if they do not like the job they can easily be replaced.

(b) Skilled workers' jobs are taken over by younger, less qualified workers.

(c) Workers who 'have problems' with the Japanese system are moved to the hardest jobs for long periods without rotation or are fired. As one worker put it: 'The open-door policy just lets them know if you're going to be a "troublemaker". What we've got there is management by intimidation'.[76] Workers even have 'to restrict their intake of liquids' to avoid having to go to the toilet during the shift.[77]

(d) Increases in productivity have, in practice, stemmed mainly from 'the old-fashioned way – through the speed-up'.[78]

(e) The workforce is broken down into small groups, which remain divided from one another and which are forced to compete with one another. Since Nissan awards merit points to groups for accident-free production, workers conceal their injuries.

Similar stories have been coming from the Nissan factory in

Sunderland in Britain.[79] It was opened in the midst of the industry's worst crisis, after the numbers of manual workers at British Leyland had fallen from 120,000 to 26,000 in only eight years and the power of their union had been broken. The 11,000 applicants for the first 247 jobs were very carefully screened. Following a strategy developed in Japan 35 years earlier, the company selected its own union and concluded an agreement which virtually outlawed strikes. It was this approach which allowed management to introduce other elements of the Japanese system of control: the just-in-time system, competitive work groups, an end to job demarcation and new technology. Not unexpectedly, there are also widespread reports of discontent.

In New Zealand, it was only after repackaging its proposals three times that Nissan managed to win the support of the Engineers' Union for a set of managerial practices it called the 'Nissan Way'. However, workers in the Stores, Clerical and Hotel and Hospital Unions remained adamantly opposed, a message which got through to management only after a long strike had demonstrated that the unity of these workers could not be broken. Today, the 'Nissan Way' is limited to members of the Engineers' Union.

One of the reasons for the staunchness of many New Zealand workers on the issue has been the long tradition in this country of a wage system which is diametrically opposite to Japan's. New Zealand's award wages system implies a *national rate for the job regardless of who does it or where it is done*. Large or small firm, urban or rural, old or young, male or female: workers all get the same rate for the job. There is thus, in New Zealand, an inducement to *nationwide* solidarity among workers to defend their jobs, an incentive structure which has been broken down by Japanese management in Japan. By pitting every worker against all others, Japanese- style management has ensured that individuals stand isolated and alone when it comes to defending their own interests. Small wonder the New Zealand system is currently under attack from the Japanese system.

Conclusion: Japan's New Imperialism

The Japanese system is, and long has been, very much like a system which has more recently been pushed forward in Britain and the United States by Thatcherites and Reaganites. The tendency towards the Japanese way in the advanced countries is clearly a reactionary development, not a move towards a higher stage of capitalism, closer to socialism. Rather, it is a move back to more primitive forms of social control which are only possible in the context of greatly weakened trade unions and increased divisions among workers.[80]

This weakening of working class power in the advanced countries is primarily a result of new forms of capitalist imperialism.[81] Capital could force this step backwards on its own workers only because it could increasingly superexploit workers in the underdeveloped countries. And, as the power of capital came to depend increasingly on such superexploitation, worldwide tendencies towards homogenising the conditions of labour gained momentum. If accelerated imperialism has been a major response to the current crisis in all the advanced countries, it is small wonder that the more backward conditions of Third World workers are everywhere being extended to the advanced countries themselves.

These developments are totally misunderstood, however, when they are seen as a transition from one industrial era to another. The move towards Japanese-style management is not a step forward, since such competitive power that Japanese capital has enjoyed over Western capital resulted from the backwardness of class struggles in Japan, and not from their leading the way. It has resulted from the fact that the conditions of Japanese workers, among those of workers in the advanced countries, already most resembled conditions in the Third World, conditions which international capital is increasingly universalising throughout its spheres of operation. The Japanese system might even be seen as a prototype of what has been called peripheral-Fordism in the Newly Industrialised Countries (NICs).[82] Most Japanese scholars reject the suggestion that Japanese capitalism is post-Fordist, referring to it instead as ultra-Fordist[83] or neo-Fordist.[84]

The notions of Fordism and post-Fordism are singularly inappropriate to understanding recent changes in imperialist capital's worldwide strategies. The package of characteristics that are supposed to go together are, in fact, increasingly being separated. For example, standardised Fordist mass production, with advanced technology and all, has been widely extended to the so-called NICs of Asia and Latin America. However, these moves have occurred with repression (rather than Keynesianism) being the central feature of social control. In the advanced countries, we still have mass production, but here Keynesianism is giving way to the divide-and-rule approach associated with Japanese-style management. The three fundamental divisions are between regular and irregular workers, between men and women workers, and between workers in 'parent' and 'child' companies, as in primitive putting-out systems. This development is occurring, not because workers have become more powerful and have forced a shift to a more progressive industrial era, but because they have become weaker and must endure a more primitive and exploitative system of class domination.

Notes

1. Kenney and Florida, 1988.
2. Murray, 1988.
3. Dohse *et al.*, 1985.
4. Kenney and Florida, *op. cit.*, 1988.
5. Murray, *op. cit.*, 1988.
6. Notably Maharey, 1989.
7. Kenney and Florida, *op. cit.*, 1988: 127.
8. *Ibid.*, p. 138.
9. *Ibid.*, p. 128.
10. *Ibid.*, p. 124.
11. See Holloway, 1987.
12. See Dore, 1974.
13. Kenney and Florida, *op. cit.*, 1988.
14. *Ibid.*, p. 124.
15. *Ibid.*, p. 131.
16. *Ibid.*, p. 137.
17. *Ibid.*, p. 145.
18. Murray, *op. cit.*, 1988: 12.
19. *Ibid.*, pp. 12–13.
20. Maharey, *op. cit.*, 1989.
21. *Ibid.*, p. 8.
22. Kenney and Florida, *op. cit.*, 1988: 135.
23. Murray, *op. cit.*, 1988: 11.
24. See Steven, 1988 and Katō, 1989a.
25. Murray, *op. cit.*, 1988: 11.
26. Ken Douglas, *NZ Tribune*, 12 June 1989: p. 6.
27. Kenney and Florida, *op. cit.*, 1988: 122.
28. *Ibid.*, p. 135.
29. *Ibid.*, pp. 132–3.
30. *Ibid.*, p. 133.

31. Kamata, 1984.
32. Kenney and Florida, *op. cit.*, 1988: 134.
33. For example, see Steven, 1983 and Katō *op. cit.*, 1989a.
34. Keizai Kikakuchō Sōgō Tōkeikyoku [General Statistical Bureau of the Economic Planning Agency], 1988: 122.
35. Cf. Steven, *op. cit.*, 1988.
36. Kenney and Florida *op. cit.*, 1988: 132.
37. *Ibid.*, p. 134.
38. *Ibid.*, p. 135.
39. Sugimoto, 1986.
40. Kenney and Florida, *op. cit.*, 1988: 129.
41. See Kamata, 1982 and Nohara and Fujita, 1989.
42. Kenney and Florida, *op. cit.*, 1988: 128.
43. See Steven *op. cit.*, 1983 and *op. cit.*, 1988.
44. Kenney and Florida *op. cit.*, 1988: 122.
45. *Ibid.*, p. 131.
46. See Steven, *op. cit.*, 1983 and *op. cit.*, 1988.
47. Kenney and Florida, *op. cit.*, 1988: 129.
48. *Ibid.*, pp. 124–5.
49. *Ibid.*, p. 133.
50. *Ibid.*, p. 136.
51. *Ibid.*, p. 136.
52. Maharey, *op. cit.*, 1989: 3.
53. Kenney and Florida, *op. cit.*, 1988: 137.
54. *Ibid.*, p. 137.
55. See Steven, *op. cit.*, 1983.
56. Kenney and Florida, *op. cit.*, 1988: 136.
57. *Ibid.*, p. 137.
58. See Katō, 1989b.
59. See Steven, *op. cit.*, 1988: 114.
60. Kenney and Florida, *op. cit.*, 1988: 137.
61. *Ibid.*, p. 137.
62. *Ibid.*, p. 130.
63. Cf. Chūshō Kigyōchō, 1989: 11.
64. Kenney and Florida, *op. cit.*, 1988: 146.
65. See Steven, *op. cit.*, 1988.
66. *Time*, 27 June 1988.
67. Murray, *op. cit.*, 1988: 12.
68. *Ibid.*, p. 11.
69. Murray, *op. cit.*, 1988: 11.
70. Holloway, *op. cit.*, 1987.
71. Kenney and Florida, *op. cit.*, 1988: 142.
72. *Ibid.*, p. 139.
73. Cf. Keizai Kikakuchō, 1989: 537.

74. Cf. Katō, 1988 and Steven, *op. cit.*, 1988.
75. Junkerman, 1987.
76. *Ibid.*, p. 18.
77. *Ibid.*, p. 20.
78. *Ibid.*, p. 17.
79. Cf. Holloway, *op. cit.*, 1987.
80. Cf. Katō, 1987a and *op. cit.*, 1989b.
81. Cf. Steven, 1990.
82. See Lipietz, 1986.
83. See Katō, *op. cit.*, 1989b.
84. See Nohara and Fujita, *op. cit.*, 1989.

5 GENDER
Equal Opportunity and Gender Identity: Feminist Encounters with Modernity and Postmodernity in Japan[1]

Vera Mackie

Modernity and Postmodernity

In recent discussions of theories of modernity and postmodernity, some energy has been expended on a consideration of the extent to which Japan measures up to, or even exemplifies, some abstract standard of modernity or postmodernity[2]. Approaches to this question have considered postmodernity as a state or condition of society. Other approaches have considered the relevance of postmodernism as a constellation of cultural phenomena, characterised by parody, irony, pastiche and deconstructive forms of critique. Postindustrialism has been considered as one of the defining characteristics of postmodernity. Postindustrialism has been defined as a particular stage of capitalist development, characterised by the dominance of transnational capital, the growth of a service economy, and the development of new technologies of information and communication, and these features have been identified in contemporary Japan.[3]

These issues have been canvassed in the Japanese context in a volume edited by Masao Miyoshi and Harry Harootunian, *Postmodernism and Japan*. Although many of the contributors to the volume concentrate on the cultural features of postmodernism, the volume also includes warnings against the limitations of such an approach. Miyoshi and Harootunian remind us that 'the most problematised of all the absences in postmodernism is a relation with politics',[4] and caution against the neglect of issues related to the legacy of colonialism and imperialism:

Thus a paradox: as postmodernism seeks to remedy the modernist error of Western, male, bourgeois domination, it simultaneously vacates the ground on which alone the contours of modernism can be seen. Furthermore, colonialism and imperialism are ongoing enterprises, and in distinguishing the late post-industrial capitalism from earlier liberal capitalism and by tolerating the former while condemning the latter, postmodernism ends up by consenting to the first world economic domination that persists in exploiting the wretched of the earth.[5]

Stephen Melville, in his postscript to the volume, laments the almost total neglect of feminist issues.[6] Indeed, such issues as the distribution of wealth, equality and inequality, repression, exploitation, gender relations and class relations, colonialism and neocolonialism receive little attention in the above-mentioned volume. Yet it is precisely at the intersection of postmodernism with the political critiques of feminism[7] and postcolonialism[8] that the most exciting debates are occurring today. Rey Chow explains the productive, but uneasy, relationship between feminism and postmodernism:

> The difficulty feminists have with postmodernism is thus clear. Although feminists share postmodernism's poststructuralist tendencies in dismantling universalist claims, which for them are more specifically defined as the claims of the white, male subject, they do not see their struggle against patriarchy as quite over ... feminists, must always begin, as the non-Western world must begin, with the legacy of the constellation of modernism *and* something more. While for the non-Western world that something more is imperialism, for feminists it is patriarchy.[9]

Such issues are obviously relevant in considering the place of Japan in narratives of modernity and postmodernity. However, Japan also occupies an uneasy position between 'East' and 'West'. We are used to a series of dichotomies which position Asian countries as 'Third World', 'under-developed', 'premodern', 'pre-capitalist', in opposition to the 'First World', 'developed', 'capitalist', 'modern' world of Europe and the United States. Japan, however, as a 'developed', 'capitalist' economy in Asia unsettles these easy habits of thought. In considering the situation of Japanese working women, for example, it is appropriate to consider issues of equal opportunity, questions of citizenship and gender, and the place of the women's movement in engaging with state institutions – questions also relevant to women in the capitalist economies of the 'West'. In this chapter I will concentrate on the conjunction of feminism and postmodernism in the Japanese context, but a postcolonial perspective can also shed light on contemporary Japanese society, shaped as it is by a history of imperialism and colonialism, and the contemporary reality of unequal relationships with other Asian countries.

Postmodernism and Feminist Politics

In order to consider the relevance of discussions on the relationship between postmodernism and feminist politics to the Japanese context, I will consider debates within Japan on the issue of equal opportunity policy – an issue which consumed much feminist energy during the 1970s and 1980s. I will examine situations where discussions on this issue were constrained within the bounds of modernist political discourses, but will also consider examples of feminist attempts to go beyond these discourses. The lessons of this experience point in one possible direction for feminist politics in 1990s Japan, which involves going beyond both liberal and socialist strategies, combining demands for institutional and structural change with an expanded notion of politics which involves paying attention to meaning and discourse.

The campaign for the creation of an Equal Opportunity Act in Japan from the mid-1970s was spearheaded by the International Women's Year Action Group (*Kōdō Suru Kai*)[10] and a group known as *Tsukuru Kai*.[11] The political strategies engaged in by campaigners for equal opportunity policy in Japan were those of a pressure group in a liberal, capitalist society: the use of publicity, petitions, demonstrations, and parliamentary politics. There were, however, some distinctive aspects of these Japanese feminist campaigns. Firstly, they used a dispersed, decentralised organisational structure. In addition to *Tsukuru Kai*, a coalition of 48 organisations contributed to the equal opportunity campaign in various ways.[12] While each of these disparate groups retained its autonomy and identity, it was able to contribute to a concerted national effort. Secondly, Japanese feminist groups were able to use international publicity, in the form of several international conferences organised under the auspices of the United Nations International

Decade for Women, in order to bring further pressure to bear on the Japanese government.

The Equal Employment Opportunity Act (*Danjo Koyō Kikai Kintō Hō*) was eventually promulgated in May 1985, to become effective in April 1986. The Act referred specifically to sexual discrimination in recruitment, hiring, promotion, training, and retirement, and thus went beyond previous legislation on sexual discrimination. While the Constitution of 1947 had encoded broad liberal principles of equality;[13] the Labour Standards Law (*Rōdō Kijun Hō*) of 1947 was somewhat more specific in stating the principle of 'equal pay for equal work' (Article 4).[14]

The campaign for the creation of an Equal Opportunity Act, then, may be seen as an example of the use of liberal feminist political strategies, in order to gain a concession compatible with liberal views of politics. It is at the point of the implementation of the Act, however, that the limitations of liberal political strategies became apparent, and the late 1980s in Japan were marked by feminist discussion of the limitations of equal opportunity policy.

Critiques of Equal Opportunity Policy

Because equal opportunity policy aims to treat all individuals exactly the same, such policy will be successful only in so far as men and women are able to participate in waged work under identical conditions. It is when these limitations become apparent that feminists move beyond liberal feminist strategies to call for the structural transformation of society. In the Japanese context, feminists faced with the limited efficacy of equal opportunity policy focused on the sexual division of labour in the home and the working conditions of full-time permanent employees which make male participation in child-rearing and other domestic labour virtually impossible.

Others brought a socialist feminist perspective to critiques of equal opportunity policy, by considering the structure of the capitalist labour market,[15] the development of a feminised casual labour force,[16] the role of state institutions, policies and practices in shaping gender and class relations, the 'gendering' of particular occupations, and the failure of social institutions to deal with the specificity of women's reproductive capacity.

Complaints to Equal Opportunity Bureaux in the years immediately following the implementation of the Act often concerned private companies which had attempted to transfer women to branches several commuting hours away, thus making it impossible for married women to carry the 'double burden' of childcare and waged work, and perpetuating the idea that full-time labour and domestic labour are incompatible. Although these complaints could often be resolved by conciliation procedures, many women resigned without calling on the services of the Equal Opportunity Conciliation Board, according to Ōta Masae, Policy Chief of the Women and Minors Bureau of the Department of Labour.[17]

The question of the sexual division of labour in the home was also raised with respect to overtime and night work: Critics argued that full-time male employees were only able to maintain a strong level of commitment to the workplace because of the support of the domestic labour provided by their wives. Similarly, married women were unable to give such a commitment to the workplace because they were unable to call on the support of husbands in domestic labour and child-rearing. The solutions proposed by feminist activists at this stage were basically institutional: a change in the working conditions of permanent full-time employees, so that men could share in domestic labour while women shared in waged labour. This institutional solution was seen to address the structural question of the relationship between the sexual division of labour in the home and the conditions of waged work in the capitalist economy. While employers' representatives argued that women's working conditions should be made to conform to the masculine standard, feminists preferred to argue that restrictions on overtime and working hours should be extended to cover *all* workers,[18] as explained by Kanatani Chieko:

The elimination of discrimination against women (*josei no sabetsu teppai*) surely does not mean that men and women should both be exposed to inhuman working conditions, at the whim of capital. The elimination of discrimination means that the possibility of full personal and human development should be guaranteed for both men and women in the workplace and elsewhere ... [W]e should not argue for putting women in the same situation as male workers – with the same inferior working conditions. Rather, the first issue to be addressed concerns the improvement of working

conditions for men who are exposed to such inhuman
conditions as long working hours, night work, shift work,
and working in dangerous conditions. It is essential for the
liberation of women that both men and women join hands
in striving for a reduction in working hours.[19]

In other words, critics of liberal discourses of equal opportunity
in Japan realised that equality of opportunity under existing conditions would simply mean equality of exploitation, an insight
which has been noted by writers in other national contexts.[20]

Several activists I interviewed for a survey of Japanese feminism in the latter half of the 1980s referred to the issue of working
hours.[21] By the end of the decade the issue of working hours had
also been taken up by labour unions, in a somewhat different
context. Despite campaigns for the reduction of working hours,
Japanese workers still work, on average, longer hours than in
most other OECD countries – around 2,100 hours a year, which
is at least 200 hours more than in comparable nations.[22]

More recently, the problems of *tanshin-funin* (so-called 'company bachelors' who have been separated from their families
through company transfers),[23] and the coining of the phrase *karō-
shi* (death from overwork) have received media attention. What
is common to all of these issues is a questioning of the ideal of the
worker as an unencumbered masculine individual free of family
responsibilities. It is at the point where it is realised that married
working women can not conform to this ideal, that the feminist
critique intersects with other critiques of modern Japanese society.
While feminists, socialists and environmentalists call for a transformation of the social relations of production and reproduction,
government and capital have responded with technocratic and
economistic solutions, including the construction of ever-more
sophisticated resort and leisure facilities.[24]

It is in these discussions that the need for an expanded notion
of politics becomes apparent, for it is not only the social
relations of production and reproduction which are at stake here,
but also the social meanings of masculinity and femininity in
capitalist society. This expanded notion of politics, which involves
paying attention to the social meanings of such categories as
'man', 'woman', 'worker', 'citizen', has been described by Nancy
Fraser:

These differences in the quality of women's presence in the paid workplace testify to the conceptual dissonance between femininity and the worker role in classical capitalism. And this in turn confirms the masculine subtext of that role. It confirms that the role of the worker, which links the private (official) economy and the private family in male-dominated, capitalist societies, is a masculine role; and that *pace* Habermas, the link it forges is elaborated as much in the medium of masculine gender identity as in the medium of gender-neutral money.[25]

Discourses of Equality and Protection

In order to explore the relationship between working conditions and gender identity, I will consider the stage prior to the implementation of the Equal Opportunity Act, when there was discussion of the relationship between equal opportunity policy and so-called 'protective legislation', for it is in these discussions that the social meanings of masculinity and femininity, and the differential locations of men and women vis-à-vis employers and state institutions become apparent.

In this analysis I will concentrate on three concepts which are crucial to these discussions: 'equality' (*byōdō, kintō*), 'protection' (*hogo*) and 'motherhood' (*bosei*). In discussions leading up to the implementation of the Equal Opportunity Act, most controversy centred on the relationship between equal opportunity and what was called *bosei hogo*, 'protection of motherhood', as codified in the Labour Standards Law (*Rodō Kijun Hō*). In preparation for the drafting of the Equal Opportunity Act and possible revision of the Labour Standards Law, a tripartite committee was formed, with a brief to report to the Diet, including representatives of the 'public interest', employers, and labour.[26]

Employers' representatives mobilised the discourse of equality to argue that equal opportunity meant equal treatment in all ways. It was argued that equality was incompatible with policies which accorded women differential treatment, and this was encapsulated in the phrases 'equality without protection' (*hogo nuki byōdō*) and 'either equality or protection'(*hogo ka byōdō ka*),[27] implying that the price to be paid for equal opportunity legislation would be the removal of those policies which accord women differential treatment. Equal opportunity activists, on the other hand, called for 'equality with guarantees' (*hoshō*).

These discussions, then, have similarities with Anglo-American discussions of 'equality versus difference'.[28] A common refrain from representatives of government and business in Japan was that women, if 'granted' equal opportunity, should be willing to work as hard as their male counterparts. For example, a report issued by a committee of the Department of Labour in 1982 defined equality of opportunity in the following terms:

> The achievement of sexual equality in employment means a situation where all kinds of opportunity in employment (the opportunity to gain employment, the opportunity to be allocated various jobs in the workplace, the opportunity for promotion, the opportunity to receive training) may be gained equally by males and females. That is, equal opportunity means to effect equal treatment on the basis of each individual's volition and talents.[29]

What is codified here is an individualist view of equal opportunity which prioritises individual effort over structural factors. 'Equal Opportunity' in employment depends on 'the individual's volition and talents'. The fact that differences of class, gender and ethnicity shape each individual's experience of education and work is ignored. Encoded in these discussions is a view of the worker as implicitly masculine: an unencumbered individual able to give undivided attention to waged labour, as becomes apparent when the failures of the implementation of equal opportunity policy are analysed.[30]

It is now illegal to designate certain jobs as 'for males' or 'for females', but many companies have circumvented such provisions by labelling jobs as *sōgōshoku* ('comprehensive', 'management track') or *ippanshoku* ('general', 'clerical'). Women who state their preference for the management track are often asked whether they intend to work after marriage, and whether they will be available for transfer to outlying areas.[31] In other words, women who hope to pursue a management career are asked to measure up to the standards of the unencumbered masculine individual, but without the benefit of a spouse to carry out domestic labour.

The issue of 'equality versus difference' becomes more apparent when we consider so-called 'protective' legislation, for much discussion of equal opportunity policy was conducted in terms of a 'trade-off' between equal opportunity and those provisions of the Labour Standards Law specifically directed at women workers. The language of this legislation is significant. Most of the provisions relating specifically to women workers are known colloquially under the generic heading *bosei hogo* ('protection of motherhood'). I will have more to say about the concept of motherhood[32] below, but I would first like to consider how women have been positioned according to what I will call, following Pathak and Rajan, the discourse of protection.[33]

While men are positioned as workers or as citizens with rights, women, according to the discourse of protection, are positioned as weak and as supplicants in need of the protection of the state.[34] The implication is that the category of 'woman' and the categories of 'worker' or 'citizen' are mutually exclusive. While men are constructed as citizens with rights, only women are constructed as supplicants in need of protection. This protective attitude has been reinforced by the institutional arrangements which until recently placed policy related to 'women' and 'minors' in the same Bureau of the Ministry of Labour: The Women and Minors Bureau (*Rōdōshō Fujin Shōnen Kyoku*).[35]

Thus, in attempting to change the situation of women in Japanese society, it has been necessary to combine institutional change with a politics of discourse which exposes the constructions of masculinity and femininity encoded in the language of legislation and the practices of employers and bureaucracy. It is in this context that we should understand the rhetorical move of feminist activists who attempted to replace the slogan 'equality without protection' with the phrase 'equality with guarantees' (*hoshō*). By describing specific policies directed at women as 'guarantees', there was an attempt to reposition women as active citizens, with rights which must be guaranteed, rather than as passive supplicants, receiving the protection of a paternal state. The language of rights and citizenship is a feature of modernist political rhetoric, but such attention to the politics of discourse is compatible with a postmodern politics. I would echo Nancy Fraser in arguing that politics must be carried out both at the level of institutions and at the level of social meanings. Fraser argues that 'any satisfactions we are able to win will be problematic to the degree we fail to fight and win the battle of interpretation.'[36]

Discourses of Motherhood

Another feature of 'protective' legislation is that all working women are positioned as mothers or as potential mothers, through the language of *bosei hogo*.[37] With respect to the Labour Standards Law, the shorthand term *bosei hogo* ('protection of motherhood') actually refers to a whole series of policies directed at working women, each of which implies a different meaning for the term *bosei* ('motherhood').

Maternity leave and nursing leave are provided by employers during pregnancy and breastfeeding. Measures such as maternity leave and nursing leave refer to the physical reality of parturition and lactation. These provisions are directed at the biological mother – the woman who faces these physical realities – and, as such, are relatively uncontroversial.

Protective provisions prevent women workers from working late at night, from working overtime, or from working in dangerous industries such as mining. Protective provisions are directed at *all* women workers, on the premise that they are *potential* mothers. This is revealed by the fact that legislation does not distinguish between married and single women, or women with and without children. *All* women are protected from shift work or late night work on the grounds that they have potential responsibility for childcare. The health of young women is protected for future childbearing. Protective provisions, then, concern not the physical reality of pregnancy for any individual woman, but rather an abstract potential.

Extended periods of maternity leave or paternity leave involve the responsibility for childcare. The failure, until recently, to provide paternity leave for male workers has reinforced the notion that childcare is a woman's responsibility.

There are several reasons for trying to disentangle the disparate meanings subsumed under the phrase *bosei hogo*. Each of the above-mentioned policies implies a different definition of the word *bosei* ('motherhood'). Where the biological facts of pregnancy are involved, it is necessary to implement policies directed solely at women. Protective provisions are directed not at an individual woman or mother, but rather at an abstract potential for 'motherhood'. This is revealed by the fact that protective legislation is directed at *all* women, not just those with children. Where childcare is concerned, this need not concern the mother alone. Several approaches are possible, including individual responsibility, communal solutions, or state provision of childcare. The use of the word *hogo* ('protection') for the above provisions is also problematic – implying that women are physically weaker than men, and therefore need the protection of a strong state. It might be argued, instead, that all workers have the right to safe and humane working conditions.

In discussions on equal opportunity and 'protective' legislation, there was little controversy over the retention of measures such as maternity leave and nursing leave, realities which must be addressed if women are to participate in waged labour. Other measures such as restrictions on overtime and night work have little to do with these physical realities, and it was these which caused most controversy. Feminists realised that, despite the rhetoric about the 'protection of motherhood', measures concerning working hours and overtime have little to do with the biological reality of motherhood. Rather, they concern the social location of women, who still bear the major responsibility for childcare and domestic labour.

While capital and government argued for the removal of restrictions on overtime and night work by women, feminist commentators argued that such provisions were necessitated by the fact that women and men came to waged labour from different situations in the home. While women still carry the major burden of childcare and domestic labour, this affects their ability to engage in waged labour on equal terms. There was thus an attempt to shift the terms of debate from the terrain of the biological role of 'mother' to the social role of 'mothering'. There has been some advance in this area with the enactment of the Childcare Leave Law (*Ikuji Kyūgyō Hō*), which provides for either father or mother to take up to one year of childcare leave. However, because this leave need not be paid for by the company, it is likely that this will act as a disincentive for fathers to take childcare leave if they are the more highly-paid partner.[38]

Debates on the relationship between equal opportunity policy and so-called 'protective' legislation thus provided an opportunity for the deconstruction of the concept of motherhood (*bosei*) – a term which collapses biological, social and symbolic meanings.

This concept is one which has received extensive attention in Japan, from the earliest days of Japanese feminism.[39] While some feminists have attempted to deconstruct this term, others have valorised the identity of 'mother' and have even attempted to use this as a speaking position in political activity. This has been true of members of consumer associations, citizens' movements, environmental groups, and pacifist organisations.[40] There is, however, a tension in this approach, for the category of 'mother' has tended to imply a passive recipient of state protection, rather than an active subject demanding rights.[41]

Differences Among Women

The social implications of modifications to the Labour Standards Law did not only concern differences between men and women, but also class differences between women. It was obvious that the modification of restrictions on overtime and night work would disadvantage working-class women, while providing dubious benefits to elite women. Japanese feminists were united in their insistence on 'equality with guarantees', and refused to be divided into elitist and anti-elitist factions. This is not to suggest that equal opportunity activists denied the possibility of class divisions between women. Rather, they made a strategic political choice to emphasise solidarity between different groups of women.

A significant proportion of working women in Japan are now married women, and many of these women are engaged in casual, temporary or part-time positions, rather than career positions.[42] Equal opportunity policy has little to offer such workers.[43] Rather, an analysis of the structure of the labour market is necessary, in order to explain capital's 'need' for a casualised sector of the labour force. However, a purely structural analysis can not explain why it is women workers who come to occupy the most vulnerable positions in the labour market.

Labour market analysis needs to be combined with an understanding of the relationship between domestic labour and waged labour, and the constructions of masculinity and femininity which make it seem 'natural' that women occupy jobs which may be more easily combined with domestic labour, such as casual clerical and service positions. It is often argued that many women 'prefer' the flexibility of part-time positions, and this is a rational choice when it is women in most households who bear the major responsibility for domestic work and childcare. It is unlikely, however, that part-time women workers also 'prefer' to be exploited at wages something like one-third of a full-time regular employee's wage.[44]

In the Japanese context, strategies for changing the conditions of such workers have included seeking state regulation of part-timers' working conditions,[45] attempts to extend the activities of some mainstream unions to include part-time workers in addition to permanent full-time employees,[46] and the development of new forms of union activity in organisations known as 'Community Unions' or 'Part-timers' Unions'.[47] As discussed above, such institutional strategies could be combined with an attention to the social meanings of masculinity, femininity and work.

New Political Alliances

In the above discussion I have argued that, through a case study of the implementation of equal opportunity policy, it is possible to see how the limitations of the liberal strategy of equal opportunity legislation can lead, first of all, to a socialist feminist critique of the structural impediments to equal opportunity, and then to a deconstructive feminist critique of the constructions of masculinity and femininity encoded in legislation and employment practices. I have argued that strategies for change must take account of all of these levels of analysis. Deconstruction, while exposing the dynamics of the social constructions of masculinity and femininity, can not, however, completely supersede the modernist narratives of liberalism, feminism and socialism, for most of the institutions of capitalist society – the law, the bureaucracy, the workplace – still operate according to the modernist principles of objectivity and rationality.[48] In a somewhat different context, Dipesh Chakrabarty invites us to imagine the consequences of an attempt to bring postmodernist narrative techniques into the courtroom:

> Can we imagine ever winning a case, however 'simple', by flouting the rules of evidence (often shared between judicial and historical narratives), by employing, say the narrative techniques of a Nambikwara myth or those of a postmodernist Dennis Potter play?[49]

Thus, while heeding the lessons of deconstructive critique, it is necessary to find ways of engaging with institutions which operate according to modernist principles.

The insights gained from the above case study in Japanese feminist politics could be applied to the study of other aspects of power relations in Japan. An obvious example concerns part-time workers who, due to their construction as 'non-workers', have been denied a status as potential unionists, thus allowing the more effective exploitation of such workers. This could be linked to an analysis of constructions of masculinity and femininity in the Japanese labour movement, and a consideration of how such constructions affect our understandings of class relations and gender relations.[50]

The gendering of roles in white-collar workplaces is underlined by the colloquial expressions used to refer to different categories of workers. Women workers may be referred to by such disparaging terms as *'O.L.'* (Office Ladies), or by terms which emphasise decorative qualities. Elite male employees, on the other hand, may be referred to as *'kigyō senshi'* (corporate warriors), a designation which emphasises masculinity. Dorinne Kondo has analysed the constructions of masculinity and femininity in small businesses in Tokyo, and argues that the roles of full-time worker and part-time worker in these workplaces are gendered roles, with the part-time worker occupying the feminine role. Gender identity in such workplaces interacts with class-based identities. In recent years there has also been an increasing consciousness of the sexualisation of the workplace, as sexual harassment receives more attention.[51]

Workers are also implicitly constructed according to ethnic categories. In addition to constructions of masculinity and femininity, the 'corporate warrior' of the Japanese company is not only categorised as masculine, but as representing a facet of Japanese identity. When we consider the exploitation of immigrant workers from South East Asian countries and the Middle East in Japan, then the question of unequal development can be considered in conjunction with local constructions of gender, race and ethnicity.[52] Such an analysis could draw on recent theorisations of 'racially-constructed class exploitation' and 'racially-constructed gender roles'.[53] In other words, a consideration of the dynamics of gender, race and ethnicity can form part of an understanding of mechanisms of exploitation in Japanese society, and can contribute to the process of formulating strategies for political change. This task has recently been receiving attention in Japan at both a popular level and an academic level.

A new understanding of politics, which recognises that class differences are experienced in 'historically specific', 'racially specific', and 'gender specific' ways[54] also implies the possibility of new types of political alliances. Union activity, for example, has traditionally been based on the common identity of 'worker' – often implicitly understood as a masculine identity – uniting workers in particular industries or companies. In contrast, the new community unions in Japan bring members together on the basis of shared membership of a local community,[55] or a common experience of marginalisation from the mainstream union movement. These new unions, then, can include part-time and casual workers, handicapped workers, illegal immigrant workers, or simply residents of the local community, brought together in a strategic alliance based on 'affinity'[56] rather than 'identity'.[57] Such alliances between disparate groups have also been a feature of the women's movement in Japan, for example in the coalition of groups who contributed to the campaign for equal opportunity legislation.

It is in the analysis of such specific, localised issues that we can begin to come to terms with elements of modernity and postmodernity in Japanese society. The implications of questions concerning political communication in the age of rapid communications, or the most suitable political strategies for dealing with centralised bureaucracy, must be played out at this local level. However, a consciousness of the international context of 'post-industrial' Japan might also lead to scepticism about this concept. While the growth of service, leisure and knowledge-related industries in Japan may be seen as a symptom of postindustrialisation (one element of postmodernity), this process is supported by the labour of part-time women workers within Japan, the use of illegal immigrant workers in construction and small-scale manufacturing, and the use of factory labour in offshore manufacturing plants. The global movements of capital are implicated in gender and class relations well beyond the Japanese archipelago. Any analysis of Japanese society should be aware of such contradictions and be sensitive to the political implications of postmodernity.

1. I would like to express my thanks to Andrew Buck, Lucy Healey, Yoshio Sugimoto and Amanda Whiting, who commented on earlier drafts of this chapter.
2. On narratives of modernisation and theories of modernity applied to Japanese society, see McCormack and Sugimoto, 1988; on postmodernity and postmodernism, see Miyoshi and Harootunian, 1989.
3. For definitions of these terms, see Hutcheon, 1989; Rose, 1991.
4. Miyoshi and Harootunian, *op. cit.*, 1989: viii.
5. Miyoshi and Harootunian, *op. cit.*, 1989: viii.
6. Melville, 1989: 284.
7. The relationship between feminism and postmodernism is discussed by, among others: Hutcheon, *op. cit.*, 1989; Morris, 1988; Waugh, 1989; Nicholson, 1990; and the contributors to *Differences: A Journal of Feminist Cultural Studies*, Vol. 3 No. 1 (1991): Special Issue on Politics/Power/Culture: Post-modernity and Feminist Political Theory.
8. The connections between postmodernism and postcolonialism are discussed by, among others: Adam and Tiffin, 1991; Spivak, 1988; Trinh, 1990.
9. Chow, 1992: 104–5.
10. *Kokusai Fujin Nen o Kikkake to Shite Kōdō Suru Onnatachi no Kai*, commonly abbreviated as *Kōdō Suru Kai*.
11. *Watashitachi no Koyō Byōdō Hō o Tsukuru Onna Tachi no Kai*, abbreviated as *Tsukuru Kai*.
12. Discussed in more detail in Mackie, 1988a: 64–73. See also 'Tokushū: Kintōhō, Hakenhō, soshite . . .' [Special edition: Equal Opportunity Act, Labour Dispatch Act, and . . .]. *Agora* No. 100 (Aug.) 1985.
13. Article 14, paragraph 1 of the Constitution of 1947 states that: 'All of the people are equal under the law and there shall be no discrimination in political, economic or social relations because of race, creed, sex, social status or family origin'.
14. The Labour Standards Law also included provision for maternity leave (Article 65), nursing leave (Article 66), and menstruation leave (Article 67). Provisions which prevented women from engaging in dangerous occupations (Article 63) and excessive overtime or night work (Article 62) were the subject of controversy at the time of the introduction of the Equal Opportunity Act, as I will discuss below.
15. Cf. Kuba, 1984.
16. The relationship between equal opportunity policy and labour market policy is explored in Mackie, 1989: 97–109.
17. Quoted in the *Nihon Keizai Shinbun*, 20 June 1988.

46. See Broadbent, 1991.
47. Surveyed in Community Union Kenkyū Kai, 1988.
48. Joan Scott, in her analysis of the Sears Roebuck case, bravely advocates that feminists employ a deconstructive political strategy, with a 'refusal of simple dichotomies', but her discussion of the court proceedings in this case shows that the legal system still operates on the basis of just such simple dichotomies. Scott, 1988a: 176.
49. Chakrabarty, 1991: 114–15.
50. Kondo, 1990.
51. For discussion of the issue of sexual harassment in the Japanese context, see Sugii, 1990; Tsunoda, 1991 and 1993: for a more general discussion of the sexualisation of the workplace in the Australian context, see Pringle, 1988.
52. The interactions of gender, class and ethnicity in the situation of illegal immigrant workers have been discussed by Mackie and Taylor, 1994.
53. Parmar, 1982: 237, cited in Bottomley *et al.*, 1991: 166.
54. Sacks, 1989: 542.
55. Takagi, 1988: 11.
56. I am borrowing this term from Haraway, 1987.
57. For a somewhat different understanding of the relationship between class politics and postmodernity, see the writings of Ong, 1987; Ong, 1991: 279–309.

6 SCIENCE
Fuzzy Logic: Science, Technology and Postmodernity in Japan

Tessa Morris-Suzuki

The approaching end of the twentieth century provokes speculation about long-term currents of history. With the spread of
industrialisation beyond the confines of the Atlantic economies,
the decline of the West, proclaimed by Oswald Spengler over 70
years ago, seems to have become a reality. The scientific and
technological world-view which sustained the rise of the Western
industrial system has also lost its hold. The words of Siegfried
Giedeon, written in mid-century, have acquired a particular resonance as the century draws to its close: 'in every sphere a revolution, arising from the depths of our mind, has shattered the
mechanistic conception of the world'.[1]

The extension of the geographical frontiers of industrialisation
has coincided with an extension of the frontiers of technology
beyond the manipulation of things to the manipulation of symbols, and even of the information code of life itself: technological
power is no longer identified with the megamachine. Within
science a more gradual development of ideas, from the theory of
relativity onwards, has eroded the simple vision of the universe
as a piece of celestial clockwork, whose microscopic and cosmic
workings conform to the intuitively comprehensible laws of the
visible world. At the same time, the criticisms of philosophers
and historians, feminists and ecologists, have challenged the image
of modern science as a uniquely valid representation of transcendent reality.[2]

It is tempting to conclude that we are poised on the brink
of some truly new order of things, some 'twenty-first century
paradigm'.[3] But, if this is true, the outlines of the new order, and
of the theories needed to analyse it, remain remarkably obscure.
In the pages which follow we shall look at some debates on the
'new paradigm' in the context of Japanese science and technology,
and try to unravel the social and political implications of these
debates.

Modernisation, Marxism and Science in Japan

Until recently, interpretations of Japan's position in the world order were dominated by two rival approaches: modernisation theory and Marxism. For Marxists, who formed a large proportion of Japan's academic community, the object of analysis was capitalism. Debate focused upon the nature of capitalist development in Japan, and upon the similarities and differences between the western model of capitalism and its Japanese variant. From the Marxist point of view, the rise of capitalism had set in motion the emergence of modern science and technology, with all its immense potential to enhance human welfare. At the same time, however, capitalism had also subverted science from its true objectives, making it a servant to the competitive greed of the ruling classes.

In the Japanese context, the central Marxist debate was the famous *Rōnō–Kōza* controversy: the *Rōnō* faction emphasising parallels between the evolution of Japanese capitalism and of its western counterparts, and the *Kōza* faction emphasising the relatively backward and 'feudal' nature of Japanese capitalism. *Kōza* historians, in particular, believed that the development of science and technology in Japan was retarded by the power of the state, the poverty of the working classes, and (after World War II) the subordination of Japan to *Pax Americana*.[4]

During the 1950s and 1960s, modernisation theory emerged as an influential alternative to the Marxist approach, and as one especially favoured by US scholars of Japanese development. In place of the idea of 'capitalism', with its unmistakable aura of ideological controversy, modernisation theory offered a supposedly universal and value-free notion of 'modern development'. Its message, in fact, was profoundly teleological. Since 'modern' also has a chronological meaning – 'pertaining to recent time' – the term 'modernisation' has overtones of a process as linear and irreversible as the arrow of time itself. How could any society ultimately avoid becoming 'modern'?

The content of modernisation, however, remained controversial. Some writers have restricted its meaning to economic or technological development. Fosco Maraini, for example, considers modernisation as 'the impact of science and technology, with all their extraordinary, precious, horrid, marvellous, dangerous, stupendous and sometimes deadly effects upon life, social and individual, human, animal and vegetable – not to mention their impact on brute matter, on the very face of our planet'.[5] Most, though, see modern development as a process encompassing changes to social systems, politics, art, religion and ideas, as well as to science and technology. Its characteristics are commonly believed to include an increasing emphasis on rationality, secularism, individual identity, achievement (as opposed to inherited status) and bureaucratic forms of organisation.[6]

Ironically, modernisation theory, despite its claims to be beyond ideology, became a powerful weapon for social and political criticism within Japan. Where many Marxists had used the ideal type of 'capitalist development' as a means of highlighting the backwardness and distortion of Japanese capitalism, many modernisation theorists used the ideal type of 'modernity' to emphasise Japan's failure to become truly modern. A common refrain was that Japan's economic and technological development had outstripped its social and political development. For all its increasing wealth, Japan had proved incapable of producing that independent, rational individualism which was the cornerstone of political modernisation. Some writers attributed the weakness of Japanese individualism to the historical circumstances of Japan's industrialisation,[7] but others related it to a traditional culture which had no concept of a transcendent creator-god and no sense of the separation of human beings from nature. In the West, it was argued, the dualism which divided creator from creation and human beings from nature gave rise to a sense of individual responsibility and of absolute moral standards. In Japan, on the contrary, humanity was seen as part of a numinous natural order, and unity and harmony were valued more than the individual conscience.

This vision of incomplete modernisation was widely used to explain the peculiarities of Japan's scientific and technological development. Group consciousness and weak individualism made the Japanese hard workers, ready to absorb imported ideas when necessary. But the survival of traditional culture stifled creativity, and helped to explain why Japan had succeeded as an imitator rather than an innovator.[8] Without a belief in a creator god, there was no stimulus to 'enquire into the divine design'[9]; without the sense of nature as something separate and challenging there was (according to physicist Yukawa Hideki) no need for 'adventure either in action or in thought'.[10] Japan, it seemed, was doomed by culture to achieve modernisation without Nobel Prizes.

Modernisation theory, as a critical tool, had its uses, but it also had several limitations. One was that modernisation as an ideal type was often confused with modernisation as a real process experienced by real societies. As a result, it was assumed that western societies had actually achieved the prescriptions of theory, and that Japan's failure to do so was in some way uniquely deviant. The analysis, consequently, could sometimes end up sounding a little like the logic of Lewis Carroll's Cheshire cat: 'A dog growls when it's angry and wags its tail when it's pleased. Now I growl when I'm pleased and wag my tail when I'm angry. Therefore I'm mad'.[11] Another problem lay in the reification of Japanese culture. Some of the more simplistic versions of modernisation theory tended to present Japan's culture as something static and fundamentally distinct from Western culture. This view ignored the complex, dynamic and ideological nature of all 'cultures', a point to which we shall return later.

Japan and the 'New Science'

By the last quarter of the twentieth century the vision of Japan as a nation of skillful but uncreative borrowers of Western ideas was becoming hard to sustain. Japanese technological innovations in areas like superconductivity and robotics were presenting real challenges to other industrialised nations, and Japan was evolving into a serious exporter, as well as importer, of industrial technology.[12] In the basic sciences too, Japanese creativity was attracting increasing international attention. A survey of the leading international science journals, for example, showed that contributions by Japanese scientists had risen from 5.4 per cent of all published papers in 1975 to 7.7 per cent in 1986, overtaking France, West Germany and the Soviet Union.[13] Japan had even obtained five of the elusive Science Nobel Prizes. (The first was awarded to Yukawa Hideki in 1949. The remaining four have all been awarded since 1965.)

There are, of course, many possible ways of explaining Japan's growing scientific and technological impact on the world, but one popular explanation goes something like this: it is not Japanese culture which has changed; rather, scientific thought itself has evolved into a new paradigm which fortuitously coincides with the traditional 'oriental' (and particularly Japanese) world-view. This argument was originally developed, not so much by Japanese scholars, but rather by a number of popular writers on science in the United States – the most influential works included Fritjof Capra's *The Tao of Physics* and *The Turning-Point*, and Gary Zukav's *The Dancing Wu-Li Masters*[14] – but it has since been taken up and debated by some prominent Japanese writers, including Kyoto University's Ito Shuntaro.[15]

The main theme of these writers is that developments in particle physics, and particularly in quantum mechanics, have led to the collapse of the mechanistic view of nature which characterised Newtonian science. In the classical Newtonian world-view, the concept of nature as a machine led scientists to believe that the whole was merely the sum of its parts, and that the best way to study a natural phenomenon was to dissect it and scrutinise the workings of its smallest component elements. In this process, the interrelatedness of the whole was overlooked.[16]

As physicists probed deeper and deeper into the subatomic world, however, they were forced to recognise that this vision of nature was no longer tenable. Matter was not made up (as school physics lessons once taught) of a mass of particles which resembled and behaved like minute golf balls. Instead, at the subatomic level, the clear boundaries between matter, energy and motion dissolved. An electron might in some respects behave like a particle, but in others behave like a wave; other particles might possess some of the common attributes of physical objects, such as spin, but lack such fundamental attributes as mass. In this world, therefore, it became impossible to separate the individual particle from its relationship to other particles: matter was formed from relationships as much as it was formed from particles.[17]

Equally disconcertingly, in certain areas of experimentation, it seemed that the very process of observing particles disturbed their behaviour in unpredictable ways. The scientist was no longer, as in the Newtonian world, an impartial, godlike observer of nature, but was part of the natural process which he or she was studying. In Heisenberg's famous words, 'what we observe is not nature itself, but nature exposed to our method of questioning'.[18]

Looking at it from this perspective, the parallels with 'Eastern' thought seemed clear. As in Taoism and Buddhism, all natural phenomena are seen as being visible manifestations of a single interrelated whole: 'this world which seemed to be Many is in

truth One'.[19] As in the traditions of Shintoism as well as Buddhism, human beings are 'immersed in the midst of nature', rather
than observing it from afar.[20] The new paradigm was, as Murakami Yasusuke puts it, a 'hermeneutic' rather than a 'transcendental' one,[21] and since the traditional patterns of Japanese
culture were also hermeneutic, the very sources of Japan's earlier
scientific backwardness and derivitiveness could now become
sources of scientific creativity.[22]

It should be said at this point that Capra's ideas on the 'new
science' are treated with some scepticism by many scientists, both
within Japan and elsewhere. However, this has not prevented his
notion of the connections between eastern religions and science
from winning a wide public following. Entrepreneur Kumaoka
Shun'ichi, for example, attributes his success in developing a new
water filtration technology to his belief that 'Buddhism contains
all the concepts of physics and therefore all the laws of nature'.
Through Buddhism Kumaoka 'reached the firm belief that
nature moves within a single great law, namely the cycle of birth
and death which holds all beings together'.[23] Besides, the notion
of a new scientific paradigm which had emerged from the world of
particle physics was soon extended to other areas of scientific
discovery. Cultural anthropologist Nakazawa Shin'ichi, for
example, draws a parallel between the new mathematics of frac-
tals and the philosophies of Taoism and Buddhism.[24] Another
particularly influential variant of 'new science' is the work of Ilya
Prigogine and the so-called 'Brussels School', whose ideas deal
with one of the major paradoxes of nineteenth-century science:
the contradiction between evolutionary theory and the laws of
thermodynamics. While evolutionary theory sees nature as
becoming steadily more diverse and complex, thermodynamics
postulates a process of entropy, whereby diversity is dissipated
into a state of equilibrium and uniformity. The Brussels School's
answer to this conundrum is to suggest that the laws of nature
do not work in a smooth linear way in either direction. On the
contrary, they are characterised by moments of crisis and radical
change. In natural systems such as chemical structures, small
fluctuations caused by environmental or other changes may ampl-
ify themselves until they throw the whole system into chaos. At
this point, the future of the system is uncertain, and very small
chance influences may push it in one direction or another. In
some circumstances, however, an external influence may set off

a process of change which, through positive feedback, will lead
to a new, more sophisticated organisational structure arising from
the decline of the old.[25]

Like the ideas of particle physics as presented by Capra and
others, this vision of the universe stresses the interrelatedness of
the natural order. It also suggests a notion of spontaneous self-
organisation: given the right conditions, the elements of nature
will form themselves into complex and self-replicating structures.
Nature tends, as the title of Prigogine's book suggests, to order
as much as to chaos.

In this sense, Prigogine's views have a close connection to a
third form of 'new science', and one which is particularly closely
associated with Japan. This is the science of 'holonics'. The idea of
a 'holon' originates with Arthur Koestler,[26] but contains powerful
echoes of a current of holistic natural philosophy originating with
Leibnitz and developed in the twentieth century by (among
others) Jan Christian Smuts.[27] In the late twentieth-century context, however, 'holonics' is the name given by a group of Japanese
researchers to research in which they seek to identify the characteristics which define life itself. They see the difference between
machines and living creatures as lying in the principle of self-
organisation. The elements (or holons) which make up living
creatures have, they argue, a capacity for spontaneous coordination which, through positive feedback, creates highly sophisticated structures. This capacity is sometimes likened to the
relationship between words and sentences: the words work
together to create a meaningful sentence, and the sentence in
turn endows the individual words with meaning.

The science of holonics is largely based upon experiments conducted on the molecular structure of muscles by Shimizu Hiroshi
and others at Tokyo and Kyūshū universities. These experiments
appear to show that there is spontaneous cooperation between
the molecules which make up living organisms. At a molecular
level, the various substances within the muscles are linked
together into a system in such a way that the movement of one
molecule transmits information to others nearby, initiating a chain
reaction of coordinated movement.[28]

Shimizu explicitly relates his notion of holonics to the traditions
of Japanese Buddhism. 'In explaining our approach, I refer to
the ideas of Buddhism. What I mean is that the basic ideas of
Buddhism – not only of Buddhism but of traditional Eastern

thought in general – are founded upon the rule of a circular relationship between the individual and the totality of things . . . An excellent feature of Buddhism is that it begins from a notion of "all living creatures" (*ikitoshi ikeru mono*) and not just from a concept of "human beings". Thus it is founded upon the premise of the existence of many individual beings. The mutual linking together of "all living creatures" into appropriate relationships is what creates the cosmic order or, in other words, creates . . . "Buddha" '.[29]

Some non-Japanese scientists, too, have accepted this link between religious tradition and Japan's contribution to the development of life sciences. Marvin Minsky of the Massachussetts Institute of Technology observes that 'many Western scientists involved in life-related research have taken a strong interest in Eastern ideas and philosophies, such as Buddhism. This is a sign that they have realized the limitations of the Western preoccupation with analysis and are groping for new approaches. As an Eastern culture, Japan could play a meaningful role in this effort'.[30]

Of Robots, Fuzzy Logic and the Japanese Mind

In order to create machines which move and reason like human beings, it is first necessary to understand the workings of the human organism. Research into the life sciences in Japan is therefore closely related to technological programmes in areas such as robotics and artificial intelligence, and this explains the substantial government support given to schemes like the Human Frontier Science Project, which aims to unlock the secrets of the human brain and related physiological processes.

It is not surprising, then, to find that themes of organic holism and spontaneous self-organisation recur in debates on these frontier areas of technology. Nor is it surprising to discover some academics and journalists attributing Japan's technological success to traditional philosophies of Buddhism and Shintoism. The robotics pioneer Katō Ichirō, for example, has developed a notion of synalysis – a combination of 'synthesis' and 'analysis' which is strongly reminiscent of Shimizu's 'circular relationship between the individual and the totality of things'.[31] More controversially, Katō has also suggested that Japanese workers' receptiveness to robotics stems from an animist notion that 'a God dwells in each individual piece of equipment', and that Japan's success in developing clean-room technology is related to Shinto traditions of self-purification.[32] The connections between religious tradition and high technology are energetically pursued by Katō's fellow roboticist Mori Masahiro, whose Mukta Institute (*Jizai Kenkyūjo*) propagates Mori's vision of the need for a uniquely Japanese form of scientific creativity.[33]

This approach has been given new impetus by efforts to develop forms of artificial intelligence which transcend the traditional binary logic of the computer, and can therefore approximate more closely to the complexity and subtlety of human thought. During the late 1980s much popular excitement was generated by the notion of 'fuzzy logic', a form of information processing in which a computer was able, not only to choose between the polar opposites 'yes' (=1) and 'no' (=0), but also between a range of intermediate positions (for example, 0.7). Fuzzy logic, which can greatly enhance the capabilities of computers and computerised equipment, became both an object of large-scale research projects, and also a potent marketing tool, with companies vying to produce the first 'fuzzy' washing machine, microwave oven etc.

Fuzzy logic fitted neatly into the debates on the new science and Japanese culture. Binary logic was readily equated with Western dualism, while fuzzy logic was identified with Japan's 'cyclical', 'circuitous' or 'vague' thought patterns.[34] Information scientist Azumi Kazuhiko, for example, argues that, where Western thought perceives truth in black and white, Japanese thought perceives it as a spectrum of black, grey and white. The recognition of this grey zone, according to Azumi, is a 'driving force behind Japanese advanced technologies . . . It's one of the reasons advanced technology has entered its Asian age'.[35]

These views might seem more convincing were it not for the fact that other writers have been simultaneously arguing that the secret of Japan's high-tech success lies in the Japanese tradition of *precision* rather than of vagueness. Shiomi Kazumitsu of the Fuji Filter Manufacturing Company, for example, relates Japan's success in filter technology and other areas of microelectronics to the exactitude and perfectionism of traditional Japanese culture: 'Japanese-made products embodying submicron technologies can, for example, be compared to the light meal served before a traditional Japanese tea ceremony. The meal, *kaiseki ryōri*, comprises a set of delicacies exquisitely and aesthetically prepared in accordance with the principles of Zen. Products manufactured using submicron design rules can by no means be achieved with rough-and-ready production techniques that can be compared to the way beefsteak is prepared and served'.[36]

Holonic Companies; Fuzzy Markets

Ideas about the 'new science' and its relationship to Japanese culture are important, not only because they are being offered as explanations for Japan's technological success, but also because they are providing the inspiration for a variety of 'postmodern' models of social organisation. Just as Darwinism gave rise to social Darwinism, so ideas of self-organising structures, holonics and fuzzy logic are being borrowed to explain social phenomena and to offer solutions to social problems.

The economist Imai Ken'ichi, for example, incorporates Prigogine's ideas into his writings in an attempt to overcome the limitations of the conventional, static equilibrium approach to neoclassical economics. In the same way that Prigogine emphasises the open, interrelated nature of physical structures, Imai argues that the business organisations of the future will be open rather than closed systems: large, hierarchical corporate structures will be replaced by networks of small bodies linked by a wide range of intangible connections. While cautioning against the use of oversimplified analogies, Imai also suggests that events like the oil crisis of the 1970s can be compared with Prigogine's thermodynamic collapse, and that Japan's recovery from crisis through the application of new technology can be likened to the spontaneous rise of self-organising structures from the chaos of the disintegrating old order.[37]

Shimizu Hiroshi similarly sees the principles of holonics as being applicable to society as well as to the molecular structure of living things. He argues, for example, that the energy efficiency of living organisms arises from their capacity for spontaneous coordination, and then goes on to draw a clear and confident analogy with the structure of society: 'People are the same. Through cooperation with one another, people create society or groups. To understand how people cooperate, we must observe their behaviour within the group. There is no way that we can take separate individuals and try to observe their cooperative behaviour. Unless we create an environment for cooperative behaviour we cannot ascertain the presence or absence of cooperation'.[38]

The ideas of Shimizu and his colleagues have been taken one step further by management consultants like Kitaya Yukio, whose notion of the 'holonic company' provided a popular buzz-word for the Japanese media in the mid-1980s. Kitaya presents the holonic company as offering a new form of management structure to meet the needs of the information age. Its overriding characteristic is that its members will be independently creative and yet will spontaneously cooperate to serve the goals of the organic corporation. In practice, this seems to mean a network structure of small, semi-independent units (similar to that proposed by Imai Ken'ichi) bound together by a strong emphasis on corporate ethos.[39]

More recently, as buzz-words come and go, the holonic company has been overtaken by the idea of the 'fuzzy market' (an extension of the concept of 'fuzzy logic'), put forward by the Japan Management Association as the key to corporate survival in the year 2000.[40] Here 'fuzzy' is used to refer to a blurring of the dualistic distinction between producer and consumer. The idea, reminiscent of Alvin Toffler's notion of a 'prosumer'[41] and Jonathan Gershuny's 'self-service society',[42] is that high technology will give individuals a creative, productive relationship rather than a merely passive relationship with the goods they consume.

One point to be made about this social theorising is that it creates what advocates of the new science would doubtless call a 'positive feedback loop', reinforcing images of society as an organic, harmonious whole. In step one, the paradigm of the new science is presented as conforming to the traditional Japanese image of universal harmony and interconnectedness; in step two, that paradigm is transferred back from science to society to give 'traditional' ideas a new patina of postmodern scientific validity.

The New Science and Japanese Culture Reassessed

There are many criticisms which can be directed at the idea of a natural correspondence between the 'new scientific and technological paradigm' and traditional Japanese culture. At one level, popular writings on the 'new science' can be criticised as being simply bad science. Yoshioka Hitoshi of Kyūshū University, for example, notes that a large section of Capra's work is based on a version of particle physics (known as bootstrap theory) which is now rejected by most scientists.[43] At a more basic level, however, it is hard to deny that important changes in scientific approach to nature have occurred during the twentieth century (though it should also be noted that, since many of these changes are the result of scientific discoveries made before World War II, the term 'new science' is a rather questionable one). The simplistic notions of a mechanistic universe *have* been undermined; science today *is* increasingly conscious of complexity, inter-relationships and unpredictable variations.

The main problem with attempts to relate 'postmodern' science and technology to Japanese culture is not so much that these attempts are based on a misreading of science, but rather that they are based upon a misreading of the relationship between science and society. Like the more simplistic versions of modernisation theory, they accept a view of 'science' as something transcendent and value-free, evolving according to its own internal laws, and a view of 'traditional culture' as something complete, crystallised and static.

A more useful starting point for analysing the relationship between science, technology and culture in modern Japan would be to recognise that science and technology are the products of society, and that their evolution not only depends on the intellectual traditions from which they spring, but is also shaped in every generation by social structures and social conflicts. If Japanese scientists pursue particular lines of enquiry – such as examining the molecular structures of living organisms – this is (at least partly) because of the economic needs, the political pressures and the science policies of contemporary Japan. If they use an intellectual framework which emphasises harmony, self-organisation and interconnections, this is not only because they are influenced by age-old Japanese views of nature, but also because they are influenced by much more recent ideologies and social experiences.

Shimizu Hiroshi, for example, may derive support for his ideas from Buddhism, but he also 'claims that the inspiration to devote himself entirely to the study of life itself came from the student rebellions that had Japanese campuses in turmoil in the late 1960s, when he was teaching pharmacology at Kyūshū University. "I

125

saw that student unrest arose as a result of the breakdown in the relationship – the harmony – between the whole and its individual components. And I realized that science, including biology and physiology, had neglected to examine the relationship between the collective whole and the individual" '.[44]

Like science and technology, notions of 'traditional culture' too are shaped by social structure and social conflict. Every generation, indeed, rediscovers and rewrites 'tradition' in its own image. In preindustrial Japan, for example, there were a number of different views of the relationship between human beings and the natural world, of which the animistic sense of total immersion in nature was just one.[45] The contemporary fascination with early animist conceptions of nature tells us as much about contemporary ideology as it does about the nature of tradition. It is important to recognise the complexity and dynamism of Japan's intellectual history if we want to acquire a balanced perspective of the background to scientific and technological in present-day Japan.

Because they rely on a transcendent, autonomous view of science and a reified, static view of culture, attempts to link the new science to traditional Japanese culture have several obvious weaknesses. One is that, for all their emphasis on 'tradition', they are oddly a-historical. Elements of 'tradition' are plucked from the remote past and inserted into the present without any sense of how they got there. This tendency is particularly evident in some recent writing on Japanese technology. As well as references to Buddhism and Shintoism, there is a current fashion for relating Japan's contemporary technological achievement to the craft techniques of the Edo period. Engineering professor Ishii Takemochi, for example, describes Japanese technology as being rooted in the Edo period, and states that 'in Japan today, if we look at LSI technology or whatever, we can surely say that the same production system and the same workplace atmosphere was already complete in the Edo period'[46] In a similar spirit, journalist Oyama Shigeo connects Japan's contemporary clean-room technology to the purification rituals of traditional swordsmiths,[47] and Sheridan Tatsuno links Japanese skill in microelectronics to the traditions of *netsuké* carving and *bonsai*.[48]

Historical research by Nakaoka Tetsurō and others has indeed shown that the technical skills and institutional structures of the Edo period were a crucial factor in Japan's success in importing

Western technology in the nineteenth century.[49] The small-scale craft workshops which earlier historians had dismissed as symptoms of 'backwardness' and 'feudalism' prove to have been vital elements in Japan's modern technological development. In this sense, it is true that contemporary Japanese technology is heir to a legacy stretching back to the Edo period. But that legacy has not been transferred intact from the mid-nineteenth century to the 1990s. On the way, it has been refined and remoulded by historical events such as the 1930s militarism, the Pacific War, postwar democratisation and the high growth of the 1960s. The influence of the Edo legacy on contemporary Japan can therefore only be understood if we also understand the impact of this intervening history.

One weakness of the 'postmodern science' approach then, is that it imposes a static, a-historical 'tradition' upon the present. Another is that it imposes ideas derived from science upon social thought in order to render it immune from criticism.[50] As in simplistic versions of modernisation theory, science is accepted as absolute truth, and its terminology and methods are borrowed to make politically debatable choices seem part of the inevitable order of things. Thus questionable images of the corporation and other social institutions as organic and nonconflictual can be sanctified by the application of terms like 'negative entropy' or 'holonics'.

My favourite example of the use of the 'new science' to remove human choices from the realms of human controversy comes from the Honda Motor Company which, in the late 1970s, faced a decision on setting up a plant in the United States. In the words of Honda's Managing Director, 'The usual approach to decisions is binary: yes or no. But the quaternary approach at Honda recognizes two additional possibilities: "both yes and no"and "neither yes nor no". In binary terms the answer to the question about setting up a plant in the United States would have been no, but I've heard that the quarternary approach gave us an answer of "both yes and no" '.[51]

Postmodern-isation or Post-modernisation?

Thomas Kuhn has a lot to answer for. His careful and thought-provoking work on scientific revolutions,[52] by popularising the idea of paradigm shifts, has given rise to a fashion of interpreting every emergent social or intellectual trend as a 'new paradigm'. Thus, in the late twentieth century we are assailed by a thousand prophets proclaiming a postmodern social paradigm, a postindustrial economic paradigm, a post-Newtonian scientific paradigm, a post-Fordist managerial paradigm, and so forth.[53] One problem with these ideas is their uncertainty about the depth of the changes which they celebrate. For example, is the new technological paradigm a change comparable in magnitude to the discovery of agriculture or the industrial revolution, or is it merely a new wave of industrial innovation similar to those of the late nineteenth century or the 1930s-1950s? Is the new scientific paradigm the end of modern science as we have known it, or is it merely one of many shifts of dominant perspective within the framework of modern science?

I would suggest that the most useful way of looking at contemporary scientific and technological changes may be to see them, not as a sharply defined break with the past, but as an extension and intensification of trends which have been occurring at least since the eighteenth century. Industrialisation is expanding from one small area of the world to become an increasingly global process. The commodification of goods and services is extending itself into the commodification of knowledge and of the processes of life. Science and technology, rather than losing their grasp on our society, are permeating more deeply into every area of human existence. These developments, of course, are new and demand new forms of social and political response, but they can only be understood if we recognise them as part of a long historical continuum.

With these thoughts in mind, it is possible to envisage two different approaches to the changing world order. One approach can be termed 'postmodern-isation'. Here the story goes as follows. The leading industrial nations have passed through a phase of 'modernity' and are now entering a new phase called 'postmodernity'. The object of research is to define the characteristics of postmodernity, and to discover which societies conform most closely to its contours.[54] The ideas which we have been discussing in this essay suggest that 'postmodernity' involves an intellectual reorientation from atomism, individualism and Cartesian dualism, to holism, interrelatedness and spontaneous self-organisation. Just as some modernisation theorists saw particular cultures as best able to adapt to the paradigm of modernisation,[55] so the views discussed here suggest that certain cultures (above all Japan's) are particularly well suited to the 'postmodern' intellectual paradigm. From here it is not a very large step to the conclusion, seriously proposed by a few cultural nationalists, that Japan is destined to provide the next great world civilisation, one which will apparently avoid all the paradoxes and catastrophes of modern Western civilisation.[56]

We could counter this by coming up with some quite different visions of 'postmodernity', which might show Japanese development in a much less flattering light. But a more useful approach may be to abandon pursuit of the mirage of postmodernity altogether, and to focus instead upon a 'post-modernisation' approach: in other words, an attempt to overcome the inherent limitations of the notion 'modernisation' itself. The first target of criticism would then be the linear historical approach which envisages societies as progressing Indian-file through 'modernity' to 'postmodernity'.

In place of this linear history, the 'post-modernisation' approach would recognise that the process of industrial and technological development produces diversity as much as it produces convergence. Not only may some regions be actively underdeveloped,[57] but various regions may become 'developed' in different ways. For example (as Michael Piore and others have pointed out), the industrialisation process has led in some countries to the emergence of an economic structure characterised by large centralised business institutions, and in others to the survival and growth of many small firms.[58] In some countries, industrialisation has resulted in the appearance of many centres of manufacturing activity, and in others it has produced the rise of a single megalopolis. These diverging patterns reflect a variety of historical influences, including the relationship between industry and agriculture and the position of the individual industrialising nation in the wider world economy. Different patterns of industrialisation, in turn, have profound implications for the development of social institutions, political organisations and ideology in different parts of the world.[59]

A second feature of the 'post-modernisation' approach is its scepticism towards the reified and static image of 'traditional culture' implicit in some versions both of modernisation and of 'postmodern-isation' theory. In tracing various possible developmental paths, the focus is on institutions and historical processes, rather than on the determining force of a preexistent culture. In this sense, it is different from the approach of writers like Murakami Yasusuke (who proposes Chinese, Islamic, Indo-Hispanic etc. variants of industrialisation)[60] and Peter Berger (who counterposes Western and 'Confucian' development paths).[61]

Thirdly, the 'post-modernisation' approach makes the notion of Japanese 'uniqueness' redundant. The history of every society is by definition unique. What is interesting, from this perspective, is the interplay of overlapping patterns of resemblance which, for example, make Japan like South Korea because the state has played an important developmental role in economic growth, but also like Italy because both countries have differential economic structures in which small firms play a vital role. 'Post-modernisation', in other words, creates a window through which we can look with interest at the distinctive characteristics of science and technology in modern Japan, without assuming some unique and culture-bound Japanese scientific paradigm.

Notes

1. Giedeon, 1948: 717.
2. See, for example, Bachelard, 1984; Goonatilake, 1984; Harding, 1986.
3. Murakami, 1986.
4. For example, Hoshino, 1956.
5. Maraini, 1988: 45.
6. For example, Hall, 1965: 20–23.
7. For example, Maruyama, 1965: 489–531.
8. Morishima, 1983, see particularly pp. 176–7.
9. Kyogoku, 1985: 269.
10. Yukawa, 1967: 55.
11. Carroll, 1946: 94.
12. See, for example, Kagaku Gijutsu-chō 1990.
13. *Ibid.*, 1990: 145.
14. Capra, 1975 and 1982; Zukav, 1979.
15. See, for example, Inoue and Itō, 1984. Itō is now a professor at the International Research Centre for Japanese Studies in Kyoto.
16. Capra, *op. cit.*, 1975: 22–3.
17. Capra speaks of modern physics as seeing the universe as a dynamic 'web of relations'. *Ibid.*, p. 192.
18. Quoted in Zukav, 1979: 136.
19. Lao Tzu, *Tao Te Ching*, quoted in Watts, 1962: 58.

20. Watanabe, 1976: 174.
21. Murakami, 1990: 1–34. Murakami notes that, even in the natural sciences, 'the old [transcendental] analytic framework seems to be facing serious limitations' with the emergence of 'the uncertainty principle; Gödel's incompleteness theorem, the notion of a particle without mass, the concept of "super vacuum", and so forth'. *Ibid.*, pp. 31–2.
22. It is interesting to note that Yukawa Hideki drew a connection between his ability to contribute to the development of particle physics and the influence of East Asian culture on his thought pattern. See Yukawa, 1973, especially p. 57.
23. Mogi, 1984: 242–3.
24. Nakazawa 1984: 246–59. Nakazawa, it should be noted, recognises that the ideas of this 'new paradigm' reflect a search for a more dynamic model of nature which draws upon Western as well as Eastern philosophical traditions.
25. See Prigogine and Stengers, 1984.
26. Koestler, 1978.
27. Smuts's 'holism' seems in places remarkably similar to the holonic view of nature. For example: 'The idea of wholes and wholeness should . . . not be confined to the biological domain; it covers both inorganic substances and mental structures as well as the highest manifestations of the human spirit. Taking a plant or an animal as a whole, we notice the fundamental holistic characters as a unity of parts which is so close and intense as to be more than the sum of its parts . . . the synthesis affects and determines the parts, so that they function towards the "whole"; and the whole and the parts therefore reciprocally influence and determine each other, and appear more or less to merge their individual characters . . .' Smuts, 1936: 85.
28. Shimizu, 1987: 199–234.
29. *Ibid.*, p. 212.
30. Quoted in Tahara, 1986: 10.
31. See Schodt, 1988: 204.
32. Quoted in Oyama, 1989: 89.
33. Schodt, 1988: 209–11; see also Tatsuno, 1990: 42–5.
34. Tatsuno, *op. cit.*, 1990: 21–2; see also *Tokyo Business Today*, Vol. 59 No. 1 (Jan.) 1991: 6.
35. Quoted in Schodt, 1988: 212.
36. Oyama, 1989: 87.
37. Imai 1984: 58–60 and 202–5.
38. Shimizu, 1987: 234.
39. Kitaya, 1985, see particularly pp. 46–7.
40. See *Tokyo Business Today*, 1991.

41. Toffler, 1980.
42. Gershuny, 1978.
43. Yoshioka, 1986: 121–7.
44. Tahara, 1986: 11–12.
45. Morris-Suzuki, 1991.
46. Ishii, 1983: 120.
47. Oyama, 1989: 91.
48. Tatsuno, 1990: 55–9.
49. See Nakaoka, 1986: 3–106; Nakaoka, 1990.
50. This point is also emphasised in Yoshioka, 1986: 112–13.
51. Quoted in Aoki, 1990: 27.
52. Kuhn, 1977.
53. See, for example, Murakami, 1990; Kitaya, 1985; Kodama, 1991, Ch. 1.
54. It should be said that many of the original theorists of post-modernism had a much more complex vision of the subject. Jean-Francois Lyotard, for example, states that 'post-modernism is not modernism at its end but in the nascent state, and this state is constant'. Lyotard, 1984: 79.
55. See, for example, McClelland, 1961.
56. See, for example, Umehara, 1976: 62–4.
57. Frank, 1971.
58. Piore and Sabel, 1984.
59. See, for example, Berger, 1980; Koo, 1987.
60. Murakami, 1986: 228–9.
61. Berger and Hsiao, 1988.

7 LITERATURE
Questioning Modernism and Postmodernism in Japanese Literature

Toshiko Ellis

In this chapter I would like to consider some preliminary questions regarding the discussion on postmodernism in the Japanese context. My intention is not to argue whether Japan is a postmodern society, nor to present a detailed analysis of the cultural phenomena referred to by some as representing the postmodern in Japan. What I believe is most crucial for any discussion on postmodernism in Japan is the examination of the context in which the term came into use in the West and in Japan, particularly in relation to the fundamentally different construction of Western and non-Western societies.

It must be emphasised that to look at the visible symptoms of each society and to argue whether or not one resembles the other is a typically 'modern' attitude. As I will discuss at length later, this preoccupation with comparing one society with another, looking for either similarities or differences, assumes the existence of a universal scale of measurement and is, after all, what postmodernists are striving to move away from. Although one can easily find numerous phenomena in contemporary Japan that appear strikingly similar to phenomena that are regarded in the West as characteristically postmodern, finding parallels in cultural and societal phenomena and claiming that the two societies are undergoing a similar historical experience are two entirely different matters. It has been argued with regard to Western societies that postmodernism can be seen as the cultural logic of late capitalism.[1] Admitting that Japanese society is showing various symptoms of a late-capitalist postindustrial society, it is nevertheless misleading to assume that postmodernism should then be its 'cultural dominant'.[2] Such a perception is potentially vulnerable to a view which positions Japan on an evolutionary ladder of progress and, using the West as the point of reference for comparison, celebrates the extent of Japan's achievement in its project to modernise and to go beyond the West. Any assessment of the state of a particular culture must involve a careful examination of the various structural forces that contribute to the making of that culture; this includes not only economic but also social and political forces. Such a study is far beyond the scope of this paper. Rather, I will take an historical perspective and discuss some of the implications of the use of the term postmodern in light of Japan's modern history; in particular, with regard to how the term stands in relation to Japan's cultural modernism and what it suggests about the West/non-West conflict that lay at the base of Japan's thrust towards modernisation.

One of the central issues raised in recent discussions on Japan's modernity concerns the relationship between Japan's modernisation and the geopolitical configuration of the world in the late nineteenth century which set the conditions for Japan's modernising project. It has been widely argued that the notion of the modern is not simply a twin concept to the notion of the premodern, indicating a temporal transition from one state to another in accordance with a linear progression of history; the term modern has also functioned to delineate a distinctly nineteenth-century Western perception of the world as divided into the modern and the nonmodern, the West being the representation of the former category and the entire bloc of non-Western cultures falling into the latter. Notably, another assumption behind this dichotomous division of the world was that the West was to serve as the universal point of reference in relation to which all non-Western nations would recognise themselves as particulars. As Sakai has pointed out in his analysis of the concept of modernity and its critique, there is no inherent reason why the binary opposition between West and non-West should determine the geographic perspective of modernity except for the following reason: 'that it definitely serves to establish the putative unity of the West, a nebulous but commanding positivity'.[3] Despite the fact that the West is itself an arbitrary construction which embraces a limitless number of geographic particularities, it has become 'a name for a subject which gathers itself in discourse', as well as 'an object constituted discursively'. Sakai thus argues:

[The West] claims that it is capable of sustaining, if not actually transcending, an impulse to transcend all the particularisations. Which is to say that the West is never content with what it is recognised as by its others; it is always urged to approach others in order to ceaselessly transform its self-image; it continually seeks itself in the midst of interaction with the Other; it would never be satisfied with being recognised but would wish to recognise others; it would rather be a supplier of recognition than a receiver thereof.[4]

Hence, through its constant efforts to become its own self by continually striving to transform itself 'reflectively' through its interaction with the Other, the West succeeded in believing itself 'to represent the moment of universal under which particulars are subsumed', consequently establishing a 'Eurocentric and monistic world history'. Sakai calls this process 'a ceaseless process of self-recentering by the West'.[5]

Japan in the late nineteenth century emerged on the modern world scene as a rapidly industrialising nation aspiring to overcome its status as a latecomer. It devoted its energies to absorbing and adopting the Western models of modernisation as efficiently as possible so as not to be frozen into the sphere of the Other, as viewed from the dominant West. The realisation that Japan had to adopt the Western pattern of modernisation to be able to compete with the West on an equal footing, while at the same time desiring to retain the nation's historical and cultural integrity, became one of the major axes of conflict amongst Japanese intellectuals in the years following 1868. Westernisation and nationalism constituted the two poles against which each individual defined his/her cultural orientation. It was also quite evident which pole was the more dominant with regard to the formation of the general intellectual trend. Following the institutional halting of Western penetration in the late 1930s and early 1940s, open opposition, which created the dynamics of intellectual currents, became submerged. What followed was the emergence of the well-known 'transcendence of modernity' debate of 1942. In this debate, a group of leading intellectuals strove to create the perception that modernity, which had been imposed on Japan by the dominating West, had been overcome, and that the war against the Allied powers was ideologically justifiable if seen in the light of its significance for future world history.

Sakai, in the above-mentioned analysis, refers to one attempt made by Japanese intellectuals to resist Western dominance. In 1941, a theory of world history was presented by a group of young philosophers who argued that the development of the monistic history of Western creation was approaching a turning point and that the time had come for a world history to emerge which would bring about a fundamental change in the relationship between the Western subject of history and non-Western others.[6] Sakai argues, however, that the fragility of this new world theory became apparent when reference was made to Japan's relationship with China. In their desire to liberate Asia from Western domination, the young philosophers spoke from a position of universalism, placing China in the position of the particular and assuming Japan to occupy the central position, in other words, defining Japan as 'the subject which determines other particularities in its own universal terms'.[7] They failed to realise that their theory was not free from a typically modern logic based on the paired notions of universalism/particularism. This implied that, in its wish to occupy the central position, Japan would inevitably have to eliminate all other 'centres'. Thus, the young philosophers' new world history was nothing more than a protest against the Eurocentric arrangement of the globe and a desire to reverse that order. In their attempt to negate the West, these Japanese intellectuals conceptualised Japan's position by employing an historical scheme developed by the modern West, and in so far as they worked within this theoretical framework they were unable to threaten the 'ubiquitous' existence of the West. According to Sakai, the weakness of the Japanese intellectuals who attempted to resist the West lay in their failure to realise that 'Japan did not stand outside of the West'.[8] Quoting from the works of Takeuchi Yoshimi who, in the immediate post-1945 period, critically examined the implications of the 'transcendence of modernity' debate as well as various other theoretical issues related to Japan's defeat, Sakai elaborates further on non-Western nations' resistance to expansion of the West and argues that this very resistance contributed to the completion of a Eurocentric and monistic world history.[9] As the only way for non-Western nations to resist Western dominance was to modernise by adopting the means of modernisation developed in the West, their resistance was doomed to failure. '[I]n its resistance, the Orient is subjugated to the mode of representation dominated by the West', therefore, no matter how hard it resists, 'the Orient cannot occupy the position of a subject'.[10] The resistance of the non-West served only to assure the West of the existence of the Other, against which the West would establish its identity as the subject. With the following quotation from Sakai's discussion of Takeuchi, I will move on to discuss the relevance of this problem to recent debates on postmodernism in Japan:

> The Orient is neither a cultural, religious, or linguistic unity, nor a unified world. The principle of its identity lies outside itself: what endows it with some vague sense of unity is that the Orient is that which is excluded and objectified by the West in the service of its historical progress. From the outset, the Orient is a shadow of the West. If the West did not exist, the Orient would not exist either ... For the non-West, modernity means, above all, the state of being deprived of its own subjectivity.[11]

With regard to the emergence of the term 'postmodern', Sakai argues that it 'possibly testifies not so much to a transition from one period to another as to the shift or transformation of our discourse as a result of which the supposed indisputability of our discourse of the historio-geopolitical pairing (premodern and modern) has become increasingly problematic'.[12] As is widely noted, one of the major focuses of the postmodern debate is its implications for the transformations of the global system. As Friedman argues, 'the crisis of modernity is a phenomenon specific to the declining centres of the world system', which he attributes to 'decentralisation of the global accumulation of capital'.[13] In support of Friedman's analysis, Featherstone also underlines the point that the current debate suggests a general global shift in 'the balance of power between the West and other nations which has forced them [the West] to consider the possibility that the other (the non-Western cultures, civilisations and traditions) could be a mutual partner in a dialogue'.[14] While it may be correct to a certain extent that the world at large is gradually going through a 'dehegemonising and dehomogenising' process bringing about 'cultural pluralisation',[15] the implications of such a tendency would be different for cultures of Western than for non-Western origin. From the point of view of the West, this suggests that the global geopolitical configuration set up in the nineteenth century, which served so effectively to secure its position at the centre of the world system, is now under threat. From the point of view of the non-West, however, it can be taken as an encouraging sign that the binary opposition sustaining the world system, which it was unable to destroy as long as it remained within the system, is finally breaking down and giving way to a somewhat less restrictive order. This transfiguration of the world system is no doubt related to the massive change in the flow and distribution of capital over the last two decades, resulting in an entirely different picture of the world economy. Japan, being one of the countries that contributed significantly to redrawing the map of the global economy, is thus included from time to time in current debates on postmodernism.

What must not be forgotten, however, is that, like many other concepts which signify a new orientation in society and culture, postmodernism as a theory was developed in certain countries of the West to challenge existing perceptions of their own culture. As the term suggests, postmodernism assumes some sort of break from the preceding 'modernist' perception. Whether the break suggests the emergence of a new paradigm in cultural theory which responds to the changing context of the contemporary world, or whether it is to be conceived of as signalling the entrance of certain cultures into a distinctly new phase of modernism, that is, seeing the break more as a division within the modernist paradigm, is still under debate. Some are also inclined to claim that modernism and postmodernism are not successive forms but are in fact simultaneous.[16] Whatever the case, the current debate on postmodernism in the West reflects the willingness of theorists to view critically the state of their own culture and position in society in relation to the social and cultural heritage of their society. That the recognition of this sense of rupture coincided with the emergence of a new type of world economy is, in that regard, secondary. The postmodernist critique of the authoritarian nature of rational discourse as shown in Lyotard's attack on the grand narratives of the modern age, or the strand of postmodernist theory that has strong ties with poststructuralism, for instance Derrida's elaboration of the notion of *'différance'* as a tool to break down the 'logo-centrism' of the Western world, can be understood as a process of self-examination by the West which throws into question the very foundation on which its culture stands. Another aspect of the postmodernist theory is that, in questioning the authority of rational discourse and in focusing attention on hidden assumptions and the ways in which theories are built up, it has lost the ability to speak for 'the Other':[17] the subject/object dichotomy which characterises the modern discourse being challenged, 'the Other', in this case, the non-West, is not the object of either incorporation or exclusion which, as we have seen, are two faces of the same mechanism.

The critical point in the discussion of postmodernism in the Japanese context is that postmodernism is once again an imported concept for Japan which is passively acknowledged and accepted, at least in academic and popular journalism, with considerable enthusiasm. The manner of reception has been undoubtedly ambivalent, unlike various other Western concepts introduced in the past. The assumption that the West possessed a ready-made model for non-Western cultures to follow was willingly abandoned by the West itself. However, the fact that the West has begun to express its willingness to decentre its position does not necessarily mean that the countries formerly excluded from the centre are no longer peripheral. The emergence of the postmodern debate in the West by no means presupposes that Japan, as one of the countries of the non-Western bloc which has succeeded in influencing the redistribution of world capital, has overcome Western dominance and thus transcended the modern.

This point is emphasised by Miyoshi, who argues that new intellectual currents in Europe and North America, the theory of postmodernism included, are promptly acquired and replicated in Japan without much critical evaluation. Japan's response often goes no further than attempts to identify corresponding characteristics in Japan itself, either in contemporary Japan or somewhere amongst its buried 'traditions'.[18] A similar point of view is presented by Ōe Kenzaburō, a novelist of the older generation striving to revive the tradition of 'modern' literature which, he asserts with confidence, is decaying. Ōe, too, refers to the Japanese pattern of reception of Western thoughts and ideas, observing that new theories and cultural criticisms produced in the West are vigorously imported, 'accepted' and soon 'discharged' as the next theory is introduced.[19] While it must be noted that Ōe speaks from a typically 'modernist' point of view based on the belief that writers should provide an appropriate human model for their age and resist trends in academic and popular journalism[20], when compared with Miyoshi's discussion, which is a critical 'postmodernist' analysis of the concept of the novel, it is clear that both writers share the view that the emergence of the postmodern debate in the West does not necessarily suggest the decline of

Western cultural hegemony. This brings us back to the question concerning the implications of the postmodern debate in the Japanese context.

In the following section, I shall focus my discussion on literature and briefly outline some key issues involved in the development of modern Japanese literature. This will provide an historical framework with which to examine the state of contemporary Japanese literature and the related question of postmodernism. We will then examine how the foregoing discussion of West/non-West relations becomes relevant to our understanding of the state of Japanese culture today.

The fact that Japan was a non-Western nation, entering into the modern world as a latecomer, conditioned the development of modern Japanese literature in a number of ways. One of the issues to be dealt with was the treatment of the pre-Meiji literary tradition, though this was gradually overshadowed by the increasing awareness that modern Western literature was an integral component of Western culture and should therefore be learned and absorbed. The acquisition of Western literature by the Japanese did not, however, mean a simple transmission of literary techniques and practices from one culture to another. As Karatani argues, this process involved a fundamental transformation in the function of the Japanese language and in the Japanese perception of the exterior world.[21] This is related to the fact that the earliest stage in the development of modern Japanese literature was coupled with the movement to unify written and spoken Japanese, which became widespread in the 1880s. The Japanese literary tradition had always guaranteed the independence of language, that is, language which is not subordinate to the subject. For the ancient poets, the exterior world was not an object to be perceived with an analytical eye but was acknowledged by means of allusion through a network of words and phrases constituted by preceding literary texts. The acquisition of modern Western literature, therefore, went hand in hand with the acquisition of a new mode of perception in which there existed a correspondence between the word and its referent. Karatani calls this process 'the discovery of the landscape' and claims that, ironically, when the West was just starting to look for an alternative to its 'logocentrism', Japan was moving in exactly the opposite direction.[22] A point made by Karatani which might offer some suggestions for the present discussion is that nineteenth-century Japanese culture, which lacked the notion of the subject and therefore of perspective, became an obstacle to be overcome in the development of modern Japanese literature. However, for the introduction of postmodern literature, it might prove to act as a catalyst.[23]

The modernisation of Japanese literature thus involved a fundamental reshaping of vision among Japanese writers and poets, not only the ones who embraced the Western style but also those who wished to retain a certain continuity with Japan's classical tradition. The latter adhered to traditional stylistic considerations but modernised their choice of subject matter and its representation. The notion of the subject, the perception of the exterior world as 'landscape', and the whole idea of individualism, were avidly absorbed and adapted by writers and poets in the development of Japanese literature, and this no doubt signified an emancipation from the way in which the human condition was framed in traditional Japan. It is beyond the scope of this paper to discuss the complex issues related to this process of literary modernisation. However, one point which must be noted is that, strictly speaking, literary modernisation did not occur in response to social, political and economic modernisation. The entire nation was thrown into the maelstrom of the modern world and put under pressure to waste no time in proving to the advanced nations of the West that it deserved full membership status. Social, political and economic modernisation was thus carried out on an institutional basis. Literary modernisation, or more broadly, cultural modernisation, was a by-product of this, but as soon as it was launched it began to take its own course. In other words, the notion of the subject, for instance, did not develop in response to the transformation of a society that nurtured the idea of the subject. In this sense we may conclude that literature was not institutionalised in the way that it was in modern Western nations.

If we call this initial stage in modern Japanese literature the 'modernising' period, the next stage could be defined as the emergence of modernism in Japan. This roughly coincides with the period spanning the first few decades of this century, when avant-garde movements which challenged the traditional notion of literature swept through Europe and North America. After several decades of enthusiastic absorption of Western literature, there emerged a stage when Japanese writers and poets began to see themselves as contemporaries of their European and North American counterparts. To identify the point at which this new awareness developed is not an easy task and is not of crucial importance to our present discussion. After the turn of the century, the time gap between literary occurrences in the West and their reception in Japan became increasingly small. The synchronicity of movements was reinforced by the fact that with the rapid growth of urban culture in Japan, wider channels for exchange of information between Western nations and Japan were opened. Various means of cultural exchange were explored on the popular level, unlike the preceding period when the introduction of Western culture into Japan was mediated by a limited number of intellectuals.

The modernist movement in Japan is therefore characterised by an awareness of contemporaneity with the West among certain groups of Japanese writers and poets. Together with their avant-garde counterparts in the West, they also aspired to free themselves from the oppression of tradition and to open new horizons for the future. There was, however, one crucial issue facing the Japanese modernists: once the near-synchronicity of literary movements was achieved, the Japanese modernists had to confront the fact that they were working in a different social and cultural context to that of their Western contemporaries. As noted earlier, the emergence of new literary movements did not necessarily correlate with the changing context of Japanese society. Therefore, even though the new concepts of the avant-garde were taken in by the Japanese, their application to the Japanese context brought about quite a different outcome from that of the West. In the present discussion I will not attempt to analyse the various types of modernist literature that emerged as a result of this. The point to be highlighted here is that, because of the unique socio-historical context in which Japanese modernism developed, the Japanese modernists were faced with a complex set of factors to take into consideration in defining their position in society. They had to define themselves not only against contemporary Japan and its modern institutions, but also against the traditional Japan which persisted on various levels of people's lives, and furthermore, against the West, which was the source of their inspiration as well as a threat to their cultural identity.

We can thus conclude that at the base of the modernist movement in Japan there lay the fundamental conflict that Japan was a non-Western nation which had acquired Western cultural principles, some of which not only contradicted Japan's societal situation but could potentially threaten Japan's cultural integrity. Writers and poets formed themselves into different groups that represented varying attitudes to the situation. Despite the conflicting ideologies and aesthetic attitudes expressed by these groups, commonly shared by them was a distinctly modern idea of self-definition. Every poet was at the same time a poet and a social being, who had to choose his/her position in society and define his/her work against Japan's past and present history. No poet could work independently of his/her social context, and this process of self-definition necessarily involved a radical exclusion of the other. On a different level, however, the Japanese modernists also shared a common awareness of their peripheral position in the world. Some negated it by claiming that the contemporaneity of their works had dissolved the West/non-West conflict, or by reverting to traditional approaches to prove that Western influence had been overcome. But in either case, they could not deny the fact that in their claims they were using the West as the point of reference: the West remained the centre in relation to which peripheral cultures defined their position.

This point relates to our earlier discussion about the intrinsic dilemma of Japanese modernity. In the specific sphere of culture as well, the modern configuration of the globe could not be challenged as long as those who wished to challenge it were conditioned to remain within the realm of the modern. Let us now move on to discuss the contemporary situation and the relevance of the postmodern debate in Japan today.

Just as it is difficult to determine when literary modernism began in Japan, it is hard to tell when, or whether or not it has, ended. Instead of attempting to draw a line at any specific point, I will approach the question from a different angle by concentrating on what appears to be a new type of writing in Japan, which presumably has challenged the preceding modernist notion of literature. My discussion will focus particularly on one author as a case study, Murakami Haruki, who is a novelist and short story writer in his early forties, often quoted as a representative figure in this new trend. Notwithstanding that the contemporary Japanese literary scene is much too diverse to be seen through the works of one writer, Murakami's case seems to represent many of the critical issues related to Japanese culture today. Firstly, his works appear to contain numerous elements relevant to the present discussion of postmodernism. Secondly, his works, which contain many pop images, lack 'serious' themes, and possess other norm-breaking features, have been received by the older generation of writers and critics in a most ambivalent manner: some ignored them completely; some criticised them as nothing more than another form of 'popular' literature; some praised them for their freshness and excellent technique in the composition of images and storyline; and some decided to reserve their comments simply because his work had such wide appeal to the younger generation. Lastly, Murakami's works have enjoyed enormous commercial success in the last decade: in 1989 his unprecedented popularity and the impact he had on the literary market was described as 'the Murakami Haruki phenomenon' in academic and popular journalism.[24] The following section gives a brief examination of his literary style, followed by some discussion of the supposedly postmodern features of his work. Then we will return to the question of the applicability of the term 'postmodern' in the Japanese context, this time focusing the discussion on the relationship between the emergence of this new literary trend and the preceding tradition of modern Japanese literature.

Some of the significant features of Murakami's stories are the namelessness of the characters, the contingent nature of the relationships that develop between them, and the pervasiveness of a vague sense of loss shared by the characters. The characters do not confront each other to create a dialogue: dialogues are immediately turned into monologues and are fragmented into a chain of images, which in turn is mingled with images of the exterior world. The following words of the protagonist in one of his early works, *A Wild Sheep Chase* (1982), well sums up the nature of human relationships in his stories:

> I turn a corner, just as someone ahead of me turns the next corner. I can't see what that person looks like. All I can make out is a flash of white coattails. But the whiteness of the coattails is indelibly etched in my consciousness. Ever get that feeling?[25]

A typical character in Murakami's works is someone who has already come to terms with the fact that positive human interaction is in vain. 'I' in *A Wild Sheep Chase* meets with a number of characters who pass through his life, providing him with vivid images that make up the succession of the present, which is his life. In other words, he lives in a state of perpetual change, the only sense of connection with the past being felt in the form of a nostalgic longing for a remote past. In the past, it seems, there was a dream, a hope and a belief that action was possible. But all this has been lost, not because one has failed in one's actions but because one has forgotten the dream itself, and lost any cause to fight for. As Aoki points out, 'to go to a resort hotel during the off-season period and enjoy a cup of coffee by yourself on a rainy morning' was a dream in the 1960s; in the 1980s, however, it has become a plain reality; you can go and have your cup of coffee, but what else?; all you encounter is an empty sense of recognition that 'you are there'.[26] In other words, the dream is too 'used up' to remain a dream. Kawamoto also points to the recurrent theme of nostalgia in Murakami's works. Referring to *A Wild Sheep Chase*, he argues how this apolitical, semifantasy novel, which does not dare use such 'raw' terms as 'revolution', or present a commentary on the student movements, is so amply suggestive of the 1960s that the reader cannot help reminiscing about 'that period'.[27] The protagonist 'I', in fact, does speak of 'exploitation', but in the following way:

> Exploitation doesn't exist. It's a fairy tale. Even you don't believe that Salvation Army trumpets can actually save the world, do you? I think you think too much.[28]

And with regard to the lack of faith in words themselves, he says:

> Sure we're tossing out fluff, but tell me, where does anyone deal in words with substance? C'mon now, there's no honest work anywhere. Just like there's no honest breathing or honest pissing.[29]

This fundamental suspicion towards words, and thereby towards action because it is deprived of a meaning, runs as an undercurrent in many of Murakami's works. A compact example of this is a short story entitled 'The Second Attack on a Bakery' (1986),[30] in which a young urban couple, who come to realise that something important is missing in their life because of a past uncompleted attack on a bakery, go through the elaborate ritual of a bakery attack, only to prove to themselves that action rationalised by words takes them nowhere.

It is obvious that there are certain elements in Murakami's works which are generally noted to be expressive of a postmodern cultural trend. The transformation of reality into images, the 'used-up-ness' of image linked with the notion of the pastiche, the dominance of nostalgia themes and of historical amnesia, all of which we find in Jameson's description of the postmodern[31], can be observed in Murakami's works as well. The manner in which Murakami deals with the nostalgia theme is also congruent with what has been argued to be characteristically postmodern: the past is not presented in its totality but is reinvented through fragmented images associated with a certain epoch: a pinball machine, an old film magazine featuring John Wayne's *Alamo*, The Beatles' 'Norwegian Wood' etc. The objects are concrete but the age which they evoke is felt to be far out of reach. In *A Wild Sheep Chase*, Bing Crosby's 'White Christmas' is played 26 times in a row, as if to reinforce the blurring effect of the distance between the present and the indefinable, imprisoned past.

Leaving aside for the moment the fact that they are all Western in origin, the above-mentioned objects of nostalgia are all products of pop culture. Murakami's stories, indeed, display abundant images of popular culture which are often juxtaposed with those of so-called high culture, thus neutralising the particular significance of both. Let us also note that the questioning of the referential function of language and the impossibility of dialogue, because of its constant 'slips' into monologue, were also suggested in Murakami's stories.

Having had a glimpse of the world created by Murakami Haruki, I shall now turn to the issue of how we can interpret the emergence of this new literary trend in contemporary Japan. The question to be raised here is, I repeat, not whether or not one can perceive parallel features in the works of contemporary Japanese literature and those of their Western counterparts. Acknowledging certain elements of a postmodern culture does not mean that the culture is postmodern, or that the writer is a postmodernist. Therefore, whether or not Murakami is a postmodernist is an entirely different question. I must also emphasise that I have only taken one of his early works as a case study, simply to detect certain elements in it which suggest a change in Japan's new literary trend. The following focuses on two major questions: how can Murakami's work be understood in relation to the modernist tradition of Japanese literature; and how do they stand in the broader sociocultural context of contemporary Japan?

One significant characteristic of Murakami's works is the absence of a sense of place. Even when specific place names are used in the text, they are used only to present an image of a certain type of place. Because these images are too fragmented to construct a three-dimensional picture of a real place, the settings of the stories take on an abstract nature. To make a brief comparison with modernist writing, one major feature of the modernist literature in Japan was that there was a clear awareness of the position from which writers and poets perceived the world. Regardless of whether or not they made it explicit in their writing, they could not write without choosing a certain perspective according to which the individual writer's position in relation to society, as well as Japan's position in relation to the West, could be determined. To put it more clearly, in Murakami's case, even if one replaces the name of a town in Japan with the name of a town in a Western country, its effect on the overall significance of the work would be minimal, whereas this would not be so in the case of modernist writing. The implication here is that the longstanding theme of conflict between West and non-West, underpinned by the conception of the West as the centre, appears to have been dismissed by Murakami as an assumption that was simply not relevant.

With regard to the sense of time, we have already seen that a vague sense of nostalgia dominates Murakami's themes and that the distance between the present and the past, which is evoked in nostalgia, is too obscure to be measured. In other words, the idea of a linear progression of history which provides a diachronic perception both of the past and the future is nonexistent. This aspect of Murakami's work is also strikingly different from the perception of history in modernist literature. As is most clearly shown in the term avant-garde itself, historical consciousness is an integral element of modernist literature. A desire to break away from tradition is accompanied by the urge to press forward and to break open a new horizon.

We can thus argue that Murakami's work does disclose certain features which are in conflict with the modernist perspective. Apart from the above two aspects regarding the sense of place and time, we can also mention the lack of confrontation characterised by monologue-like exchanges in conversation and the contingent nature of human relationships as anti- or nonmodernist.

The next question, then, is how the emergence of writers like Murakami can be explained in the context of contemporary Japanese culture and society. As mentioned earlier, the response to the emergence of this new stream of writing by writers and critics of the older generation has been ambivalent. The undebatable fact is that Murakami's works, together with those of other writers with more or less similar tendencies,[32] have thoroughly penetrated the literary market and have demonstrated the diversification of literature in recent times. This phenomenon has also contributed significantly to the breaking down of the hierarchical distinction between high culture, represented by modernist literature, and the popular culture and its product, the so-called popular literature, which until recently had been largely neglected by literary critics. The emergence of this trend and its wide acceptance by the general readership also testifies to the fact that there has been a significant change in the Japanese perception of the West. As suggested earlier, the conflict between West and non-West is no longer a crucial element in the thematic composition of Murakami's works. Rather, the West in Murakami's works is simply a part of the characters' everyday lives. Also, the West is represented by its pop culture, which contemporary Japanese readers can easily assimilate: his work does not present the West as the cultural centre that provides a model for Japanese to emulate.

All of these facts seem to suggest that Japanese society is currently evincing a break from the past and that this is strongly related to the transformation of Japan from a belated moderniser to a society which no longer requires a model for its social, political and economic progress. But does this hold true for culture as well? The visible signs of progress in the economic sphere and its consequences seem insignificant in comparison with the fundamentally contradictory nature of Japanese modernity. Even though it may be argued that certain aspects of contemporary Japanese cultural products indicate that Japanese society today renders a typical picture of a late-capitalist society and attests to the decentralisation of world culture, this is not to say that Japan has overcome, or transcended, the problems it encountered in its process of modernisation.

In this regard, Karatani's remark that the absence of a Japanese equivalent of the Western notion of the subject in pre-Meiji Japan may facilitate the development of 'postmodern' tendencies is revealing.[33] The introduction and popularisation of theories of postmodernism from the West may have even further accelerated this process. It is ironic that Japanese society, which has followed a typically 'modern' path of adopting Western cultural criticism, is at the same time exemplifying an arguably 'postmodern' phenomenon. However, as long as this cultural criticism, developed in the context of Western society and culture, remains the only available means for understanding the condition of its own society, Japan will remain firmly within the modernist paradigm. Just as the Japanese modernists of the early decades of this century were trapped in the complex position of having to define themselves against a plurality of opposing forces, adopting a postmodernist stance in Japan will give rise to a fundamental contradiction in terms. The 'deconstruction' of subjectivity will have no effect if subjectivity is yet to be established.

In concluding this working paper, I would like to mention some implications arising from the present cultural trends in Japan. Putting aside the point that postmodernism in Japan cannot be discussed by using frameworks provided by the West, it is still possible to use some suggestions from the Western theory of postmodernism to further our understanding of the cultural situation in contemporary Japan. It has been argued by many that postmodernism can be viewed in two ways: either as 'a culture of incorporation' that is 'fundamentally complicit with the socio-political status quo', or as a culture that is 'open-endedly subversive and paralogistic'.[34] Ryan, who stresses the latter, draws on the postmodernist critique of the classical theory of representation which held that meaning preceded and determined the representations, and attempts to present the progressive possibilities of postmodernism.[35] He contends that, when the reversal in the equation of sign and thing, or the cultural and the social, the political or the economic, occurs, culture would be granted 'a power it could not possess when it still was accountable to a determining materiality',[36] and in this way cultural signs can become 'instruments of the creation of new grounds, new meanings and new institutions'.[37] Opposed to the classical theory of representation which he describes as a metaphorical idealisation process, Ryan proposes the potentially emancipatory quality of metonymical contingency.[38] Taking a slightly different angle,

McGowan sees in postmodernism 'the attempt to forge effective strategies for intervention in the social'.[39]

Our question is whether or not the new type of literature as we saw in the works of Murakami possesses any subversive quality of this kind. One Japanese critic has pointed to the increasing tendency of writers in Japan today to abandon the effort to resist the existing system of representation.[40] Another critic has questioned why Japanese writers have so thoroughly lost the capacity to address the question of negativity.[41] Murakami's name was mentioned by both. And yet, the undeniable fact is that Murakami's works have attracted a remarkable following, which suggests that the general readership in contemporary Japan is willing to endorse the sentiment and the sensibility expressed in his writing. Are they reading it as a 'background novel' as they would enjoy harmless, nonengaging background music, as one critic cynically put it?[42]

In contemporary Japan, the critical faculties on the part of both writers and readers are put to question. As Ōe mentioned in the paper quoted above, it is indisputable that modernist literature as fundamentally oppositional art is in decline.[43] The shock of the new, characteristically defined in modernist literature as the experience of estranging oneself from the familiar world and establishing a critical distance, no longer seems to work in a society in which everything, or anything, can become a purchasable commodity. As Eysteinsson illustrates in the context of the modernism/postmodernism debate in the West, in a society where commercialism pervades, 'shock' ultimately becomes affirmative. The intended shock effect of TV commercials is one such example; or in the case of punk, 'the material objects that the radical practices of punk had sought to empty of meaning are again turned into marketable commodities'.[44]

In contrast to the oppositional, and therefore exclusionist, character of modernism, postmodernism in theory aims at radical decentralisation. Furthermore, the elitist aspect of modernism associated with high culture is negated by postmodernism, which claims to break down cultural hierarchy. However, when 'popular culture' is absorbed by 'mass culture' the self-critical function of society is threatened. Mass culture, while it is not exclusionist or hierarchical, is potentially incorporationist and could work to effectively minimise differences that would create critical viewpoints. To quote Stauth and Turner on this point, mass culture embraces an 'incorporationist ideology' or 'institution which has the effect of pacifying the masses through the simulation of false needs via the "culture industry" '.[45]

As the modernist discourse of opposition becomes increasingly threatened by the emergence of nonexclusionist, mass-consumable texts, the modernist question of self-definition, too, loses its dominant position in the thematic construction of literary works. As we have seen in Murakami's work, the question of where the individual stands in relation to his/her society or to history is suspended. The West/non-West confrontation also loses its relevance; therefore, the West is naturally decentralised and dispersed in the text in the form of consumable images which constitute the everyday life of the characters. It is misleading to assume, however, that this nondefensive attitude toward Western culture suggests a path toward emancipation from the persistent dilemma of Japanese modernity. If nonmodernist writing is to dismiss the idea that an external centre exists as the supplier of a model to emulate or to oppose, the only alternative would be for it to create a model for itself. A mere evasion of the historical question would leave the modernist conflict unresolved. And when the contradictions are suspended and dissolved into fragmented images of everyday life, literature will gradually lose its capacity to maintain a critical stance from the existing system of signs and will only contribute to inundating society with complacent discourse.

It must be noted that postmodern phenomena and the theory of postmodernism are two separate things, and therefore, even in the West, where the theory of postmodernism emerged as a critique of the modern, its cultural products may not necessarily possess the critical edge that the theorists are striving to maintain. In the case of Japan, the theory of postmodernism will be effective only when it is accompanied by a fundamental reexamination of the dilemma of Japanese modernity. Introducing a second-hand Western theory and looking for parallel symptoms in that society is a procedure all too familiar in Japan; and it is the procedure that has always secured Japan's position in the world as an efficient moderniser which can never become a subject in its own right.

Notes

1. Jameson, 1984: 57, 78.
2. *Ibid.*, pp. 55–6. This expression was used by Jameson to distinguish it from 'style'.
3. Sakai, 1988: 476.
4. *Ibid.*, p. 477.
5. *Ibid.*, p. 497.
6. *Ibid.*, p. 490.
7. *Ibid.*, p. 495.
8. *Ibid.*
9. *Ibid.*, p. 498.
10. *Ibid.*
11. *Ibid.*, p. 499.
12. *Ibid.*, p. 476.
13. Friedman, 1988: 457.
14. Featherstone, 1988: 213.
15. *Ibid.*
16. See Eysteinsson, 1990: 127–30.
17. Featherstone, *op. cit.*, 1988: 205.
18. Miyoshi, 1987: 116.
19. Ōe, 1989: 203.
20. *Ibid.*, p. 193.
21. Karatani, 1989a: 618. For further discussion on 'the discovery of the landscape' see Karatani, 1988: 9–50.
22. *Ibid.*, p. 620.
23. *Ibid.*, p. 621.
24. Kawamura, 1989: 2.
25. Murakami, 1989: 31.
26. Aoki, T. 1986: 147.
27. Kawamoto, 1986: 56.
28. Murakami, *op. cit.*, 1989: 48.
29. *Ibid.*, p. 49.
30. To my knowledge, this work is not available in translation. The original is 'Panya saishūgeki', in *Panya saishūgeki*. Tokyo: Bungei-shunjū, 1986: 9–31.
31. Jameson, 1983: 111–25.
32. Yoshimoto Banana is a female writer who has been enjoying popularity together with Murakami. See Fussel, 1990.
33. Karatani, *op. cit.*, 1989a: 621.
34. Milner and Worth, 1988: xii.
35. Ryan, 1988: 559.
36. *Ibid.*, p. 560.
37. *Ibid.*, p. 561.
38. Ryan, 1987: 208.

39. McGowan, 1991: x.
40. Watanabe, 1991: 2.
41. Kobayashi, 1991: 5.
42. Arai, 1986: 139.
43. Ōe, *op. cit.*, 1989: 203.
44. Eysteinsson, *op. cit.*, 1990: 223–4.
45. Stauth and Turner, 1988: 510.

8 FINE ARTS
The Conditions for Postmodernity in Japanese Art of the 1980s

John Clark[1]

A. Postmodernism

The rhetorical constructions of postmodernism have found quite a place in recent general understanding of cultural life,[2] of that of Japan in general,[3] and to some extent that of recent Japanese art.[4] There have also been attempts beyond Euramerica to see in what discourses various conceptions of postmodernism might construct meaning in recent Asian art.[5]

Debate has often revolved around the issue of whether postmodernism is a further ideological and formal complex beyond and in contradiction to modernism. Or, whether it is a shift into a different register, a variant trope within a now established rhetorical discourse, that of modernism itself. I adopt the latter position because I see postmodernism as an inversion on itself of the self-critical logic of modernism.[6] Perhaps what typifies the postmodern is a questioning of how image becomes material form, and whether the bounding codes of the material form are more, or less, plastic to both meaning and formal origin as any initial image or underlying image-signifier/signified relations were.

Rather than seeing postmodernism as a new, overarching ideological paradigm that has displaced that of modernism, I see it as a state in which this questioning exists in a more intense, possibly more radical form than the earlier modernism, of which postmodernism is itself an extension. I thus refer to the conditions for postmodernity, by that implying that postmodernity is a late or developed kind of modernity, a situation or phase-state within social and artistic contexts governed by that set of intellectual and artistic paradigms called modernism.

I think we must distinguish between discourses of interpretation and discourses of forms in the world. Too often have discussions of postmodernity assumed that the former can be simply read out from or read into the latter. It is as if modern understanding of visual perception has lead to an atavistic quest for a materialist nominalism. Signs have become things. This is due to the advent of photographic media, but also to the recent, complex consequences of more highly-controlled, technically-advanced and, to modern people, more powerful types of visual reproduction. The ideological jump has been from the knowledge that 'we can make images', to that of 'we control what images do because we can make them'. Even if the questioning of how images become form is intrinsic to postmodernity, those forms have their own specific characteristics which, in turn, indicate peculiar conditions of generation and dissemination.

I will here initially outline some categories for the kinds of form produced in the 1980s, and will do so in ways that are not always dependent on the interpretive codes used by contemporary Japanese critics. I will then look at changes in the structure of the Japanese art world, for which some statistics are available. This will be followed by a brief examination of types of legitimation, and of the interpretive codes applied in legitimating art. I shall then suggest some new hypotheses about postmodernity.

B. Types of Form

It is premature to produce any completely descriptive set of form-types for Japanese art of the 1980s, about which there will necessarily be disagreement over terms that should be conceptually as precise as possible, but which cannot always be so in practical application. For introductory purposes, and to provide an analytical direction, I will now establish some categories or, more accurately, penumbrae. The proviso should also be made that these categories are in part based on the prior selection for exhibition by Japanese critics, although not always in groupings they would recognise. I have also included several artists who are not on the Japanese critics' habitual selection lists.

These categories are:[7]

1. Decorative painting

1.1 Decorative painting as neo-figurative, metaphysical trace: Asashina Yasuto, Tatsuno Toeko, Hori Kōsai, Yamada Masaaki, Nakanishi Natsuyuki, Maki Tomoko, Yamada Junko, Akioka Miho, Yoshida Katsurō

1.2 Decorative painting as site which orders raw chaos: Ōtake Shinrō

1.3 Decorative relief as paint-processable field: Hikosaka Naoyuki, Hirabayashi Kaoru, Okazaki Kenjirō, Masuda Satoko, Suwa Naoki (Plate 1)

1.4 Dream decoration, somnambulist, phantasmagoric haptic fields: Odanaka Yasuhiro, Matsumoto Yōko, Yamabe Yasushi, Katayama Masahito, Ueno Keiichi, Ara Atsuko

This category denotes painting which deploys the effects of pure decorative pleasure, sometimes in ways that can be interpreted quasi-figuratively; one which sets up a visual field in which the lineaments of some unspoken desire may be traced. Quite frequently the viewer feels that visual sensation is deployed to sign the existence of a world of sensations beyond the visual which would not otherwise find external form [1.1]. There are many variations; one finds the establishment of visual fields that seem to be boundary zones for an absolute and visceral disorder comprised within [1.2]. This disorder can be overcome by using reliefs as a decorative zone that displays control by extending two-dimensional planes into a thickness. It is here that a kind of technological immanence elides with a fairly self-willed technological replication of references to the past of Japanese painting [1.3]. There is also a purely infantile field of decoration which creates fields into which the viewer is absorbed, as if, in the old Freudian metapsychology, there was nowhere fore-pleasure could not substitute surplus gratification for end-pleasure [1.4].[8]

2. New classicisms

2.1 New classic opticalism:[9] Nakamura Kazumi, Sakurai Hideyoshi

2.2 New classic imagism: Arimoto Toshio, Funakoshi Katsura (Plate 2),Usami Keiji

2.3 New classic conceptualism: Suga Kishio, Fukushima Noriyasu, Lee U-fan, Koshimizu Susumu, Kiyomizu Kyūbei

By the early 1970s, Japanese art had produced its own minimalist art called *Mono-ha*, associated with a reassertion from within

Japanese art discourse of relations between *objet* and site which did not depend on North American minimalism for their conceptualisation.[10] This was to produce a reaction against the authoritarianism and puritanism of *Mono-ha* perceived on the part of younger artists, several of whom identify with 1.3 above. But the *Mono-ha* artists went on working. Together with certain early conceptual/minimalists, those interested in 'optical' effects of geometrical replication in painting, and even quite distinct and different artists fascinated by Renaissance figurative art, they continued within a penumbra of given styles to produce work which was a reworking and extension of their earlier concepts. In its retrospective foundation this work was classicising, in its tentative to silent uniqueness within a known stylistic code, this work did not relinquish its authority as of being the new.

3. Negative, interstitial, and positive aggrandisement of the *objet*

3.1 Chic, impoverished minimalism: Nagasawa Hidetoshi, Funakoshi Naoki, Haraguchi Noriyuki, Wakabayashi Isamu (Plate 3)

3.2 Installation as trace; Kashihara Etsutomu, Mika Yoshizawa, Hoshina Toyomi, Kitayama Yoshio, Nishina Shigeru

3.3 Giganticism by replication and extension: Kuniyasu Takamasa, Toya Shigeo, Ebizuka Kōichi, Kawamata Tadashi, Endō Toshikatsu, Kenmochi Kazuo, Chiba Senzaki, Aoki Noe

Objet is the work made to be seen as thing, not the thing as dumbly-seen object. Here the critical distinction is in the being seen, for these works gain their impact from the aesthetic of display: the work performs. Aggrandisement against the world with a replicated or vast parade of scene-dominating forms is, for me, the most powerful categorising metaphor. Of course, the scene can be interiorised or externalised, or even considered as constituting some interstitial place between inner and outer worlds.

Sometimes the scene is considered as a space interior to an imagination, in which a resonance is sought from placement of bruised, 'poor' small *objets,* whose very control of effect results in a kind of chic display. Sometimes the effect sought is within an immense but enclosed imaginary space dominated by one or two massive *objets,* where the resonance feels like a roaring akin to the 'white noise' found in Tarkovsky's films [3.1]. There are also installations where discourse consists in tracing, often quite literally by the making and placement of an *objet* which is no more than a trace, the implosion or explosion of interior and exterior worlds upon each other. Here the aggrandisement comes with the performer's domination of his/her own skill in displaying this interface, rather like shop-window design that makes the most pressed main street shopping crowds stop and gawk [3.2]. Finally, there are a group of artists who, from often quite different artistic and intellectual positions, reverse the scale of interiority and make their assertion against the world. They make *objets* on a scale in the world, or on a scale in the scene for which they are intended, which completely overcome that space. With works of this category, it is often difficult any longer to perceive who the viewer of the *objet* might be, or indeed if there is any more a scene for the *objet* to be viewed in [3.3].

4. New narratives

4.1 Installation as field of narrative forces: Takubo Kyōji, Sekiguchi Atsuhito, Yano Michiko, Sugiyama Tomoko, Matsui Chie, Nakahara Kōdai (Plate 4), Nagasawa Nobuho (Plate 5)

4.2. Image re-[de-]contextualised: Morimura Yasumasa, Complesso Plastico, Idemitsu Mako, Kawamura Katsuhiko, Kon Michiko, Fukuda Miran, Kamiyama Akira

4.3 Hard totems and congealed paradigms: Sugano Yumiko, Nomura Hiroshi, Matsui Shirō, Kawashima Keijū, Kaitō Kon, Yano Michiko, Nishimura Yōhei, Sakaguchi Masayuki, Akiyama Yō, Kasahara Emiko

4.4 'Ero-guro' objects of metaphysical dread and delight: Maemoto Shōji, Katsura Yūki, Kusama Yayoi, Tsubaki Noboru, Nakanishi Manabu, Tashima Etsuko, Hashimoto Masayuki, Maemoto Yōko

If placement of *objet*(s) in a scene implies the mobilisation of forces in a performance where often the position or even the existence of the audience may be called into question, one of the common characteristics of works in the 1980s across many categories is the search for new narratives which will give order to, or enable the artist to control such performances.[11]

Fairly clearly, one category of such works are those which control the narrative by treating the *objets* in an installation as a field through which narrative forces flow, and which the viewer learns to interpret, in ways which can lead to multivocal or open interpretations [4.1]. If the field is closed, or tends towards univocal interpretations, I tend to place these works in one of the sub-categories of 3 above.

New narratives can be sought, not only with narrative fields demarcated by *objets* as such, but also by images as *objets*. Here the narrative play is often between the associations between images, particularly the variable interpretation of an image made possible by the new association given in a new narrative of location. Thus another control on narrative forces which allow different fields of possibility to be explored is the scene in which the image is to be enacted. This scene can be found by the co-location of images, or the co-location of different *objets* within an image or image series [4.2].

Play can also be made by the dislocation or tricky shift of connotation in the *objet* itself, which is presented as a determining key in some narrative of which the viewer may be barely aware, or which the *objet* suggests as a totem or fetish [4.3]. The totemic *objet* is often hard or crystalline to suggest some subterranean structure of desire which has congealed in it.

The totemistic *objet* suggests a modern narrative guise for quite ancient Japanese aesthetic discourses, such as in the aniconic and unsullied *objets* of Shinto ritual or wabi/sabi Tea Ceremony utensils.

There is also an adjacent category which is its inverted pair, the *objet* as raucous, coprophiliac, squandering, grotesque, perverse polymorphic enactor of a popular narrative of energetic force. Here *objets* do not require a scene; they are self-legitimising to the audience of their own spectacle. The giganticism or forcefulness does not dominate the viewer who enjoins or enjoys a spectacle of play. For if the viewer is not a participant, he/she is allowed to remain an onlooker, rather like Prince Hal's relation with Falstaff before he was turned by the cruel necessities of a different narrative of state [4.4].

5. Technological parameters

    5.1   Techno-effect as new media-field: Ishii Setsuko, Yamaguchi Katsuhiro, Mikami Seiko, Sakuma Toshirō

    5.2   Techno-effect as metaphysical sign: Miyajima Tatsuo (Plate 6)

In 1970, I twice experienced the laser art works by the then-young Usami Keiji in collaboration with the electronic music of Takemitsu Tōru for the Steel Pavilion at EXPO'70 in Osaka. I felt then that new light and audio technology were being harnessed to hitherto understood and accepted concepts of the art or musical work, in a way which effect felt revolutionary. Perhaps the innovations of those works were premature, as indeed the efforts to create them artistically exhausted Usami.[12]

They made clear that new technological applications to art had two major directions in which to go, although this was not really followed up in Japan until the late 1970s and early 1980s. Firstly, technology could be used as a way of creating new media fields for the exploration of artistic creation, where the technical possibilities of the new media were simply devices with and within which art practice could be carried forward [5.1]. The medium in the traditional sense thus constituted the art practice, although one without inherited tradition or form-types of its own.

A second, and more problematic, direction was to use the technical possibilities of applied technology as a way of creating new types of signs, ones which the viewer had to refer to their own background technical or scientific knowledge in order to interpret [5.2]. For example, that a digital counter did not count zero, even though basic scientific knowledge told one that it should, forced the viewer to include this fact in their interpretation of the work[13]. Here one might also find at the level of the play of signs a drive to aggrandise the space between sign and its encoding discourse, that is, the same implicit domination of the relative freedom of the viewer to make multivocal interpretations, as was suggested for 3.3 above.

How do these five categories and their subsets relate to notions of modernity or of a postmodern condition? If postmodernity is about a reworking or repositioning of the discourse of modernity, then form-types of category 1 must be intrinsically postmodern because they are articulated on the basis of prior knowledge of the modern. The actual references to codes of interpretation of earlier modern painting become only indirectly relevant because they have been internalised by the artist, and integral to the appreciation or understanding of the work by the viewer. This is whether we presume reference to Abstract Expressionism with 1.1, Constructivism with 1.3 or Symbolism or Surrealism with 1.4.

The form-types of category 2 indicate a different condition of postmodernity. They assume a knowledge about past works of art, not necessarily modern ones, because the artist works from a position which has gone beyond yet still carries forward those formal discourses.

This, of course, can involve a kind of self-willed display of art historical knowledge, and here one might see some works in categories 3 and 4 as a logical extension.

The substantial difference between categories 3 and 4 comes, I suppose, from a different kind of inter-textuality, a different notion of the play between artistically-conceived con-texts. In 3, the con-texts are forms manipulated to pull the viewer into the work or push out over and dominate those who see. This may be described as internalised or externalised aggrandisement, some-times for the sake of a complex aesthetic in which the viewer is imbricated, sometimes for a new kind of primitivism, a return to 'authentic artistic roots', which, of course, finds place in other personal or nationalist discourses of aggrandisement.

One may, in parentheses, wonder why much of the Japanese work exhibited abroad in recent years as typifying the 1980s has fallen into categories 3.3, 4.3 and 4.4. Is this because one kind of postmodern condition is a nostalgia for domination, or the being dominated, and selects Japanese forms which manifest this, or, alternatively, seeks to express it through the selection of such forms for exhibit abroad? A feminist might glimpse the not-so-concealed ghost of patriarchy here.

The new narratives of category 4 are more complex because, by their very positioning between con-texts which are open to interpretations other than the artists', they allow for a kind of 'play'. Here there is a surplus of pleasure, both from enjoying the artists' knowing manipulation of expectation, and from the viewers being left to make their own interpretation in response. This kind of interpretation is open, multivocal and a genuine extension of that flexible self-mapping of cultural forms which otherwise would be self-dominating, which we find in Dada and Surrealism.

As to category 5, I am unsure whether works here are intrinsically postmodern, unless we assume that the radicalism of new techno-effects found in 5.2, and indeed in many works of 4.2, 4.3, and 4.4, indicates the need for interpretive codes predicated on the modern. Techno-effects in art have, after all, always been available for use to found a different kind of medieval authority where there is only one logos and the artist is its theocrat.

C. The Institutional Structure of the Art World

The development of the art forms above has taken place in parallel with a change in the structure of the Japanese art world in the 1980s. In all forms of social life and particularly in that specialised mode of production devoted to artistic forms, it is too difficult to make direct aetiological attributions of variations in form to changes in the structure or function of institutions. Nevertheless, those institutions legitimate the types of art form produced, in certain cases by securing finance for that production, and also physically constitute a principal means of distribution. Thus, understanding their structure is at least to begin to comprehend both part of the social context of art production and to see one of the principal mechanisms by which a society gives meaning to art in general, and also to particular kinds of art which it may define as 'modern' or 'contemporary'.[14]

Conceptually, at least, I think one must distinguish between producers, distributors, and receivers of art. Part of the production of art involves production of the producers themselves, namely of artists by art schools and similar institutions. Distributors include institutions, from museums to commercial art galleries, which mediate art products to the wider society, or critically intervene in their production and circulation. The 'receiver' is the most ideologically neutral term for a complex of roles which include public appreciation at exhibition, private consumption by purchase, direct patronage through the commissioning of production, and more widely diffuse or secondary functions like the establishment of notions of taste which communicate to and influence other receivers.[15]

Several hypotheses about the development of postmodern art forms and changes in the structure of the art world may be posited, but, to anticipate, few of these will find empirical corroboration. One may, first of all, suppose that there is some connection between the scale and type of production of artists – the overproduction of role-specialised practitioners for whom there is little or no actual demand – and forms which are increasingly defined as artistic by the art world, rather than these forms being held in common by popular or even 'aristocratic' notions of taste. Another hypothesis about the postmodern condition comes from the basic codes for formal innovation in the Japanese art world. These have been historically positioned since late Meiji by a synthetic notion of tradition, formulated on a latently nationalistic base since the nineteenth century, and by the discourse of the 'new' as defined by assimilations and reformulations of late salon realism followed by Euramerican modernism in various waves. This hypothesis would suppose that the metaphor of innovation by 'new' forms has become exhausted, and needs now to be worked out by 'new' discourses about forms which themselves have no longer to be 'new'. Metonymy at the formal level is located within, or subject to codes of interpretation at, that level of discourse which is metaphorical.

To test these hypotheses, we need to understand as far as possible what the structure of the art world is and how it may have changed.

The number of graduates in the sectors of fine arts, design, music, and others has increased by around 19 per cent between the university and short-term college sectors of higher education, from 16,347 in 1975 to 20,217 in 1989. There has also been a major shift to design from 4,331 in 1975 to 11,124 in 1989 in certain specialist or vocational colleges.[16] If one simply takes fine arts graduates at universities and short-term colleges, there were 3,605 graduates in 1975 and 5,404 in 1989, an increase of 33 per cent.

These graduates were obviously not all destined to become professional practicing artists. My own rough estimates for the year up to August 1990 indicate that there were around 18,800 active artists who were affiliated with 97 art groups, as well as about 2,400 nonaffiliated artists,[17] figures which tally quite well with the 22,800 given in government census figures for 1985.[18] But it is interesting that the number of fine arts graduates at around 5,000 should be about 23 per cent of the total practicing artists for 1989. Thus, if we make the large assumption that the same number annually become artists as move out of art production by retirement, death, or change to other occupations per year, these figures tend to indicate that an artistic generational cohort is about four to five years long. This is the periodicity one might expect to find in other changes in the art world, apart from the production and recruitment of artists. Although I will not corroborate this here, there are, in fact, empirical grounds for seeing generations of Japanese artists roughly periodised by style and other criteria as 1978–82, 1982–1986, and 1986–90.

Perhaps the most telling indicator of the structure of the art world is, however, a synchronic not a diachronic one. For 1990 the ratio of artists affiliated with groups to those nonaffiliated is about 7.8:1; in other words, 13 per cent of artists are active outside the large groups that hold exhibitions. These groups control the exhibitions, *dantaiten*, which completely fill the schedule at the Tokyo Metropolitan Fine Arts Museum.[19] Their own members can become exhibiting, candidate and full members over a number of years, and the groups resemble closed medieval guilds which preserve a restricted market and clientele, as well as operate feudal recruitment procedures. It is this social structure, as much as stylistic criteria and self-consciousness as a member of an artistic avant-garde, which keeps younger artists nonaffiliated.

Personal experience and a brief check of artists against their affiliated groups indicate that this 13 per cent equate fairly closely to those active in modern art. But there is a lack of correlation with the art market, since those affiliated with groups have within certain limits guaranteed access to sales at prices which are publically set, and published in numerous art annuals. Self-avowedly modern and unaffiliated artists must either themselves finance exhibitions at loan galleries, *kashigarō*, through art teaching, or must increasingly work in design and advertising, or at a later stage be recognised by a commercial gallery who will hold a contract or 'planned' exhibition, *kikakuten*, for them.

Despite repeated inquiries in Tokyo in late 1990 and early 1991, I was unable to discover any estimates for a breakdown in the sales on the commercial market between sales of foreign art works, including 'modern masters', Japanese art works sold by

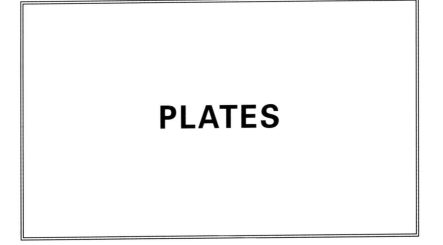

PLATES

Category 1/1.3 Decorative relief as paint-processable field.
1. SUWA Naoki. *Endless chain painting*. 1988, 180 x 1440cms, acr/c.

Category 2/2.3 New classic imagism.
2. KATSURA Funakoshi. *Sand and City.* 1986, ht 81cms,
camphor wood, marble.

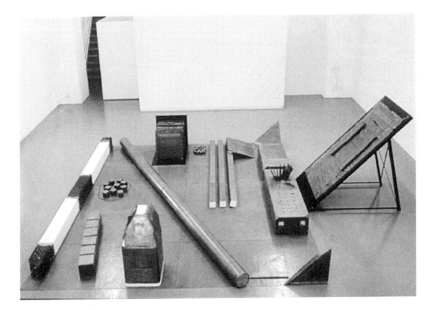

Category 3/3.1 Chic impoverished minimalism.
3. WAKABAYASHI Isamu. *Something belonging to the Green
in the Air I.* 1982. 400 x 474.5 cms, lead, wood.

Category 4/4.1 Installation as field of narrative force.
4. KODAI Nakahara. *Katakuritogifucho II*. 1988, 260 x 300 x 150cms,
bronze, marble.

Category 4/4.1
5. NAGASAWA Nobuho. *Earthwork Process 7* (at Valencia, California).
800 x 530 x 530cms, mixed media.

Category 5/5.2 Techno-field as metaphysical sign.
6. MIYAJIMA Tatsuo. *It Fucks Everything (Nachi Falls)*. 1987,
300 x 187 x 30cms, TV monitor, cassette, water, light, wire.

group-affiliated members, and modern art works sold at commercial galleries by artists unaffiliated with groups.[20]

I will now turn to the nonmarket distribution of art works, chiefly through publicly and privately owned museums and art galleries. The growth in the number of such museums in the 1980s has occurred in the context of an extremely low, not to say minimal, degree of government support for cultural activities. The Cultural Affairs Agency, whose budget is part of that for the Ministry of Education, only received 0.13 per cent of general government expenditures in 1975 and, despite quite large annual increases in the national budget, this share had actually been held down to 0.11 per cent by 1988.[21]

An even greater relative lack of priority in budget allocations is true for The Japan Foundation, perhaps the most prominent of several government organisations, including the Cultural Affairs Agency, which are active in international artistic exchanges. Despite a doubling of its expenditures between 1984 and 1989, The Japan Foundation in fiscal 1988 still had a budget which was 43 per cent that of The Goethe Institute and 15 per cent that of The British Council.[22] Even though it had an overall expenditure increase of about 17.5 per cent between 1984 and 1988, its budget stayed around the same ratio as that for The Cultural Affairs Agency, at about 14 per cent in 1984 and about 15 per cent in 1988.

There is also no evidence for The Japan Foundation having increased its activities in the support of overseas exhibitions in order to give prominence to certain contemporary artists. The Foundation's own budget for exhibitions and performing arts had remained almost constant, and even declined between 1984 and 1988 as a percentage of the whole from about 16 per cent to about 14 per cent.[23]

The above tends to indicate that, if the art styles which developed during the 1980s might be thought – in whatever distant reworking of a substructure/superstructure reflection theory – to be in part due to a cultural excess generated by a particular form of advanced capitalism, this was clearly not a result of governmental intervention in the zone of cultural activity.

Despite the insignificance of government activity in culture, the 1980s did see the advent of a large number of distribution points for art at museums. A rough estimate of the number of public museums and private museums open to the public in Japan is 330 in 1990, with the number of museums and galleries wholly or partly devoted to the exhibition of fine arts being somewhat lower. The 1980s had seen a major structural change in the distribution of art works through the opening of new museums. Clearly, 1984/5 and 1989/90 were major turning points in the increase in the number of museums, but this in itself does not indicate major changes in acquisition policy or of exhibitions of modernistic or avowedly contemporary art.

The number of visitors to fine arts museums doubled from around 11 million in 1977/78 to about 21 million in 1987/8.[24] Seeing art was thus increasingly part of leisure activity, but most of the exhibitions seen were of other than modern art. This is corroborated by the exhibitions planned by fine art museums having increased from 251 in 1976 to 382 in 1986, whilst the number of open submission exhibitions for prizes only having increased from eight to twelve in the same period.[25] Perhaps the same may be said for the increase in one-person shows at galleries, from 4,741 in 1976 to 6,679 in 1986. Although, if we retrospectively apply the roughly 13 per cent figure derived from the number of artists as crudely indicating those engaged in some kind of modernistic art, this does produce the estimate of an increase in such exhibitions of the order of around 500 in 1976 to around 700 in 1986. For a population of about 2,000 artists active in modern art, that produces an exhibition on average once every two to three years, which roughly corresponds with known frequencies for actual artists.

Thus if the structure of the art world indicates anything about postmodernity, in the context of a modern, formal stylistic discourse, it would be via the pressure on artists to identify themselves with a certain frequency as producers of 'innovation'.

This process of identification itself may, or may not, be positioned through the pressures of a kind of 'market'. This is not likely to be one of simple material sales through commercial galleries to a public, or to museums and art galleries, since the scale of either 'market' is thought to be very small, particularly for works sold outside the exhibitions of established art groups by artists not affiliated with them.

The true scale of the market for 'modern' art by living Japanese must remain at this point unknown, where the definition of 'modern' is necessarily a rough-and-ready one by producers and distributors. But this cannot in the discourse of works have had a scale or a dynamic through the direct operation of surpluses of material in the simple 'market' of sales. These cannot have constrained the production of forms that in the discourse of interpretation involve the kind of ideological surpluses of meaning thought as indicating a postmodern condition.

Neither did sales to public museums and art galleries at any point indicate an intervention of any significance on the material level.[26] If we are to look for conditions of postmodernity in the generation of forms, we must do so in the ways artists and their works were legitimated and, in parallel, at the material discourses which conditioned those formal selections or made survival strategies available to the artist. The latter also indicate new formal positions in discourses of interpretation, both of which intervene in the artist's production and in the process of legitimation.

D. Types of Legitimation

It has been hinted above that artistic changes are mapped over generational cohorts of about four to five years. This means that one might have expected to see some kinds of identifiable stylistic change associated with groups every five years. This may seem crude, but it has a certain purchase on reality. We may date *Mono-ha* to around 1969–73, an anti-*Mono-ha* tendency perhaps symbolised but certainly ideologically lead by Hikosaka Naoyuki from 1973/4 to 1979, a new kind of installation work from around 1980–5, and the advent of a kind of simulation art around 1985–1990.[27] These tendencies all, of course, continued in parallel, but one can see that: one, they became prominent in the periods mentioned; two, they were associated with a particular set of artists who were largely affiliated by age; and three, they had begun since the anti-*Mono-ha* tendency not to be directly identified with or mapped by any given international or non-Japanese tendency. This was particularly clear in the early 1980s, when the various tendencies in Europe and North America called New Painting, New Expressionism and Bad Painting were not directly followed in Japan, with one or two inferior and short-lived exceptions.[28] This could have been said of earlier movements, and occured despite the quite widespread exposure of New Painting in the Japanese art press.

Most modern artists do not live by their work, and the market for modern work is restricted, as shown above. I think one must question what kinds of patronage allow artists to be legitimated in their practice and so feel they may keep on working, even if they do not obtain economic support directly by sale of work. One may distinguish broadly several kinds of patronage which keeps modern art being made and displayed: patronage of family and friends which provides for rental of loan-gallery space; educational patronage by the provision of teaching work for artists who can then periodically finance their own rental of a gallery; aristocratic patronage via a fairly limited number of critics and museum curators who write reviews and sometimes ensure exhibition space is provided; patronage via the opportunities for decorative or graphic work provided to favoured artists from the main commercial activities of the gallery owner – who, in many cases, may run the gallery as a tax loss- in exchange for assistance in mounting exhibitions which do not make money. Recently, there has also been more direct enterprise patronage by the provision of rental gallery space or direct sponsorship for its rental from named corporations to whom application is made for support.

The kinds of artists legitimated by the aristocratic patronage mentioned are important, for the critics and curators involved often serve as a kind of primary reference for gallery and corporate patronage. There is even an intermediate stage between curator or critic sanction and the exhibition in a loan gallery. This is for the artist to be chosen at one of the three major annual shows for work by younger artists, themselves curated by younger curators and critics on a guest basis.[29] Knowledge about such artists forms part of a cycle of information exchange in the art world. In so far as gallery visiting has become more widespread than it was even in the early 1970s, information about such exhibitions, even opinions about such art works themselves, has been disseminated by urban news or 'town' magazines, and has become part of a life style of urban spectacles.

But anyone who has been to the modern art galleries in and around Ginza can count barely more than ten critics and curators at one time who write catalogue introductions for artists, or who serve as referees and jurors for the corporate support applications. So the increased circulation of information and the broader strata beyond the art world where it is circulated does not mean that more people produce and control this information, or that their opinions are in any sense more broadly formed.

168

The critics and curators are involved by their selection in confirming their own value judgements. But they are also linked with quite narrow peer group evaluations, given their limited recruitment from the art history and foreign literature – usually French-departments of Keiō, Waseda, Gakushūin, Tokyo and a few other metropolitan universities. Given their place in the Japanese educational elite, they are often very sensitive to evaluations which privilege a particular artist because of his or her selection for exhibition by an overseas commercial gallery or *Dokumenta*. It is their awareness that there is such – albeit limited and infrequent – a source of evaluation outside their peer group and outside Japan, which seems to come into play in the selection of artists to represent Japan at the São Paolo or Venice Biennales. Selection by an overseas gallery or thematic exhibition, or as a Japanese representative, is not insignificant for the reputation of either the artist's work or ability to make a living by selling work.

It is only such selection abroad, or their work being sent abroad, which seems to allow artists to begin to sell their work on any scale. Thus the perception of that limited group of critics and curators of the international art movements and the correct or necessary place of art works created in Japan at home and abroad becomes crucial in the legitimation of artistic practice, a point to which I will return shortly.

E. Codes of Interpretation

Perhaps the most significant aspect of the situation of postmodernity in Japanese art of the 1980s is how little direct critical literature this seems to have produced. True, there has been a great deal of discussion of major poststructural thinkers who have been frequently translated into Japanese very soon after publication in France.[30] There have also been very interesting analyses of the role of images in mass society by writers who have had access to foreign theory but write in a Japanese which has already assimilated those concepts and does feel constrained to continually refer to its translated originals.[31] But the major texts of post-structural theory seem to be more concerned with a late-Hegelian exploration of the parallels between early Shōwa history and the Japan of the later 1980s when the Shōwa Emperor died, or with the way various intellectual positions adopted in the 1980s' cultural situation were a kind of rerun of the 1930s and 1940s debate about 'overcoming' the West.[32]

Of the texts by thinkers about the postmodern which deal with art, perhaps two stand out: those in 1990 by Asada Akira[33] and in 1986 by Kurabayashi Yasushi.[34] True, the arrival of new painting had been recognised in 1983 by Hayami Shō, amongst others, as having two tendencies:

1. art which, belonging to the modernist context liberates itself from modernism, and
2. art which refers to an individual internal space and to the past, that is, history.[35]

But most discussions of postmodernism were entirely abstract and conducted in terms of works by foreign artists, as if indicating the access of the thinkers to an exclusivity, the very snobbishness criticised by Asada among others as a feature of modern Japanese culture itself.[36]

Kurabayshi identifies the postmodern with the death of the myth of the avant-garde, and that its mental approach is one, 'where behind phenomena one can find no abstract class system at all. Postmodern thought indicates a freedom from the targeting that brings the difference into being which makes things clear'.[37]

This absence of a discriminant thought-system in postmodernist work is also symbolic of any system of fashion where what produces style is unquestioned, only that the dictates of its inner transformational logic are followed absolutely. The anarchy which Kurabayashi also refers to is part of a semiotic situation where the referent-free signifier floats haphazardly, or according only to the imposed logic of an economy of consumption. The contradiction for art is that, inasmuch as the set of regular formal properties we call style distinguishes one artist from another, so art criticism is based on the notion that the work is interpretable as having been the result of thought, that it is a meaningful entity. If the work has no such meaning, then one strategy of resistance may be to adopt the forms of, say, new painting, and produce a form of slick illustration underneath which is a hidden message about the work's fundamental lack of meaning. Asada notices this and criticise resistance as a naive strategy that will only result in self-satisfaction in a corner of the art world. Asada anticipates that the meaninglessness of postmodernism in the 1980s will produce a reaction so that its real impact will be felt in the 1990s.

Perhaps I may make a few comments here from my own general observation on how modern art works were interpreted in Japan in the late 1980s. The proliferation of galleries which would rent space to exhibit modern art or would, for certain featured artists, organise an exhibition on their behalf, has increased the need for artists to have their work identified as in a style peculiar to themselves, whatever common concerns they might have with other artists of the same generational cohort. This has meant that the artist must be identified by the various systems of patronage as having an exclusive ability to explore a particular formal or intellectual direction. The competition for attention from the legitimator-patrons I have mentioned above, and the pressure on them to be able to identify and be identified with particular artists has thus increased. It comes as no little surprise to see various artists as associated with a particular legitimator-patron who is often tied to a gallery. This can even be seen in the limited number of artists who have been introduced abroad in the 1980s, either at long-standing venues like São Paolo and Venice but also at new spectacular events like *Europalia* in Brussels or at the various 'representative' exhibitions organised in the United States, Germany and Sweden in the late 1980s.[38]

Of course, two forms of distinctiveness operate at once: against other Japanese artists and against artists abroad. Given the peculiarly critical role foreign recognition has played in domestic recognition since the early 1970s, national distinctiveness has been built in to the postmodern system of evaluation. This could disadvantage, or inculcate wilful ignorance of, artists who worked well in a style which was seen to have had its day, like optical painting for example. For some such distinctiveness might have been advantageous in the short term, but in the long term it meant that the artist could be co-opted into reproducing mannerisms of the styles which had brought them recognition. This was not only a Japanese problem, but was given a certain severity, if not always an explicitly recognised one, by the position of Japanese artists until the 1980s in having been regarded as imitators of current international styles.

The reiteration of the word *tsuyoi* or 'strong' by many Japanese curators and critics in 1990 led me to enquire where this work had come from. It would appear, according to a conversation with the painter Usami Keiji, to be a Japanese-style variation of a character compound *kyōdō*, which was originally used to translate the French word *intensité*. What seems to have been a common feature of disparate codes of interpretation applied to art works in the 1980s was whether the works involved had the intensity to attract the viewer and, if necessary, hold their own as an existence against the world. Is this not the keynote in art of the 1980s, involved in holding the value of artistic creation in a society based on such dense patterns of production, consumption and information-manipulation?

F. New Hypotheses about Postmodernity

The problem of art in a postmodern situation is that it does not exist in a context-free market; there is no great supermarket of cultural goods in the sky which can be entered where goods can be purchased that are all priced in the same currency. Postmodern or, as I have chosen to see it, late-modern art has either commercial or aristocratic systems of legitimation to see that it is produced and distributed. But it requires a trained group of legitimators to ensure this. In a sense, they fix the demand.

Postmodern art has too often been seen in the pure, formal terms of its ostensible aesthetic properties, or its situation in series which transform or react against early modern work. Its play with systems of signification and use of decorativeness almost as a kind of revenge against more thickly or formally-defined signification, has led many to ignore, or abstract out of consideration, the fact that this in itself is a kind of appreciation. Postmodern art in Japan, as elsewhere, is highly institutionalised. It requires specialist museums of modern art, commercial dealers, critics, academics, and a trained public. It needs, as I have suggested, a new type of aristocratic patronage as a pre-fix to market success. In the postmodern era, the belated awareness abroad that Japan has a distinctive and richly generative modern art will, I hope to have shown, be more fully grounded if we understand its institutional base.

Notes

1. This is a version of a paper presented at the 7th National Conference of the Japanese Studies Association of Australia, held at the

Australian National University in Canberra in July 1991. In this presentation, original statistical tables, not shown here, were included. It is based on research done in Japan from November 1990 to February 1991, when I was the recipient of a Professional Fellowship from The Japan Foundation. I would like here to gratefully acknowledge the financial support of The Japan Foundation, and also the assistance of many Japanese colleagues, beginning with those at The Museum of Modern Art, Kamakura.

2. Among some basic texts in English are: Foster, 1985 [originally 1983]; Habermas, 1981; Harvey, 1989; Huyssen, 1984; Goldstein and Jacob, 1989; Iversen, 1989; Jameson, 1984, 1989, 1991a and 1991b; Lyotard, 1984; Kruger and Marianai, 1989.

3. See, *inter alia*, Miyoshi and Harootunian, 1989 [except for two additions by Arata and Oe, the content is largely the same as Miyoshi and Harootunian, 1988]. For critical reviews, see Pollack, 1989; Asada, 1983; Hiromatsu, 1989; Karatani, 1989b, 1990.

4. See *inter alia*, Kobayashi and Matsuura, 1984; Ijima, 1986; Akita, 1984; Isozaki and Tagi, 1984; Isozaki and Yoshimoto, 1985; Kurabashi, 1986; 'Aato Shinseiki', [Special Issue] *WAVE*, No. 22 (April 1989); 'Haipaa Aato', [Special Issue] *UR*, No.1 (January 1990); Asada, 1990.

   Standard catalogues in Japanese on the art of the 1980s are Nakajima and Ozaki, 1990; Ogura, 1990; Nakahara *et al.*, 1990; Hasegawa and Terakado, 1990.

   Standard catalogues in languages other than Japanese are Nakahara *et al.*, 1989; Sourgnes and Homma, 1989; Halbreich, Sokolowski, Kōmoto and Nanjō, 1989; Okada and Namba, 1990; Nanjō and Weiermair, 1990; Hara and Fox, 1990.

   See also, in English, Koplos, 1989; Gumpertz, 1990; Chapman, 1990; Lufty, 1990.

5. For a review of certain concepts of postmodernity, see Clark, 1991. Papers in Clark (1993) by Laing on China, Yomota on Japan, and Poshyananda on Thailand also address these issues.

6. Although the formulation is highly reductive, and raises many problems of comparability across culturally and historically discrete art discourses, I think the inversion is of a kind quite familiar with earlier transitions in art discourse, an analogue of such series in oil painting as Early Renaissance, Late Renaissance, Baroque, Rococo, or, in East Asian ink painting, such series as Song/Yuan, Muromachi, Momoyama/Early Edo, Late Edo/Bakumatsu. One may also make both macro- and micro-parallels with the series Romanticism, Impressionism, Modernism, Postmodernism, and that of Late Impressionism/Cubism, Dada/Surrealism, Abstraction, Postmodernism.

7. These categories and the artists therein listed are largely based on the catalogues listed in Note 4 above, together with personal experience of the works and meetings with a number of the artists concerned in Japan in 1974–6, 1983, 1987, and largely in 1990–1. Obviously, many of the artists did works before the 1980s, and their work during the 1980s could itself fall into several categories, sometimes in different periods, sometimes at the same time. Although one could point to several complex cross-relations, for reasons of brevity and clarity I have not identified them here.

8. Or, in the language of Freud's late disciple, Ferenczi, nowhere the auto-plastic could not dominate the allo-plastic.

9. Some of the interconnections between a new classic opticalism and somnambulist decorativism may be glimpsed through Minemura, 1990.

10. See, *inter alia*, Minemura, 1987; Murata, Fujieda and Tatehata, 1990; Lee, 1971 and 1986. (I am grateful to Lee for giving me his books and for an interview.)

11. This is a fairly common predicament for artists in many cultures, and is often theorised as a 'crisis of representation'. See, for example, Goldstein and Jacob, *op. cit.*, 1989: 32; 'Anyway, is that which exists only in reproduction not truthful? Of course it is. The subject, the origin is always masked by language, by its own representation, condemned to it too, to be the object of its other. By "other" I mean its reproduction'.

12. He confirmed this to me in a January 1991 interview. Usami was to hold a retrospective in 1991 at the Sezon Museum of Art, the catalogue for which would include recent formulations of Usami, 1985. (I am grateful to Usami for the interview and a copy of his book.)

13. On Miyajima's non-use of zero, see Kurabayashi, 1989, and his interview in *UR* No. 1, 1990, Note 4 above *ibid*. For Yamaguchi's thinking in the early 1980s on the relation between technology and art, see Yamaguchi and Murakami, 1981, and Nakahara and Yamaguchi, 1982.

14. Unfortunately, there is no comprehensive survey of the institutional history of postwar Japanese art and so the following argument inevitably has a speculative quality, except where supported by statistics or oral corroboration.

15. On the sociological understanding of art and taste, see, in general, Woolf, 1981, and Bourdieu, 1979 and 1989.

16. According to unofficial estimates kindly provided by the Cultural Affairs Agency.

17. Rough estimates from *Bijutsu Techō Nenkan '91*.

18. Japanese National Census for 1 October 1985, given in Bunkachō, 1988: 459.
19. It is a measure of the strength of the established groups and their institutional rigidity that the postwar successor to the old official exhibitions, Niten, whose selection procedures are dominated by those admitted without inspection, had a 30 per cent increase in submitters from 1975 to 1987, but the number of exhibitors and works exhibited increased by only around 17 per cent and 14 per cent respectively.
20. See Note 18, *ibid.*, p. 456.
21. The Japan Foundation, 1990: 53, 63. The broad lines of Japan Foundation participation in international exhibitions are discernible in Nakahara, Yaguchi, and Sakai, 1990.
22. Cultural Affairs Agency Total Budget [¥ million]
    1984: 36, 304; 1988: 37, 823.
    The Japan Foundation Total Expenditures [¥ million]
    1984: 4,552 1988: 5,346
    Note 21, *ibid.*, p. 135, 139.
23. Bunka Seisaku Kenkyū kai, 1990: 1912.
24. *Ibid.*, p. 1222.
25. *Ibid.*, p. 1222.
26. See Chiba, 1986: 208–22.
27. See Chiba, *ibid.*, p. 212–16.
28. These are the Hara Annual at the Hara Museum in Tokyo, the Konnichi no Sakkaten at the Yokohama Shimin Gyararii, and the Aato Nau exhibition at the Hyōgo Kenritsu Kindai Bijutsukan in Kobe.
29. Already the incorporation of poststructural concepts into debates about postmodernity was clear in the discussion between Kobayashi Yasuo and Matsuura Toshio in 'Taidan: Geijutsu no postumodan Jōkyō', *Geijutsu Hihyō* (Summer 1984).
30. See Ishiko, 1987; and Yoshimoto, 1984.
31. See Karatani, 1989b and 1990.
32. Asada, 1990.
33. See Kurabayashi, 1986.
34. See the group discussion in Tani, Hayami and Mangi, 1983: 81.
35. Note 32, Asada *ibid.*, p. 7. Such texts which discuss postmodernism or related phenomena almost without reference to Japanese examples are those cited in Note 4 above for Isozaki and Tagi in 1984, and Isozaki and Yoshimoto in 1985.
36. See Kurabayshi, *op. cit.*, p. 151.
37. See Note 32, Asada *ibid.*, p. 7.
38. See the catalogues listed in Note 4, above.

9 COMMUNICATION
Modernisation and Postmodernisation of the Japanese System of Communication

J.V. Neustupný

Introduction – Two Personal Notes

Modernisation of Japanese – a view of the 1970s and 1990s

In 1971, at the Japan PEN Club International Conference in Kyoto, I had the opportunity to present a paper on the 'Modernization of the Japanese System of Communication.'[1] Modernisation was originally announced as the main theme of the conference, but I was practically the only participant whose paper dealt with it. I remember John W. Hall telling me that scholars in the United States were no longer interested in a topic which belonged to the past. Today I see that this statement signalled paradigmatic changes taking place in Japanese studies in the US: the topic of modernisation which was one of the mainstays of the structuralist approach to Japan – consider the Princeton series – was in the process of being thrown on the rubbish heap. It took more than fifteen years before the issue of the modern returned in the form of discussions on the postmodernisation of Japan.[2]

The refusal to deal with the concept of modernity was not a position I could take. As someone who had been educated in a branch of the Prague School, where poststructural features were not a novelty, I had a strong interest in variation,[3] and the concepts of premodern and modern had, for me, a different significance. Unlike Hall and others, I was interested in the possibility of theoretically explaining some aspects of variation through the concept of modernisation rather than in claiming that Japan should quickly adapt to the 'modern' type (as the Princeton series de facto suggested). I have always believed in what I call 'developmental typologies' and I still believe in their validity. It makes a lot of sense to say that a society is modern. Today, as we have entered further into the new postmodern paradigm of science, the issue of modernisation, including the modernisation of Japan, has returned to the foreground. Moreover, we discuss not only modernisation, but postmodernisation as well.

In the paper referred to above, which was a sequel to Neustupný 1965, I analysed the category of nonfunctional variation in the Japanese language, the issue of conversational language in literature and other domains of communication, the communication of social distance and appeal, contact meanings such as those embodied in *aisatsu*, hierarchy in networks, speech particularism, and other issues which all seemed to support the conclusion that the Japanese communication system was somewhere between the Early Modern and the Modern type.[4]

Today I can see that at the time I was writing the paper, the pendulum had already swung and the process of modernisation had practically been completed. However, by the end of the 1960s and the beginning of the 1970s, this fact was not yet easily seen. When we now approach the *postmodernisation* of Japanese society, we should not repeat the error I committed in 1971 of underestimating its developmental status. Friends have repeatedly asked me whether I have not overemphasised the postmodern features in a society which, as I admit, includes premodern and modern features as well. However, we should accept that when paradigms change, the change may not be easily and immediately apparent and that we should try to carefully identify the hidden features that testify against the status quo. One of the reasons why the postmodern features may not be immediately observable can be differences in strategies of postmodernisation between Western and other societies. All societies, in the East or in the West, include older features: we usually notice those that happen to differ from the premodern and modern features we ourselves are used to; on the other hand, it is easy to fail in discerning the older features in our own back yard. On the whole, Japan today may not yet have crossed the boundary that could be described as the boundary between modern and postmodern society, but the process of transition has undoubtedly commenced.[5] It is our duty to acknowledge the path to postmodernisation, to the extent that it is accessible to a sympathetic observer at this moment.

Postmodern paradigms in linguistics and Japanese studies

While language as such was one of the sources of my interest in modernisation, most of my first contact with postmodernisation was connected with work on the history of linguistics and Japanese studies.

None of us who lived through the 1960s and 1970s could avoid seeing the far-reaching changes in linguistics of the period. Structural linguistics was replaced by poststructural trends – either grammatical (such as generative linguistics) or non-grammatical (such as sociolinguistics). It was obvious that structural linguistics was modern, but what were the new varieties of post-structural linguistics? For want of a better term (and 'postmodern' was then still unavailable), I called them 'contemporary'.[6]

A paradigmatic change from modern to the postmodern, similar to that which had taken place in linguistics, was also asserting itself, with some delay, in Japanese studies. It is possible to distinguish three paradigmatic stages of our concern with Japan: Japanology, Japanese Studies, and the Contemporary Paradigm. Japanology could be classified as the early modern system, the discipline-oriented Japanese Studies as the modern system, and the newly emerging postmodern system as the Contemporary Paradigm.[7] On the basis of previous analyses of linguistics, I postulated five features of the Contemporary Paradigm of Japanese studies:

A. Systematic attention to variation
B. Interest in conflict
C. Concentration on processes rather than structures
D. Interest in interdependence of various processes in society and
E. Interest in determinants of sociocultural behaviour.[8]

This list of features is significant because it can be applied to the analyses of other phenomena which vary along the modern-postmodern axis.

Modern and Postmodern as Types

It is very unlikely that society could be composed of features that are unconnected. As each group of members builds up their own sociocultural habitat,[9] they use the same or similar principles for the task. All features that are based on the same principles are therefore related. These form what we can call a 'type'. Society can be analysed as a set of intersecting networks of interrelated features, that is, as types.[10] The components of a type mutually support each other.

There is no doubt that modernity forms a type in this sense. *Strategies* of modern societies derive from more general principles that can be called *maxims*. Among such maxims are, for instance, the maxim of modern unity (reduction of variation), the maxim of orderly structure (reduction of conflict), the maxim of individuality (individuals occupy relatively independent positions), the maxim of alliance with other modern societies (leading to the strategies of borrowing from such societies), and a number of others. In turn, these maxims are generated by a number of *determinants*, principles of a still higher order, which are particular patterns of production (of material goods) and some very basic principles of social structuring.[11]

Much of the earlier literature on postmodern culture was interested in the identification of the strategies and maxims of the postmodern and in the question of their determinants. For example Jameson listed 'pastiche' and 'textuality' (fragmentation of time into a series of perpetual presents) as features that correlate with 'the emergence of a new type of social life and a new economic order – what is often euphemistically called modernization, postindustrial or consumer society, the society of the media or the spectacle, or multinational capitalism'.[12] The features identified by Jameson can be considered as strategies active in the domains of culture which he examines. However, if we want to use the term postmodern in reference to society in general, it becomes obvious that such features lack the generality of what I termed above maxims; a generality that transgresses the boundaries of a single domain or a group of domains. Neither pastiche nor textuality as such can be easily applied to explain the postmodern in areas such as society or language.

In my view, the *determinants* of the postmodern type are, among others, a high degree of technical development (including computerisation), extensive industrial production, a high level of development of services, consumerism and globalisation. At the level of *maxims*, these determinants produce, among other things, acceptance of variation, acceptance of conflict (social problems) as a natural state of affairs, management of such problems (especially at the micro-level), attention to processes, because it is processes (not structures) in which variation and conflict occur, and a high degree of interconnectedness between sectors of society and between societies at the international level. *Strategies* resulting from these maxims vary in different areas of activity. In the area of language, we see strategies such as the wide-ranging acceptance of ethnic minority languages or dialects, attention to language problems through management at various levels (replacing the previous attitude of 'leave your language alone'), emphasis on the effectiveness of linguistic processes rather than the correctness of structure, increased attention to second and foreign language acquisition, and many others.

The future elaboration of the theory of postmodernity must take the route of producing an explicit list of determinants, maxims and strategies of postmodernisation and clarifying their mutual relationship. What is the process of generating maxims from determinants and strategies from maxims? Maxims combine to produce strategies and sometimes produce strategies which are contradictory. For example, when the maxim of acceptance of variation prevails, speakers are free to use any language they choose and a strategy, for example, of relaxing constraints on the romanisation of Japanese can appear. However, the application of the maxim of rational management prevents anarchy and produces strategies such as adherence to a unified system of romanisation.[13] Both strategies derive from postmodern maxims.

One further point must be mentioned. Only features that can be connected with the whole matrix of strategies, maxims and determinants belong to the type. For example, Miyoshi[14] lists a number of strategies of traditional Japanese culture that could appear on any list of postmodern features, including demise of subjectivity, pastiche, modularity and devotion to simulacra. However, as he himself suggests, this list represents only surface phenomenon. Let us not forget that the modernists also identified individual features of Japanese culture which, to them, appeared to embody the modern principles. However, unless the strategies in question can be shown to be connected with postmodern maxims and determinants, they will form an interesting collection – but not a collection that would be immediately relevant to the issue of postmodernity.[15]

I believe that the determinants of the developmental types and most of the maxims (and, therefore, the types as such) are universal. Perhaps some maxims, and certainly many strategies derived from developmental and other maxims, are culture-specific. This may be the answer to Sugimoto's problem of the ethnocentric nature of the concept of the postmodern:[16] although the base of the developmental types, represented by the determinants and central maxims, is universal, under the influence of other (culture-specific) maxims, the strategies of postmodernisation may differ depending on the base culture. The study of postmodernisation in Japan is thus of paramount importance for the study of postmodernisation in general.

One or several types within the same society?

In the traditional developmental typologies one type was characteristic for any single society. Japan was either early modern, or modern. The typological theory used in this paper accepts the fact that one of the types can become dominant and that this dominance can be achieved within a relatively short period of time ('the pendulum swings', as I said above). However, it is equally important to accept that developmental types coexist within the same system. Japan can be a basically modern society but also include extensive networks of features which belong to the early modern or postmodern type. It is the specific combination of the three (or more?) that is of interest to our understanding of the dynamic character of Japanese society. A system in which all facts would be governed by one single type would be a static monster, incapable of any movement – in reality, societies of that type do not exist.

Rather than trying to establish whether Japanese is modern or postmodern, we should establish a 'typological profile' that will show in which way different types are mixed to build up the structure of the language.

Developmental types and interest types

Scholars whose theories were established within modern societies often considered the modern as the most desirable type in which the interests of all strata of society were satisfied. This was the dream of 'democratic societies'. This was also the American dream underlying the theories of the modernisation of Japan.

It is interesting to note that a similar attitude exists with regard to the postmodern. Some of those who study the type speak of the postmodern as if it were a principle that automatically solves social problems. A postmodern society is conceived as a system in which no conflict exists and in which social barriers are wiped out. Harvey[17] noted that 'the rhetoric of postmodernism is dangerous for it avoids confronting the realities of political economy and the circumstances of global power'. Some postmodernists *de facto* suggest that the differences in interests between the First and Third World can simply be ignored. In this context, Miyoshi and Harootunian have observed that 'in distinguishing late post-industrial capitalism from earlier liberal capitalism and by tolerating the former while condemning the latter, postmodernism ends up by consenting to the first world economic domination that persists in exploiting the wretched of the earth'.[18]

In fact, the developmental types simply provide frameworks in which the battle of interests takes place. We must clearly see that this struggle between different strata and groups within society develops at any point of history and is not removed by switching from one developmental configuration to another.

In other words, developmental types intersect with interest (functional) types.[19] An interest type is a network of features that favours one particular stratum or group. A modern society contains a network of related features that represents the interest of the dominant stratum. These features relate to economy, politics, culture etc. Premodern types also contain similar 'interest types', as does the postmodern typological configuration. Of course, the interest type of the dominant group normally becomes very strong, but this is not the only set of interests connected with a particular developmental type. All dominated groups also have their interests and these are represented in the structure by a number of features. There is, for instance, the political ideology of the working class, their trade unions, their popular culture which corresponds to their particular needs etc. All these are features of the modern type, as much as other features connected with the interests of the intelligentsia or the industrialists.

To believe that a developmental type *per se* is simply representing the interests of a single stratum of society would be unrealistic and would lead us nowhere. It is tempting to assume that the previous type (for example, the modern type) represents an inimical social group while the new type (for example, the postmodern type) belongs to the society at large. It is a fact, however, that both the modern and the postmodern type retain a clear distinction between groups with different interests.

Language, Communication and Management

In order to map the issue of modern and postmodern in language, we need to be aware of three important circumstances. First, there is a need to distinguish between linguistic and metalinguistic facts. Second, we must distinguish between the use of such systems and behaviour in which these systems are the object of maintenance, evaluation etc. I shall call the latter, systems of 'management'.[20] Thirdly, there is the question of linguistic, sociolinguistic and socio-cultural behaviour.

Linguistic and metalinguistic postmodernity

What matters in the case of linguistic facts is the language itself, its unconscious use or unconscious management. In contrast to this, in metalinguistic systems (such as the science of linguistics or of language planning) the linguistic facts are reflected in our consciousness, and our attitudes and knowledge are systematised. On one hand, we want to know how language itself – its use and management in unconscious processes – changes in the postmodern paradigm. On the other, we also want to understand the conscious reflection of language in the system of linguistics and in language planning. With regard to postmodernity, Bauman[21] has pointed to the importance of distinguishing between the postmodern in the social world and the reflection it receives in various systems of cultural form and precept. This is a distinction similar to the linguistic/metalinguistic dichotomy.

The linguistic and the metalinguistic do not necessarily go hand in hand. For example, the system of personal reference (use of given names etc.) may change without the community being aware of the change. On the other hand, one could claim that the contemporary (postmodern) high esteem for variation in language, the positive attitude to the dialect or ethnic minority languages, is simply a metalinguistic phenomenon and has little relevance for the linguistic arena, where variation is evaluated negatively and is systematically reduced.

In the case of Japanese, metalinguistic processes of postmodernisation may be weak, but this does not necessarily imply that postmodernisation does not take place at the linguistic level.

Use and management of language

Management of language is what Fishman referred to as 'behaviour towards language'.[22] It includes noting language, evaluating it and adjusting it. Such behaviour can be unconscious, purely linguistic in the sense of the preceding paragraph, as when we struggle to find a missing word, change the plan of our utterance or correct a slip of tongue. Management can also be highly conscious, accompanied by metalinguistic attitudes or theories, as in systems of language teaching or language planning.

In assessing the postmodernisation of a linguistic system, the management of language has great importance. Either consciously or unconsciously, features of language are noted, evaluated (positively or negatively) and adjusted. For example, a feature of the postmodern system is the negative attitude to 'sexist language' and attempts are invariably made at its removal. This can take place unconsciously, without metalinguistic intervention. An example is when we remove the word 'girl' in reference to adults, or with much discussion, supported by well formulated arguments.

As far as metalinguistic management is concerned, some of the typical postmodern trends connected with the maxims of postmodernisation are:

- acceptance of variation and conflict in general
- positive policies toward ethnic, social and regional varieties
- policies opposing sex variation in language and other forms of linguistic discrimination
- the plain language movement
- policies with regard to restricted literacy
- policies towards languages of wider communication
- language rights of speakers.

With regard to Japanese, the presence of these management processes must be assessed.

Linguistic, sociolinguistic and sociocultural rules

In linguistics, the word 'language' traditionally refers only to grammar, vocabulary, pronunciation and sometimes script. It does not cover all the phenomena which in the everyday idiom are normally called 'language' and which include a wide selection of rules we use in communication.

Linguistics, in the narrow sense of the word, thus explores only a limited area of what we would call communication. The whole of the process of communication is pursued in a discipline often called sociolinguistics, pragmatics, or something similar. Some 'linguists' have recently pointed to the necessity to broaden the scope of their inquiry to deal not only with communication but with human interaction in general.

In this paper I am concerned with the process of communication, rather than with language in the narrow sense of the word. Communication, in this sense, presupposes linguistic and sociolinguistic rules and cannot but take account of sociocultural rules. The widest model available for the consideration of sociolinguistic rules is a model originally suggested by Dell Hymes.[23] It has undergone a number of revisions, and the form used here is an adaptation produced for the study of Japanese communication in my book *Communicating with the Japanese*.[24]

From Modern to Postmodern in Japanese Language

The mechanism through which postmodernisation takes place is simple. In the process of postmodernisation, the modern rules which contradict the maxims and strategies of the postmodern type are negatively evaluated and a process of adjustment (correction) takes place, affecting the area of sociocultural, sociolinguistic and linguistic regularities. Some of these changes are unconscious, while others are accompanied by conscious perceptions and attitudes. In the following I shall limit my attention to some selected issues of the postmodernisation of Japanese. This paper should be considered as the first part of a series – a series that will hopefully not be authored by a single person.

In some European societies, the process of modernisation has lead to the substantial reduction of regional dialects. This is true, for example, of French or Czech. However, in the case of German, dialects were still vigorous after World War II.[25] In Japanese, as in many other languages, we can witness two different processes: one affects the written language, the other spoken. In the written language, dialects were ruled out early, with few dialectal features surviving into the Taisho and Showa period. However, literature with a strong spoken-language base (such as the poetry of Kōtanō Takamura and Mitsuharu Kaneko) for some time retained dialectal features. Today, Shūsaku Endō can be identified as a non-Tokyo writer by a linguist, but non-standard features in his narration are few, and they are likely to escape the attention of most readers (we say that they are 'covert'). On the other hand, in terms of the spoken language, Japanese dialects did not suffer much until after World War II. The question is whether this process resembles that of the German, where regional dialects continued to be used in a basically modern society, or whether it is a testimony that Japanese society was late to modernise. I believe we should not jump to the latter conclusion, at least not with regard to the postwar period. Since the 1960s, regional dialects seem to have lost ground to the Tokyo type of the Common language. However, what remains may be available for incorporation into the postmodern matrix.

The process of the reduction of dialects cannot be understood without reference to their management by society. We already know that in the Meiji period the standardisation of Japanese did not proceed without overt policies hostile to regional dialects. Active metalinguistic management took place. Such overt hostility to dialects is known from early modern systems (that is, systems in which the early modern type is dominant) and it seems that they used the same maxims and strategies as the process of unification of the modernising nations. In a modern system, dialects are no longer the object of language policies. Their negative evaluation is left to treatment by individuals in discourse. In this period upward social mobility is connected with the strong personal correction of dialectal features in speech, and many jobs in the public sphere are only available to those who have purged dialectal features from their language.

As mentioned above, this process of gradual individual removal of dialectal features remains characteristic for contemporary Japan. How can we decide whether it is a component of the modern type in Japanese? I believe that this can only be proved if we find that it is connected with modern attitudes to language. We need evidence that speakers, when correcting their speech, do so in order to use a modern strategy. The methodology of research in this area is still underdeveloped, although the introspective method of follow-up interviews[26] promises to lead to a breakthrough.

While overt hostility to dialects and an individual negative evaluation is typical for the early modern and the modern type respectively, the postmodern attitude to regional dialects is basically positive. This is connected with the maxim of positive attitude to variation in general. In Britain we can witness the use of regionally-flavoured speech in BBC newscasts, while in Australia attitudes to the Australian accent have also changed. However, some amount, if not a great deal of reduction, probably still takes place.

To gauge the situation in Japan, we need to closely watch changes in the positive attitudes to dialects. Tokugawa[27] reports a number of facts which seem to indicate that the negative evaluation of dialects is receding. He also reports on 'dialect festivals' and other phenomena of the 1980s. The poet Makoto Ōoka also points to the strongly increased interest of the Japanese public in local speech forms and claims that it is indicative of 'people's sense of crisis and their intuitive resistance against the control and standardisation mechanisms of the computer-age society'.[28] We need more evidence that these attitudes are components of the postmodern typological matrix.

With regard to other than regional variation, Japanese speakers seem to have assumed few postmodern attitudes. Ethnic variation in Japan (Korean, Ainu etc.) has been ignored by the government. It remains to be seen what are *in fact* the conscious as well as unconscious attitudes of the population at large, and to what extent they have recently changed. How widely spread is the postmodern principle of acceptance of minorities, and what are the attitudes to the 'guest-workers' from Southeast Asia, South Asia and Iran? A sensitive analysis of linguistic and metalinguistic management, not just an overall face value assessment, is needed.

While the above comments concern internal variation in Japan, an issue relevant to the problem of international variation is the changing status of Japanese in the world.[29] Although the phenomenon itself is connected with postmodern attitudes within other communities (for example, the US, Australia etc.), the fact that the Japanese government, as well as the general public, show a great deal of interest in this phenomenon may be significant. In the 1960s and 1970s, neither the government nor the general public were interested in enhancing the position of the Japanese language in the world. Admittedly, the emergence of the post-modern maxim of globalisation may not be the only factor which has caused the change of attitude. However, its contribution should be seriously considered.

There are other facts of Japanese communication that deserve a test of postmodernity. I believe that the principle of *seiyō kabure* (West-worshipping) was a typical modern strategy, consonant with the maxim of alliance with the developed world. I suspect that the present trends in Japan, sometimes evaluated as a wave of nationalism, may, in fact, signal the arrival of postmodern attitudes. What may be meant is the acceptance of variation, the acceptance of the fact that *Japan itself* is acceptable. This attitude was absent in the case of typical Japanese intellectuals of the last four or five decades, for whom the fact that Japan was different, was embarrassing. While in Australia globalisation means that foreign cultures are accepted, in Japan it may mean (along with other facts) that *Japan itself* becomes acceptable.

Perhaps some of the attitudes to language of Takao Suzuki,[30] a man who himself went through the period of strong (modern) Western influence, can be explained in this way. Both the attitudes of those who do not mind loan words and those who, like Suzuki, assume puristic attitudes, may represent postmodern strategies: the former because they accept the maxim of interconnectedness (globalisation), the latter because they acknowledge the right of Japanese language to an independent existence (the maxim of the acceptance of variation). As Field[31] has noted, the novel *Nan to naku kurisutaru*, published in 1983 and acclaimed as an example of postmodern writing, contains a high percentage of loan words. Since most of the loan words are brand names, apart from the maxim of cultural globalisation we can also observe the maxim of commercialisation at work. On the other hand, another postmodern novel, *Tsugumi* by Banana Yoshimoto[32] has hardly any loan words. In these two novels, both the abundance and lack of loan words may be attributed to the application of postmodern maxims and strategies.

Field has also pointed to the preponderance, in *Nan to naku kurisutaru*, of the present tense, where a modern novel would be expected to use the past tense. She tries to connect this strategy directly with consumerism, saying that 'it presents the ideology of the brand name, of consumer culture, as quasi-scientific information, resistant to discussion'.[33] The observation of the preponderance of the present tense is correct, but I wonder whether the connection with consumerism is defensible. The impression the use of the present tense gives is emphasising an ongoing process rather than reporting the results of past processes. The postmodern maxim 'emphasis on process' seems to be asserting itself.

For obvious reasons, the language of fiction must be watched for the use of postmodern strategies. While in the domains of daily life and work factors such as the practical function of speech may reinforce structural strategies leading to a completely different distribution of the tenses, in literature such pressure is weaker, and cultural factors (including modern or postmodern maxims) can fully assert themselves. On the other hand, precisely because the language of fiction and poetry is void of the practical functions, as far as its developmental type is concerned it can 'float' and predate other domains of society under the influence of foreign systems. In the past Japanese poetry has certainly been developmentally ahead of fiction and of the development of social institutions.

An interesting and relatively recent phenomenon of Japanese language is the reduction of the difference between male and female speech in the plain style (*futsūtai*) of honorifics. While men and women in the past attached different sentence-final particles and attached them in a different way, the usage in informal speech has practically levelled out, with the originally-masculine forms being adopted by both male and female speakers. However, in connection with postmodernisation, at least two facts must be considered. Firstly, the distinctions seem to be retained in less formal speech, for example, when girls are speaking with senior visiting relatives. Secondly, we need evidence that the reduction (which is not accompanied by widely accepted metalinguistic processes) is connected with the postmodern matrix. Such a confirmation can only be provided by extensive studies of users, including follow-up interviews.

One further feature we should test is the process in contemporary Japan of lifting the postwar restrictions on language usage in the official domain. From the list of *Tōyō kanji*, the system has proceeded to *Jōyō kanji*, the application of which – at least in theory – should be much more discretionary. The same trend can be observed in the recent changes which allow the use of syllables containing the foreign consonant *v*, formerly not acceptable to the Ministry of Education.[34] The maxim which seems to be working here is the postmodern acceptance of variation, rather than the modern maxim of reduction of variation. Again, whether this is, in fact, a modern or a postmodern phenomenon depends on how successfully we can establish a connection with modern or postmodern strategies, maxims and determinants in areas other than language.

The connection can be proved if features which are the target of analysis are studied in discourse. When management of communicative features takes place – for example, when the speaker decides to use pronominal reference rather than a name – is this decision based on a strategy, maxim and determinant that is basically modern or postmodern? We know from informal experience that speakers say 'I hate this expression because it is old-fashioned', or that they correct a word in their manuscript from a *gairaigo* to a Japanese word because they believe that 'there are beautiful Japanese words which can serve the same purpose'. How can we find the underlying strategies? In a structural system of social science, the examination of the question would be abandoned before it could even begin. Today, we are more hopeful.

In the area of the use of language one matter that deserves proper attention is the question of Japanese literacy. Although two surveys of literacy, which were very advanced for their time, were conducted after World War II, we know very little about literacy at present.[35] Metalinguistic attention to the problems of literacy has not been characteristic for Japan at large in the first years of the 1990s. This is a modern rather than postmodern feature, and we should carefully watch for a change in perceptions.

Another matter to examine is the influence of computers, fax machines, photocopying and other recent communication techniques on sociolinguistic and linguistic structuring. These technical developments are obviously connected with postmodernity. For one thing, it seems that original expectations notwithstanding, computers have reinforced rather than restricted the use of characters (*kanji*) in Japanese. What other consequences have these techniques for the detailed communication of Japanese? It is easy to postulate wide-ranging implications, but difficult to capture the process as it functions in discourse. If other conditions of postmodernity do not yet operate in Japan, this one should. Yet we know very little about the process from the point of view of postmodernity.

Finally, the question of 'internationalism',[36] as it is called in Japan, or 'globalisation' in general,[37] is vital for communication and language. Have international networks really radically widened, and what new types of content are being transmitted? How do the language varieties used in the process change? I have already mentioned the role of Japanese in the world. A similar issue is that of the role of English and other languages in Japan. This area, too, promises a rich range of research problems.

Towards the Study of Postmodernisation of Japanese in Interaction

What defines modern and postmodern had mostly been established, in the study of communication as well as in other areas, on the basis of macro-analysis and informal observation. In this paper, while adopting the same approach to show that the issue of postmodernity applies to the Japanese language, I have also attempted to claim that in the future it will be more and more necessary to commence with establishing what processes of management take place in specific interaction and which of these processes of interaction are connected with the overall matrix of postmodernisation. For example, we might want to know how language variation (for example, the lack of knowledge of Japanese) was noted, evaluated and adjusted in a particular discourse between a Japanese speaker and a foreign worker, and how, within that discourse, these processes correlated with other modern or postmodern strategies of the Japanese speaker.

The study of postmodernity must not only apply to the point of view of variation (in what way does the postmodern vary in different social groups) or conflict (what is the relationship of the postmodern in language and contemporary social problems), but also to the perspective of the processes in which it is created and reproduced. The issue is an empirical one: in what interactive encounters does modernity operate and how? From such encounters we must proceed to generalisations, but we should not generalise before the basis for the study of postmodernity in actual interaction is well developed.

One of the next stages of the present project will be a series of case studies, based on the analysis of actual interaction encounters in which language postmodernisation can be directly identified. New methodological approaches must be developed. Preliminary explorations such as those presented above are useful, but the project is necessarily in its very beginnings.

Notes

1. The paper was later revised and published in 1974 in the journal *Language in Society*. It has been reprinted under the title 'The Developmental Type of Japanese' as chapter 9 of Neustupný, 1978.
2. Cf. Miyoshi and Harootunian, 1989.
3. Cf. Neustupný, 1978.
4. *Ibid.*
5. See Kishida, 1988: 2–8.
6. This term, it seems, was a translation of the Japanese word *gendai*, which I used in my 1976 article on sociolinguistics in the Japanese journal *Gekkan Gengo*. *Gendai* 'contemporary' has a structural similarity with *kindai* 'modern' and can be used as a noun as well as an adjective.
7. See Neustupný, 1980: 20–8.
8. *Ibid.*
9. For the term 'habitat', see Bauman, 1991: 33–46.
10. Neustupný, 1989a.
11. See Neustupný, 1989a.
12. Jameson, 1985: 113.
13. See Neustupný, 1991: 15.
14. See Miyoshi and Harootunian, *op cit.*, 1989: 148.
15. Sugimoto (1990) points to three other familiar features: dearth of individualistic self-orientation, interest in own history and living in harmony with nature. Sugimoto suggests that these featues are, in fact, premodern in their nature. Of course, when such features are extant at the moment of postmodernisation, they can be incorporated into the postmodern matrix.
16. *Ibid.*, pp. 56–9.
17. Harvey, 1989.
18. Miyoshi and Harootunian, *op. cit.*, 1989: viii.
19. See Neustupný, 1989b.
20. See Jernudd and Neustupný, 1987: 69–84.
21. Bauman, 1989: 35–63.
22. Jernudd and Neustupný, *op. cit.*, 1987.
23. Hymes, 1962.
24. See Neustupný, 1982 and 1987.
25. See Leopold, 1968.
26. See Neustupný, 1990.
27. Tokugawa, 1990.
28. Ooka, 1992: 4.
29. See Coulmas, 1988.
30. Suzuki, 1990.
31. Field, 1989.
32. Written in 1989.

33. Field, *op. cit.*, 1989: 183.
34. Cf. *Asahi Shinbun* 23 October 1990.
35. Cf. Neustupný, 1984: 115–28.
36. See Befu, 1990; Hook and Weiner, 1992.
37. See Featherstone, 1990.

10 SOCIAL STRATIFICATION
Changing Status Perceptions in Contemporary Japan: A Debate on Modernity and Postmodernity

Kenji Kosaka

Introduction

In Japan, while literature on postmodernity is seen more in the fields of art, architecture and philosophy than in sociology, interest in postmodernity – understood either as referring to recent social changes within a capitalistic framework or as a reference to criticism of modernity – now seems to be shared by a wider range of sociologists (for example, Ōmura *et al.*, 1990 on religion; Takeuchi, 1991 on education; Ueno, 1991 on feminism; Satō, 1991 on networking). However, nowhere – except perhaps in the works of Imada (1987, 1989, 1991) – has any monograph fully explored the meaning and significance of postmodernity. Imada emphasises the need to 'deconstruct the modern' (in images of science, society and humanity) in order to understand the nature of ongoing social change or understand the metamorphosis of the modern into a 'completely different society' (which might be called postmodern society). Tominaga (1989, 1990) on the other hand, partly in response to postmodernists such as Imada, stresses the 'backwardness' of Japanese society in the modernisation process, while he admits that contemporary Japanese society is a triumvirate of elements: the premodern, the modern and the postmodern. These writers have never directly contradicted one another in any publication or engaged in 'debate', but as we shall see, they have provided quite contrasting views of Japanese society and its current historical stage. Consequently, I am tempted to say that their works in total constitute a 'debate'. We will attempt to evaluate this debate in its empirical, theoretical and practical aspects, with particular emphasis on the topic of stratification and status perception in contemporary Japan; for it is in this topic that we find the widest divergence of these writers' views of the modern.

The Debate

Overview

Tominaga distinguishes three dimensions of modernisation: economic, political and sociocultural.[1] Economic modernisation simply means industrialisation, while political modernisation means establishment of democracy. Sociocultural modernisation involves values; in particular the realisation of freedom, equality and rationalism. An overall process of modernisation in Japan began with the Meiji Restoration, as is generally understood, but Tominaga emphasises that modernisation did not proceed at the same speed along those dimensions. Indeed, while industrialisation (technological development, in particular) advanced greatly under the protection of the Meiji Government, there remained even so premodern elements such as *zaibatsu* in the economic system. Industrialisation was followed by political and sociocultural modernisation in that order. Political democracy, however, was restricted by the traditional framework of the Meiji Constitution and the Imperial Rescript of Education. The traditional *Iye*-system and rural systems were so enduring that sociocultural modernisation was far from being fully realised. In sum, modernisation before the end of World War II was a 'limping' one which zigzagged among different subsystems of a societal system. To this 'backwardness' in modernisation Tominaga attributes a rise of fascism in prewar Japan.

Full-scale modernisation, then, did not proceed until the end of World War II. It was brought about through a series of reforms including: 1) the New Constitution, which proclaimed that sovereign power resides with the people; 2) freedom of thought, speech and association; 3) women's suffrage; 4) dissolution of the *ie*-system; 5) reformed local government; 6) educational reform; 7) labour reform; 8) land reform; 9) dissolution of *zaibatsu*; and 10) the Anti-Monopoly Law.[2] Indeed, there emerged elements of the postmodern, such as the development of advanced technology, microelectronics and a 'consumer society' during the period of high economic growth.

Imada, on the other hand, finds societal changes in Japan to be similar in scale to those in the West. The modern period followed the medieval period, as in the West where the Catholic Church had had exclusive authority. Just as, in the juncture between the Medieval period and the modern, there was a considerable period of fluctuation and chaos, the kind of fluctuation and chaos experienced since the 1970s shows that we likewise are experiencing a stage intermediate between the modern and an approaching 'different society' which might be called postmodern. Modern society gives primacy to function, efficiency and rationality, whilst postmodern society places an emphasis on 'meaning' and difference.

The advancement of information technology goes beyond the existing framework of modernity; through self-organisation processes similar to those of the metamorphosis of a pupa it leads into a new stage. Transitions take a variety of forms and directions. Imada describes these in somewhat peculiar and idiosyncratic terms; the gist of his account is as follows: 1) The 'scarcity motive' is replaced by a 'difference motive'. At a time of affluence in any industrialised society, very few suffer from scarcity – from poverty and lack of material goods. Currently, Japanese people are more eager to see difference as a sign of individuality and autonomy, even if the appearance is illusory. 2) In the field of production, 'added value' supplants productivity and efficiency as the primary goal, emphasising the difference motive. People no longer desire consumer goods merely for their increased functionality. Thus more attention is paid to consumption than production. 3) The expectations of employers have changed. Where previously diligence and efficiency were desired (values typically required in any industrialised society), ability to contribute to 'value adding' is sought. 4) The idea of control solely for the purpose of preserving order is replaced by the concept of support (to promote added value and self-organisation). 5) The idea of the integration of a system through consensus is now obsolete, and is replaced by the idea of 'editing' competing individualities. 6) The mode of organisation will shift from that of a network to a rhizome-type – an open-ended movement comprised of a body of differences.

Views on stratification and status perceptions

As stated earlier, Imada and Tominaga differ concerning what is meant by modernity and postmodernity, when modernisation started, and the stage contemporary Japanese society currently is at. Their differences with respect to the topic of stratification and status perception are even more evident, although, in the past, their views of changes in stratification and status perceptions have been to some extent similar.

Tominaga postulates that modernisation in the sphere of social stratification exhibits the following features: 1) equalisation of differences among strata; 2) increase of social mobility; 3) decline of the old middle class and increase in the number of white-collar workers; and 4) advancement of the structure of status inconsistency.

Before World War II there were eight social classes: the aristocracy, capitalist class, new middle class, landlords, farmers, urban old middle class, working class, and urban lower class. Only after the end of World War II did modernisation of this structure begin in Japan. In the 1950s and 1960s, Japanese society grew as a mass society, with the structure of social stratification becoming onion-shaped or diamond shaped, that is, swelled around the centre. A greater proportion of the population now regard themselves as belonging in the middle bracket; but they do so because of the increase in the number of those whose statuses are inconsistent with prewar social classes.

Imada characterises Japanese politics since the end of World War II as consisting of three stages: class politics (1950–64), status politics (1965–79), and quality politics (1980 onward). During the class-politics stage, class ideology was a factor in the labour movement. During the status-politics stage, people sought a middle position in the status hierarchy. From the 1980s on people have pursued quality of life instead of status. In the sphere of stratification and status perception, this last stage is leading to the postmodern.

Imada suggests three indicators of the movement toward a postmodern society in the sphere of stratification and status perceptions:[3] 1) Unfairness, or the issue of distributive justice (rather than inequality), is now seen as a social problem requiring solution. Even when the principle of achievement has become dominant in a society, some sort of inequality remains which cannot be overcome within the modern social framework. Problems of distribution of wealth and income will be replaced by problems of life style. A growing sense of unfairness or injustice is claimed to be related to these emerging problems. 2) 'Quality politics', politics arising from a striving for quality of life, is now dominant. The term is coined to contrast with the 'class politics' and 'status politics' referred to above. People are interested less, or no more, in maintaining or raising their status (or in building a career), than they are in self-realisation, around which political dynamics will be organised. 3) Variables of income, property or assets, and educational background are now less relevant, both as dependent and independent variables of social distinction. According to Imada, there may emerge a new type of social division and rank-order based on life style; but in a postmodern society, conventional socioeconomic variables will no longer govern behaviour. These three features, Imada suggests, are aspects of the final stage of the modern.

Points in dispute

Tominaga criticises young postmodernists (presumably including Imada) in many ways. Postmodernists claim, he believes, that Japanese modernisation is already complete or is near its completion, but in his view modernisation has just begun. Indeed, while some of its elements could be characterised as 'postmodern', Japanese society is mainly industrial rather than consumptive. Japan is now outstanding in the economic sphere, but is far behind in its degree of modernisation in the sociocultural sphere. These gaps or 'lags' between subsystems with respect to their degrees of modernisation are the cause of so-called 'Japan problems'. The more critical that postmodernists are of the modern, the 'less critical of the remaining premodern elements they are'. The enduring institution of the emperor system, and Japan's repeated political scandals, are examples of remaining premodern elements which Tominaga believes stand more than ever in need of criticism and which must be overcome by the people no less than by postmodernists.

On the other hand, according to Imada, Tominaga is among those modernists who view the problems of stratification and status perceptions mainly within the conceptual framework of transition from ascription to achievement. Modernists are too optimistic. As long as they stick to a dichotomous way of thinking, they will never elucidate the remaining problems of inequality, even if the principle of achievement were to be fully realised. Indeed, in the period of highest economic growth, hypotheses concerning the impact of industrialisation upon stratification appeared to be confirmed: equalisation, increase of openness or of social opportunities, and status inconsistencies were all evident. But these occurrences were no more than byproducts of industrialisation and the decline of agriculture, and, as such, will proceed no further once a certain level of industrialisation is attained by society. While one may feel that some degree of equality has been achieved and the amounts of social opportunity and status inconsistency have increased, one tends to fail to see the hidden reproductive mechanism of stratification. The modernists' picture is shown to be a pleasing illusion, since inequality and difference actually appear to have increased, and the stratification system has now become more rigid. The modern way of thinking would overlook this actuality.

Evaluation of the Debate

Since the debate between Imada, as a postmodernist, and Tominaga, as a modernist, has several aspects – empirical, theoretical and in praxis – it must be evaluated according to several criteria. In the following, we concentrate upon the empirical adequacy, the theoretical significance and the practical implications of the two positions on stratification and status perception.

Empirical adequacy

The literature on postmodernity has a proclivity towards empirically untested speculation and philosophical discussion. Imada's works are quite exceptional, in that they always refer to empirical data when it is available. Let us therefore investigate whether any empirical data, for example, those collected by the Social Stratification and Mobility (SSM) project,[4] betray indications (however fragmentary) that contemporary Japan is undergoing a transition from a modern to a postmodern society, as suggested by Imada.[5]

Emergence of a sense of unfairness?   During the 1980s, according to one of the three largest Japanese newspapers, *Asahi Shinbun* (January 1, 1988), 'unfairness' (or 'injustice': *fukōhei*) was popularly chosen as the word which best captured the key attribute of contemporary Japanese society. The SSM study introduced a question concerning this sense of unfairness for the first time in 1985. Unfortunately, therefore, comparable SSM data

Table 10.1 The sense of unfairness

(a) overall unfairness			
fair	3.3		
mostly fair	34.1		
not so fair	40.4		
not fair at all	19.5		
DK/NA	2.3		
Total	100.0 (N = 1239)		

(b) unfairness because of:

	Yes	No	DK/NA
(1) sex	40.2	58.1	1.7
(2) age	28.2	70.1	1.7
(3) school education	64.3	34.0	1.7
(4) occupation	50.8	47.5	1.7
(5) wealth	56.3	41.8	1.7
(6) family stock	36.1	62.2	1.7
(7) residential location	35.0	63.3	1.7
(8) ideology/creed	24.3	74.0	1.7

Note: Question (a) read: Generally speaking, do you think that society is fair?
Question (b) read: Apart from an overall evaluation of fairness, do you think
that fairness exists in the following aspects of contemporary [Japanese] society?

which could indicate possible changes in perceptions of unfairness
are unavailable. Nevertheless, the available data are revealing.
Part (a) of the SSM survey question asked about the respondents'
judgement of overall unfairness, whereas part (b) asked respondents whether they thought that society was fair or unfair for
specific reasons. It is remarkable that the greatest proportion of
respondents regarded school education *inter alia* as a source
of unfairness. Since school education is assumed to function in
realising the achievement principle, this result is rather puzzling.
If school education functions to cancel the ascription principle,
why do people in an industrial society regard it as a source of
unfairness? What exactly is thought to be unfair about it? Why
do people believe that unfairness due to school education exists?
A breakdown of Table 10.1 by level of education attained by the
respondents (Table 10.2) provides answers, as well as posing
further questions. The distribution of respondents who believe
that school education is unfair is trimodal, and suggests a hypothesis that people believe too much importance is attached to
school education, hence that society is unfair to those who are

Table 10.2 The sense of unfairness due to school education by the level of education

| | level of education | | | | |
	1	2	3	4	5
not exist	33.3	41.0	32.6	49.1	26.8
exist	66.7	59.0	67.4	50.9	73.2
Total	100.0	100.0	100.0	100.0	100.0
N =	42	356	516	53	250

Note: level 1 = graduation from elementary school, or none; level 2 = graduation from secondary school; level 3 = graduation from high school; level 4 = graduation from two-year college; level 5 = graduation from university.

deprived, or do not receive education. However, this hypothesis does not completely explain the trimodality.

Although the survey question itself is concerned not with the individual's situation but rather with a societal situation, respondents may have regarded their personal situation as resulting from unfairness due to school education. The earlier hypothesis could apply to those with the lowest education, but it does not explain why the largest proportion is among those with the highest education. A further breakdown of Table 10.2 in respect to income shows that this tendency is stronger for the lowest income earners than for the highest income earners. It is probable that the former are frustrated with their situation because they are not earning the income they believe their education deserves. This would indicate that the sense of unfairness due to education is coupled with a sense of income inequality as linked with a sense of relative deprivation. However, an appropriate hypothesis to explain the greater proportion for those with the middle level of education, or to explain the trimodality, is still lacking.

Furthermore, school education and achievement are conceptually independent of each other, though they are closely intertwined. What has been noted in most industrialised societies is the rise of 'credentialism' or 'degreeocracy'[6], where school education is evaluated only in terms of degrees awarded, or is used as a means of screening for upward mobility. The sense of unfairness due to education may be caused by the tacit assumption that formal degrees do not reflect one's actual professional abilities and accomplishments.

Unfairness itself could mean a variety of things to different people. Analytically, and from a social science perspective, unfairness may be distinguished from inequality. But many people use the two terms interchangeably, Japanese people being no exception.

In summary, it is true that unfairness is regarded as a key attribute of contemporary Japanese society. We do lack relevant data over time, but generally speaking the term does seem to be used more frequently now than before. Frequent use of the term should not be seen as implying any historical stage of society, whether it be the end of the modern or the beginning of the postmodern, until we know more about the mechanism underlying the creation of the sense of unfairness. It should also to be noted that, in Table 10.1, the sense of unfairness due to causes of a premodern type, such as family heritage and gender, is not negligible either.

Greater emphasis on quality of life? In the literature, many authors[7] emphasise the tendency towards 'privatisation' in postwar Japan. It is also held that this tendency is particularly marked among the younger generations.[8] On the basis of surveys conducted by Tōkei Suiri Kenkyūsho on the national character of the Japanese, Miyajima claims that the advancement of privatisation is one of the most remarkable changes in the consciousness and life style of people in Japan, and that this happened during the period between 1953 and 1973, when Japanese society experienced unsurpassed economic growth. During the period surveyed, the proportion of those who endorsed value orientations such as 'live an honest and righteous life' (down from 29 per cent to 11 per cent), and 'dedicate one's whole life to one's society' (down from 10 per cent to 5 per cent) declined remarkably, while there was a correspondingly remarkable increase in the proportion of those who endorsed such value orientations as 'live in accordance with one's taste' (up from 21 per cent to 39 per cent) and 'lead an easy life without worrying' (up from 11 per cent to 23 per cent). Miyajima describes these changes as a shift from collectivity-oriented to self-oriented values. Does this finding support Imada's hypothesis that 'status politics' is now being replaced by 'quality politics' and quality-of-life orientation? The answer is in the negative. The reality is that the tendency towards privatisation does not necessarily preclude an orientation towards climbing a status ladder in order to be successful in life. Although the idea of upward mobility is regarded somewhat negatively among the younger generation, it does not follow that they themselves are losing such an orientation.[9] It may well be that the motive for rising in the world has always been dominant for the entire period of postwar Japan. The first life style category in Table 10.3, 'work hard to become rich', is the only one whose proportion remained unchanged between 1953 and 1973.

Table 10.3 Changes in life style

	1953	1973 (%)
1. work hard to become rich	15	14
2. study industriously to win fame	6	3
3. live in accordance with one's taste	21	39
4. lead an easy life without worrying	11	23
5. live an honest and righteous life	29	11
6. dedicate one's whole life for the sake of one's society	10	5
7. others, DK	8	5
Total	100	100

Katase and Tomoeda[10] also conclude, after comparing the 1985 SSM data with the data cited by Kadowaki,[11] that status-seeking orientation is not attenuated even in the tendency towards privatisation (see Table 10.4). The value orientation 'to achieve higher status' increased substantially in proportion. Status-seeking orientation is even more marked among the younger generation, as seen in Table 10.5, which shows changes in status-seeking orientation by age groups.

Table 10.4 Changes in value orientation

	1973	1985
Status-oriented:		
achieve higher status	31.4	34.1
earn a larger income	76.2	75.4
meet competition with others successfully	45.9	40.3
QOL-oriented:		
serve for the sake of others	79.7	75.6
enjoy leisure time	79.2	67.7

Source: Katase and Tomoeda, 1990: 129.

Table 10.5 Changes in status-oriented value by age group

	20–29	30–39	40–49	50–59	60–69
achieve higher status					
1973	32	32	30	34	29
1985	46	32	34	31	30
earn a larger income					
1973	76	80	77	72	65
1985	81	78	80	74	56
meet competition with others successfully					
1973	47	48	45	42	36
1985	40	38	42	42	40

Source: Katase and Tomoeda, 1990: 130.

Is class/status irrelevant as a determinant of behaviour?   Imada, as a postmodernist, claims that class will lose, and is actually losing, its importance as a determinant of behaviour. Even in a postmodern society, differentiation will exist along the lines of class and/or status (possibly based on life style), but in their daily lives people will not be concerned about class or status as differentiated by socioeconomic variables such as income, property and school education. If Imada's assumption were true, people would care less than previously about class/status in its conventional sense. This must be examined against the empirical data.

The 1975 and 1985 SSM provide comparable data on whether people take into consideration the factor of class/status when selecting a marriage partner, intimate friends, schools for their

Table 10.6 Importance of class/status

		important	unimportant	DK/NA	Total
marriage	1975	67.1	32.4	1.5	100.0
	1985	71.1	23.7	4.6	100.0
friends	1975	49.5	48.8	1.7	100.0
	1985	47.8	48.0	4.2	100.0
school	1975	62.2	35.5	2.3	100.0
	1985	62.3	31.2	6.5	100.0
pol.	1975	54.0	42.0	4.0	100.0
support	1985	48.7	44.7	6.6	100.0

Samples: 1975 data (N = 1296) from project B of SSM; 1985 (N = 1239) from project A. Both sets of data are drawn from male respondents.

children, or the political party they will support. In the selection of the first three examples (see Table 10.6), it showed (assuming the samples are sufficiently homogeneous) that people were more conscious of class/status in 1985 than in 1975. There is no single sign of decline of class/status as a determinant of behaviour, despite the postmodernist argument.

One further interesting finding, as I see it, is the remarkable gap between respondents' perception of how people in general rate the importance of class/status, on the one hand, and their own rating of the importance of class/status, on the other. To be specific, in the 1985 SSM study it was asked 'To what extent do you generally take elements of class/status into consideration?', after which respondents were asked about their perceptions of people in general. The results were very interesting. There was a considerable gap between the subject's own rating and their perception of people in general. The general tendency was that respondents saw class/status as less important than previously. Even so, most thought that people in general took class/status more seriously than they did themselves.

Two possibilities suggest themselves in explanation of this gap. People in their interactive situations are not free from their perceptions of others. If one actor thinks that another takes class/status into account in forming friendships, that actor cannot ignore the other's orientation, even though tempted her/himself to ignore class/status. The result is a kind of group ignorance, where both actors are ignorant of the other party's true orientation and define the situation in a way quite contrary to their original orientation. So, even if an individual respondent placed less importance on class/status, as a result of aggregation or unintended consequences, all people will come to overemphasise the elements of class/status.

Another possibility is that people might believe that most others are actually not as conscious of class/status. Then a 'group ignorance' would not occur. In this case, the importance of perception of class/status is lessened. A close examination of those who put less emphasis upon class/status, shows that they are people who identify themselves with the 'lower lower' in status terms, or 'working class' in class terminology.[12] The probability exists that, the higher one's status is, the more importance one puts upon class/status. Thus, whether or not class/status is losing its importance at a societal level would hinge upon whether there is an increase (or decrease) in the relevant segments of the population. Has the number of those who identify themselves with lower-lower or working class increased? Although the percentage of those who locate themselves in the lower-lower status category has increased from 3.9 per cent in 1975 to 5.9 per cent in 1985, the increase is not particularly remarkable, and the present percentage is still low. The proportion of those who regard themselves as belonging to the working class is 64 per cent, but this is likely to decrease over time. All of which suggests that the second possibility is the least likely.

Theoretical dimension

As we saw earlier, in Tominaga's definition of modernisation, particularly in the realm of stratification, the indication of development is a matter of degree; once a society has started the modernisation process, we can discuss its level of advancement or backwardness only in relation to modernisation. This perspective was common to the so-called industrialists who judged the situation in terms of the principles of ascription and achievement. For instance, Blau and Duncan noted the processes by which individuals became located (or located themselves) in positions in the hierarchy: 'At one extreme, there exists the situation where the circumstances of a person's birth assign him unequivocally to a ranked status in a hierarchical system; at the opposite extreme his prospective status would be determined based on the exercise of the achievement principle'.[13] Roughly, ascription corresponds to the premodern, while achievement corresponds to the modern. There is no intermediate principle, and no principle which follows that of achievement. Indeed, as Imada points out in his criticism of industrialists, the dichotomous pair of ascription and achievement cannot describe the reality of the stratification system. We have no proper typology which could include a central organising principle for an impending postmodern society (if this ever eventuates). Imada's criticism of industrialists sounds quite reasonable.

Imada attempts to provide a possible third principle around which a coming postmodern society is organised; this is 'meaning'. In medieval times, primacy was given to structure, while in modern society it has been given to function. In the postmodern, Imada claims, great importance is attributed to 'meaning' and 'difference'. He even speaks of a 'mechanism of meaning' as determining processes. But 'meaning' seems to stand at a different level from ascription and achievement, which are both concerned with the allocation of people or personnel among statuses or ranked positions. It is pertinent that he criticises a dichotomous way of thinking and conceptualisation as a 'modern' way. But he himself, in my opinion, does not succeed in preparing the relevant third category.

The problem is, however, not only a matter of inventing a relevant typology which allows the discussion of the postmodern. It is generally understood that in the realm of stratification and social mobility, ascription/achievement is (among other things) a matter of the principle or processes by which individuals are located in socioeconomic statuses. As such, the dichotomy is constructed along quite individualistic lines. This idea puts more emphasis on procedures and formality than on contents and results of, say, education. As Karabel and Halsey put it, however, there are many unsolved problems which concern themselves with contents and results.[14] These problems will never be solved solely by introducing the principle of achievement as long as it is given the meaning of the allocative principle of individuals. Problems of equality of results, as opposed to equality of opportunity, might well be raised along similar lines.

The theory of modernisation somehow assumes that the prevalence of achievement dispels ascription. Those principles are treated as if they were mutually exclusive. A closer examination of any society will disclose more complex processes at work. For instance, increasing numbers of foreign labourers are currently entering the Japanese labour market, some of whom are forming a lower bracket on the stratification ladder. What happened is this: rapid economic growth and industrialisation has violated the principle of ascription (for example, with regard to gender and family heritage). But it has also drawn the incoming labour forces from less developed countries. This created a problem in relation to the ascription principle of ethnicity of a type which was not salient before. A dialectical way of formulating the problem is illustrated in the discussion of 'achieved ascription' and 'ascribed achievement'.[15] I believe this discussion contributes towards clarifying the possible mechanism which determines social change.

For a moment we should carefully look back at Blau and Duncan's definition of ascription/achievement.[16] Achievement is defined in terms of the mere negation of ascription, ascription being determination by 'the circumstances of a person's birth' of his/her location in an hierarchical system.[17] That is, any allocative principle can be characterised as achievement in so far as a person's 'prospective adult status would be wholly problematic and contingent at the time of birth' (although Blau and Duncan's subsequent analysis suggests that educational attainment is the criterion of achievement). Conceptions of ascription and achievement may be not only mutually exclusive but also comprehensive; however, they are so because 'achievement' is treated as a kind of residual category. This is too broad. Furthermore, the ascription/achievement distinction is involved not only in the allocation of individuals to statuses, but also in the allocation or distribution of rewards and facilities among individuals.[18] Within an overall principle of achievement, a number of different subprinciples or criteria are conceivable.[19] Here again, achievement is not unequivocal.

As we saw earlier, Imada points to three empirical problems (emerging sense of unfairness, 'quality politics', and irrelevance of class/status) as indicators of the emergence of a postmodern society, or of the conclusion of a modern society. Whether these actually are observed or not, we considered earlier with reference to relevant empirical data. Yet these concepts should be examined also with respect to their theoretical significance and relevance, particularly in their relation to 'achievement', whatever it might imply. For example, how is fairness related to the achievement principle? Is fairness equivalent to distributive justice? How is objective (un)fairness related to the sense of (un)fairness? How is the sense of overall unfairness related to the sense of unfairness broken down into divisions (such as gender, location, school education, and so on) of a societal system? While much literature since the time of Aristotle has discussed problems of distributive justice, very little has dealt with the problems above in relation to stratification and social mobility, or to postmodernity.

Practical dimension

The present debate between Imada and Tominaga somehow reminds me of the debate between *Rōnō-ha* and *Kōza-ha*, which concerned the nature of Japanese capitalism, and was carried on in the 1920s and onwards.[20] The point of disputation between the two groups within Marxism was whether Japanese society should be regarded as having succeeded in modernisation (*Rōnō-ha*), or as one which had not yet modernised and still contained premodern or feudalistic elements (*Kōza-ha*). The debate was primarily theoretical, but it also had a strategic aspect. The political strategies and practical aims of the two sides differed. Proponents of the *Rōnō-ha* view were eager to pursue a socialist revolution which they called 'proletarian revolution', while proponents of *Kōza-ha* sought a 'bourgeois revolution' (only through which, they thought, could a 'proletarian revolution' be accomplished) to dispel the feudalistic elements remaining in Japanese society. The emperor system in Japan was thus regarded by *Rōnō-ha* as a mere institutional instrument of class domination by the bourgeoisie, while *Kōza-ha* viewed it as a semfeudalistic and absolutistic authority.

The debate between Imada and Tominaga parallels, in its practical aspect, that between *Rōnō-ha* and *Kōza-ha*. Imada and Tominaga are, it seems to me, pursuing different political strategies, whether or not they are aware of this. For the modernist, the most important aim is to take modernisation to its limit by expelling any premodern elements. No newer society, postmodern or otherwise, could emerge without the thorough realisation of modernisation. For the postmodernist, the modern (view of society, science and humanity) is the very condition to be overcome. As long as we stay within the modern way of thinking, Imada says, mechanisms of self-reflexivity and self-organisation cannot be captured. The modern way of organising societies rests on the notions of control, function and efficiency, which must be overcome.

Socialism was once a symbol of postcapitalism or postmodernity; but it has lost credibility world-wide, through the very implications of its one-party political system and totally planned economy. Today, the argument for postmodernity is a functional substitute for the socialism of the past. In this sense, the debate between modernity and postmodernity is destined to be a matter of praxis.

As mentioned earlier, the main focus of criticism for the modernist is different from that of the postmodernist. In the case of the modernist, the focus is the premodern, while for the postmodernist it is the modern. In other words, as Tominaga points out, the postmodernist is paradoxically less critical of the premodern which, even in contemporary Japan, still governs economic and political spheres of life.[21] On the other hand, as Imada points out, the modernist is less critical of the modern, which involves, for example, destruction of the environment and pollution as concomitants to industrialisation. The debate again is not independent of one's actual practice.

Concluding Remarks

Tominaga views Japanese history since the Meiji Restoration as a sequential but not necessarily linear process of modernisation. Imada, in contrast, sees a universal process of historical development which could apply to most industrialised countries, Japan being simply one such example. Despite their apparent differences, modernists and postmodernists both rely upon a common epistemology within the framework of which contemporary Japan is characterised and evaluated. Within their respective analytical frameworks, both are strongly oriented toward Western societies as representing 'ideal types' of modernity. Tominaga is currently devoted to examining conditions through which any non-Western society could modernise itself; but the final state of modernisation is conceptualised upon the model of highly industrialised Western societies. Imada's grandiose program of 'deconstruction of the modern' also falls within a Western-centered paradigm, in that it investigates consequences of the recent history of industrialised Western societies. When Western societies (which, in my view, are not at all homogeneous) are established as an ideal example of modernisation, the important question must be asked: how close is the Japanese experience to that ideal; or even, how does the Japanese experience conform to, or deviate from, the ideal type? The point may be that a new perspective is needed from which we can analyse historical processes both generally and historically.

The present review of this debate (in the light of the SSM datasets and other empirical data) may not wholly deny that contemporary Japan is undergoing a transition from the modern to the postmodern. However, there is very little empirical evidence to support this thesis. Tominaga's view is that Japanese society is now a triumvirate of the premodern, modern, and postmodern. Even Imada might not deny that, to some extent, inequalities of ascription (due to sex and family heritage) still exist. The problem, however, is not simply one of determining the state of a given society, but also of identifying the direction in which it is progressing, and the mechanisms which determine the course of its alteration.

Modernist arguments lack the clarity of definition found in postmodern views. Electronic and high-technology industries are viewed as symbols of postmodernism, as are 'super-big business' and the rapidly developing information industry. Yet no definition of the postmodern is provided by Tominaga. He insists upon the coexistence of three elements, or the 'contemporaneity of the non-contemporaneous', to use Mannheim's expression. While there is nothing wrong with such a statement, the more important question is whether or not that triumvirate is undergoing alteration and just how the non-contemporaneous elements are intertwined (sometimes leading to frictions among themselves and sometimes accelerating changes in social stratification and social mobility).

Postmodernist argument gives the clearer picture of the modern and the postmodern. Since Imada himself admits that postmodern society has not yet been fully realised in Japan (or anywhere else), the very characterisation of postmodern society might currently be seen as a fabrication. Imada's discussion neither describes the concrete historical processes and mechanisms which transform the modern into the postmodern nor even suggests what they might be. Great social theories such as those of Marx and Weber include theories about such mechanisms.

Notes

1. Tominaga, 1990.
2. *Ibid.*, p. 224.
3. Imada, 1990: 212–24.
4. SSM survey research was conducted in 1955, 1965, 1975 and 1985. The head of the research committee of the fourth (1985) SSM was Atsushi Naoi, Osaka University. See Kosaka, 1994 for details.
5. For a comprehensive delineation of changing stratification and status perceptions, see Kosaka, 1994.
6. Collins, 1979.
7. Miyajima, 1983.
8. NHK Yoron Chōsabu, 1985.
9. Kadowaki, 1978.
10. Katase and Tomoeda, 1990.

11. Kadowaki, 1978.
12. Kosaka, 1994.
13. Blau and Duncan, 1967: 163.
14. Karabel and Halsey, 1977.
15. Kajita, 1988.
16. Blau and Duncan, 1967.
17. Parsons (1951: 118) suggests two types of allocative principles, both of which are associated with the primacy of achievement-orientation over the ascriptive: appointment and competition allocation. This distinction is made with reference to the procedural aspect of allocation.
18. See Parsons (1951: 114–32) for a detailed discussion of 'allocation'.
19. Boudon (1982: Chapter 6) discusses the internal relations of competing distributive principles such as Rawlsian indifference, the Pareto criterion, the equality principle and the utilitarian criterion from a normative theoretical perspective. Under the concept of distributive justice, Deutsch (1985) distinguishes three further criteria such as equity, equality and need.
20. See, for example, Koyama, 1953 for a general review of the debate between *Rōnō-ha* and *Kōza-ha*.
21. Tominaga, 1989.

11 POLITICS
The Japanese Postmodern Political Condition

Paul Harrison

The invention of the term 'postmodern' has clarified nothing. As a way of 'doing sociology', postmodern sociology has barely got off the ground. As a way of 'thinking social change', a sociology of postmodernity falls prey to the postmodern critique of historicism in its attempt to demarcate two quite distinct, successive historical stages. Used this way, the term tends to give both some sort of reassuring name ('modernity') to our new perplexities and also to exacerbate those fears that these new perplexities give rise to with a prefix that is redolent of apocalypse ('post'). However, I remain unconvinced that the problems of modern society have been superseded, and that our new problems can be defined as those pertaining to postmodern society. The significance of the prefix 'post' in 'postmodernity' rests, not in the meaning of 'after' that can be given to the term, but in the meaning of 'relay' that is also present in the term. Hence, what is now in the mail, what we have just received in the post, is not something new. The news that now haunts us when we receive our post is, first of all, simply the letters that we thought we had lost in the 'dead letters office', but which have turned up after all; and, secondly, those letters that were already in the post, but have only now just arrived. In sum, if modernity involves atavisms, delayed developments as well as novelty and transformation, then it makes little sense to one-sidedly emphasise discontinuity and rupture. The task is not so much to underplay change, however, as to explain change in terms of changing balances within longer-term processes and forces. Hence, if I retain the term 'postmodern' it is a purely provisional retention and the content that I give to the term is minimalist. I define 'the postmodern condition' to simply mean those changes that have arisen since the end of the social consensus that underlay the period of long-term growth that ended in the early 1970s. I further define 'the postmodern political condition' as the newly-created field of disputation that arises from the collapse of this consensus. The letter that we thought we had

213

lost and have only just received from the 'dead letters office' brings us the news that everyone had simply forgotten; namely, that economic growth is not inevitable, but a remarkably fragile product of a series of political compromises and cultural accommodations. The letter that we have only just received, but which was always en route, is that the central modernist conflict between labour and capital, socialism and liberalism, has tended to hide an equally central conflict between enlightenment and romanticism, or between the proponents of the modern condition (those with so-called materialist value-orientations) and their adversaries (those with so-called postmaterialist value-orientations).

Hence, there is a change of condition and we are 'living after', but what we are living after is not the 'end of modernity'. However, the curious thing is that, what we are 'living after' is clearer to spell out in detail than it is to encapsulate in a concept. At a global level, what we are 'living after' can be summarised under four points. We are living, first of all, after the equation of modernisation with Westernisation, and we live, as a consequence, in a world where there has been a pluralisation of models of development. We are also living, secondly, after the '30 glorious years' of uninterrupted economic growth. However, the interruption of growth in the West has not resulted in a global crisis of capital accumulation and economic development, but in a crisis of Western economic growth. We are also living after the 'economic pax Americana' that has seen a period of remarkably high and remarkably sustained economic growth. What we are moving toward is an economically multipolar world that will only be partly Western. We are also living after the end of the great Western ideological invention of socialism which, as an alternative to capitalism labelled communism, had little impact on the West as compared with Asia and the 'Third World'. Hence, we are living after the foundering of the two superpowers and the respective end of their self-imposed '*civilising missions*'. At a societal level, what we are living after can be summarised under four points. We are living, first of all, after the end of the great central 'distributive conflict' of industrial society between labour and capital that grew out of the nineteenth century, which is, of course, not to say that we are living after the end of all conflict per se. What may be emerging is a new type of social conflict that does not divide worker from boss, but one type of middle-class professional from another. This entails that we are also living after the end of class-based political parties and in an era of a passionless politics of the centre within the official political scene. We are also living in a society of new social conflicts centering on questions of life and the management of life-threatening risks that range from nuclear destruction and environmental devastation to access to medical care, nursing homes and the like. We are also living in a society of new technologies that radically accelerate the rate at which old technologies and old skills become obsolete. As a consequence, the societies that do best will be those societies that can best manage the process of their own continual self-transformation. In this context, the ideology of the free market that has dominated Anglo-American type societies in the 1980s is one that has masked the lack of institutional resources these societies possess to manage their future due to the ideological rigidity of the opposition between planning and the market. We live, furthermore, in a society of fractured subjectivities populating 'drifting cities', where mediatised culture has replaced the oedipal family as the fulcrum in which personalities and ethoses are shaped. The fact that these changes, and many more could be added to the list, have been named 'postmodernity' is a testament to the fact that the perception of an 'epochal shift' is a real one that will have real consequences, even if the term itself can be shown to embody an overly-exaggerated sense of the novelty or epochal character of these shifts.

The question of how to reconstruct the phenomenon of postmodernity varies in relation to which dimension of social existence is to be examined. What I want to do in this essay is to reconstruct the term 'postmodernity' in relation to the political system; and to compare developments in Western political systems to developments in Japanese politics and society. The general approach is to treat postmodernity, firstly, not as a set of epochal shifts, but rather as a set of intra-epochal changes; and, secondly, as a set of political reactions to those changes that vary from a hyperliberalism, to a neocommunitarianism and a postindividualist romanticism. This means, firstly, that we have yet to 'overcome modernity', and, secondly, that in the context of Western political systems, it has been the hyperliberal reaction to the set of intra-epochal changes that has been most influential in the 1980s, but both the romantic and neocommunitarian reactions have been a prominent countermotif. In relation to Japanese politics and society, what is of interest is both the differing nature of these changes and the differing ways that they have been handled, and also the differing political reactions that they have called forth, as compared with the West. The differences at both levels between Japan and the West can be traced back to long-term differences in processes of political and cultural development.

I

In the West, the postmodern political condition has encompassed four aspects. The first two aspects constitute together the reconstituted left axis of the contemporary field of political disputation. The first aspect is summed up by the term 'difference', which in this context refers to the tolerance and even celebration of all forms of heterogeneity. The idea that a society does not need to have any substantive basis for social membership is one that stands squarely within the liberal tradition. It is one, however, that even the most liberal societies have never fully realised through the usage of principles of racial and political exclusion, but which contemporary hyperliberalism has made intellectually and politically redundant. From a poststructuralist and psychoanalytical perspective, this hyperliberal defence of difference takes the form of a plea for the acceptance of foreigners within the social body on the grounds that each and every individual psyche is foreign to itself, in so far as it contains the opaque otherness of the unconscious.[1] From a poststructuralist and philosophical perspective, this hyperliberal defence of difference takes the form of a plea for the necessary inherence of nonidentity or difference within every culture against those who assert that the identity of a culture depends on its principles of exclusion, of closure.[2] The second aspect involves the re-emergence of non-economistic notions of civil society and the renewed concern with reformulating notions of democracy.[3] These have emerged out of the political practice of the new social movements of the 1980s that have formed a political counterweight to the shift towards the centre within the official political system. These movements are not so much concerned with questions of distribution, but the question of the management of risks (nuclear or environmental) and, hence, their demand is for the broadening of participation in decision-making, as these are risks that affect entire populations. Although the substantive demands of such movements may be romantic, the demand to expand participation incorporates a liberal dimension even when it goes beyond this toward types of neocommunitarianism. The next two aspects constitute together the reconstituted axis of the right field of political disputation. The third aspect is summed up by the term 'market'. The return of the market and the critique of state planning and state intervention has reversed a half-century of economic and political practice that began in the wake of the Great Depression. The renewed appreciation of the market is also squarely in the tradition of modern liberalism, with its distaste of administrative law and *dirigiste* forms of social co-ordination; and its advocacy of civil law and voluntarist forms of social co-ordination. This return of the market has occurred not only in Anglo-American-type societies, but also in continental societies that have been typically *dirigiste*. In France, the renewal of economic and political liberalism has been variously referred to as a 'silent revolution' and as 'the end of French exceptionalism'.[4] The fourth aspect involves the increasing globalisation of both economies and political systems. At one level this has meant the emergence of so-called global 'third cultures', which are cultures that are neither national nor supranational, but are autonomously functioning markets and media that maximise the free circulation of money, people, ideas, etc.[5] These could also be described as nomad cultures. At another level this does involve the construction of supranational entities such as the European Community (EC) and the North Atlantic Free Trade Agreement (NAFTA), within which the possibility of such free circulation is obviously maximised. At one level, it is the old liberal economic utopia of the peaceful nature of commerce that is being reinvoked. At the other level, it is the old liberal utopia of 'perpetual peace' emerging out of an association of free republics that is being revived. Hence, all four notions contain strongly liberal elements that either continue or radicalise the unarguably central political ideology of Western political development; namely, liberalism. Hence, the redrawn field of political disputation sees the replacement of the old political conflict between a market-driven, social investment project and a state-driven, social consumption project being replaced by a market-driven process of internationalisation, on the one hand, and by a difference-driven process of pluralisation, on the other hand.

When one compares this new field of disputation in the West

with developments in Japan, the picture that emerges is markedly different from the one that emerges out of an analysis of Western developments. The hyperliberal component of the Western variant of postmodernity makes Western postmodernity a form of hypermodernity, whereas the Japanese variant of postmodernity has a strongly antiliberal component that makes it a form of antimodernity due to its negative evaluation of the culture of Western modernity. However, such a stark formulation overly-polarises a difference that may be better understood as a differential weighting of elements, even if it has the advantage of delineating two quite clearly separate trajectories. In this context, I define liberalism quite broadly as the political philosophy of Western modernity which developed out of the political revolutions of the seventeenth and eighteen centuries; and which radically puts into question the prevailing political institutions and opens up the political space to new social forces and to new types of demands. What distinguishes modern hyperliberalism is the bifurcation of what was formerly held together; and the perhaps temporary predominance of economic over political liberalism is evident in the contemporary triumph of slogans like 'rolling back the state', 'market forces', 'consumer sovereignty', 'privatisation', 'getting government off people's backs' etc. Along with these slogans, but subsidiary to them until the recent visible failure of the neo-classical model, came a conservative refrain that has moved from the return of mainstream conservative themes to more extreme forms of radical right-wing rhetoric. What distinguishes Japanese political development is, of course, the failure to autonomously develop such a liberal tradition of political philosophy. Indeed, seventeenth-century Japanese political philosophy saw the construction of a 'state ideology' that stabilised a warrior-dominated political order from above; and the post-Meiji Restoration era is notable for the erection of a nationalist ideology and the subordinate status of the more liberal current in Japanese political life.[6] The attempt by Japanese liberals at the beginning of the twentieth century at a Taisho *ishin* as the democratic complement to the Meiji *ishin* that opened the way to a specifically Japanese version of capitalist modernity was fraught with ambivalence from the beginning.[7] The significant feature of the liberal postwar Japanese Constitution is that it is an imposed constitution with fewer roots in Japanese civil society than the similarly imposed postwar German Constitution. The peculiarities of the postwar political

system, as compared with the political systems of other consti-
tutionally liberal-democratic regimes, have their roots in this tor-
tured political history more than in any institutional peculiarity
of one-party-dominant political systems.[8] This kind of normalising
perspective remains blind to the cultural and institutional unwillingness of the post-Meiji elite to create an autochthonous reshaping of the Japanese political system along Western liberal-
democratic lines in the same way that they were able to do for
the Japanese economic system. Japanese modernity still remains
marked by its failure to autonomously institute the other element
of Western modernity's 'dual institution'; namely, democracy, or,
in more controversial terminology, the project of autonomy.[9]
Indeed, it remains remarkable because of its conscious refusal
of it.

Given this political history, it is not surprising that the slogan
of 'overcoming modernity' has a quite distinctively antimodern,
anti-Western and antidemocratic ring to it in recent Japanese
history. The 1941 symposium on 'overcoming the modern' (*kindai
no chōkoku*) articulated a threefold rejection of the key elements
of modernity: the Western notion of history as progress was
rejected in favour of a notion of a timeless Japan; the Western
notion of cultural differentiation was rejected in favour of a
purportedly specific Japanese notion of the wholeness and unity
of knowledge; and, finally, the instrumental notion of rationality,
which was further equated with Americanism, was also rejected.[10]
What is important here is not so much what is rejected, as all
these notions have been subject to internal criticism within Western thought itself, but the lapse into a remythicisation of national
tradition that is its upshot. This antimodern remythicisation of
national tradition can be also found in the work of the most
important progenitor of contemporary postmodern thought,
namely Martin Heidegger.[11] What is new about the second
attempt to overcome modernity launched by the Ōhira government in the 1980s, is that it explicitly recognises the destruction
that the development of commodity production and the usage of
media-steered communication have had upon tradition; and the
way in which it functionally adapts culture to the imperative of
control that guides both the state and private business. Hence,
the aim is not so much to rehabilitate a disappearing national
culture, but to instrumentally mobilise its 'simulacrum' – 'the
"Japanese thing" (*Nihon tekina mono*), rather than "tradition" '.[12]

The difference between the two moments is, therefore, that the earlier romantic motif of national tradition could be cannibalised by ultranationalist political movements, whereas the simulated romanticism of the second attempt to 'overcome modernity' is itself the product of the normal and rational functioning of the political system. It is less dangerous because it is more under control; and it is more under control precisely because it is less real. The danger that besets such a system is not the irruption of irrational forces that derail political normality, but the simple intrusion of reality itself.

Administrative attempts at an 'overcoming of modernity' must not be mistaken for an 'overcoming of the reality of modernity' itself. In the Japanese case, the assimilation of modernisation with Westernisation has always entailed a partial rejection of the former, as evident in the early Meiji slogans about combining 'the moral and spiritual values of the East, with the technical skills of the West.[13] The Japanese state has always tried, therefore, to define itself as separate from Western modernity, even as it actively pursued a path of Western industrialisation. This strategy is by no means an oriental peculiarity, as there is a direct parallel that can be drawn between Japanese and German developments that goes beyond the more limited parallel I have drawn between the 1942 symposium and Heidegger's *Rektoratsrede*. In this context, Murakami has spoken of 'late-developer conservatism'.[14] His argument is that late-developers like Germany and Japan need to balance processes of cultural differentiation with the need for political integration in order to pursue a catch-up industrialisation policy that compensates for the culturally destabilising effects of industrialisation through the reaffirmation of national traditions. This is a rather anodyne way of saying that capitalist industrialisation is incompatible with democratisation outside of a small number of countries in the West European tradition of political development. It raises the question of whether a 'delayed', as opposed to 'impetuous', introduction of democracy would be possible at all, given the missing cultural, historical and institutional prerequisites. When this question is raised, the concept of late-developer conservatism breaks down due to its inability to differentiate countries in terms of such prerequisites. The notion ends up with an apologetic justification of the similarity of the 'predominant party' political system of Japan to other such systems in Europe. The problem with such an approach is that, as with the contributions in the volume edited by Ishida and Krauss,[15] it also normalises the exceptionalism of Japanese political development.

II

When I speak of Japanese exceptionalism, I do not refer to the self-proclaimed and culturally-defined exceptionalism of *nihonjinron*, but to the different path that Japan has taken into the modern world and the way in which that path still affects contemporary society despite the political normalisation that the imposition of a liberal-democratic constitution may seem to have brought. What I want to show, in particular, is how the four elements that I have defined as essential to the Western postmodern political condition are only partially present or take on a vastly different character in the Japanese context. The aim of such a comparison is not, of course, to measure Japanese political developments against a normatively prescribed Western model, but to test whether Japanese exceptionalism in the sense that I have defined it, is not simply a product of a one-party-dominant political system, but of long-term differences in political development. I will begin with a discussion of what I have described as the left axis of political disputation; namely, those aspects involving difference and democratisation. These aspects embody the most politically-left liberal aspects of the postmodern agenda, but shade off both into anarchic libertarianism and neocommunitarianism. What I have described as the postmodern political condition of the acceptance of difference and of the emergence of new forms of social action that emerge out of civil society is, of course, not an uncontested political fact in the West. The 'difference agenda' and the 'protest movements' in the West were a product of a postmaterialist generation of the 1960s and 1970s, which, in either its hyperliberal or hyperromantic variants, has been partly 'turned back' in the 1980s by, on the one hand, a neoliberalism that focuses on markets and internationalisation and, on the other hand, by neoconservatism.[16]

At first glance, there are quite clear parallels with regard to Japanese political developments. The politics of the 1960s in Japan was marked by the growth of new demands that emerged out of extraparliamentary social movements. What is usually suggested as peculiar about the Japanese case is the failure of such movements to leave their mark on the official political system through the drift of their membership and their agenda into the mainstream parties of the left. The fact that the Japan Socialist Party's working-class base was unsympathetic to the employment cost of the new agenda is not a complete explanation, given the fact that this was an obstacle successfully overcome by several Western socialist parties, nor is the conservatism of their nonurban constituency, given the similar religiously-based conservatism that also had to be overcome in several Western socialist parties.[17] Furthermore, explanations that point toward the ideological rigidity of the JSP, which stands in stark contrast to the increasing flexibility of Western socialist and even communist parties from the 1960s to the 1980s, as an explanation for the continued conservative dominance that has shut out the 'difference agenda', have to come up with an explanation of this rigidity itself.[18] In order to answer this question we have first to ask whether the Japanese movements of the 1960s through to the 1980s were really similar to such movements in the West? This will, in turn, raise the question of whether the 'difference and democratisation agenda' was one that was there for the opposition parties to pursue? If it was not, then the ability of the dominant party to 'buy back' support through 'compensation politics',[19] and the continuing rigidity and the concomitant lack of electoral success of the parties of the left, becomes more understandable.

What strikes one about Japanese social movements is, firstly, that the movements that stem from the epoch of industrialisation die later and yet more abruptly than they do in the West; and, secondly, that there is a persistent recrudescence of traditional patterns of revolt that results in the presence of some forms of social movement typical in the West that are, however, taken up and acted out in different ways. What follows from this is the conclusion that this recrudescence and transformation of traditional patterns results in some typically Western social movements being absent or only weakly present. With regard to the first point, the year 1960 is a crucial turning point. If a simplistic notion of a Japanese postmodern political condition made sense, then the year 1960 would have to be taken as the year of its birth. The failure of the movement against the renewal of the American-Japan security treaty and the failure of the miners' revolt at Miki mark the end in Japan of the kind of socialist project that Touraine has defined as the attempt to exercise politi-

cal control over an essentially state-directed process of modernisation through political action. The Japanese version of this
socialist project re-emerged in the early days of the American
Occupation; and suffered a long period of decline until its final
defeat. The need to turn away from this type of socialist project
was quite quickly realised in the reformist movements of labour-
ism in England, Germany and Australia, but periodic outbreaks
of paleo-socialism in the 1930s, the immediate postwar period,
and even in 1980s Britain, show how long this model took to die,
even in the West. The delay in the case of Japan can be quite
easily explained, using Touraine's framework, as a consequence
of the prolonged utilisation of a state-directed form of industrialisation that was only partly and incompletely transformed in the
post-war period. What happens after 1960 is the almost complete
acquiescence of the post-Miki union movement to its incorporation into the corporate ministates of internationally-orientated
business; and their almost complete absence from the competitive,
small-scale units of the domestically-orientated economy. This
state-created dualisation of the Japanese economy has left room
for a 'corporatism without labour' in the advanced sector.[20] It
is a state-created corporatism that has its roots in the prewar
bureaucratic development of right-wing corporatist models that
were pursued by differing means in the differing political context
of postwar Japan. At the political level, the de-alignment of political parties from their class constituencies that has affected both
sides of the political spectrum in the West has only really affected
the left-of-centre political parties in Japan.[21] The resultant political system does not much resemble the 'split top' postulated by
systems theory, both because the pervasive Japanism acts to mor-
ally impugn the political suitability of leftist parties for office;
and also because, at another level, the electoral system constitutes
a mirror in which only the level of political clientelism, rather
than the level of public opinion, is reflected.

The recrudescence of traditional patterns of revolt is a theme
taken up in a recent article on contemporary Japanese social
movements.[22] The starting point of Kajita's analysis is the differing
basis of political organisation in the West as compared with Japan.
The contrast he makes between the voluntarist forms of social
organisation typical of the West and the communalist forms typical of Japan casts a sceptical light on approaches that emphasise
the conflictual nature of Japanese society in so far as they suggest

that conflict is not incompatible with a certain kind of mobilis-ation of tradition. However, the more radical point that Kajita makes is the way that consensualism can be turned back on the state and become a principle of radical mobilisation. Yet, this means that the most vigorous of contemporary social movements are not the ones that are evident in the West. Hence, citizens' movements and students' movements are weaker than in the West and have not survived the 1960s; and hence, also, the continuing weakness of antigrowth coalitions and the women's movements. These 'Western-style' movements are a priori hostile to the ideol-ogy of Japanism, but this very rejection explains the weakness of the movements. On the other hand, Kajita points out that move-ments against the state over the question of pollution conducted at the communal level were far more successful in achieving their objectives than were the movements that organised at the local level to secure improvements for the village. The result of this pattern is that the state not only fosters certain kinds of consen-sus, but that it tolerates also only a certain kind of conflict. Hence, the presence of conflict in Japanese society cannot be taken at face value as an indicator of the nonconsensual nature of Japanese society. And, secondly, the absence of hyperliberal forms of postmodernism typical of the West is rooted in the absence of a mobilisable, individualist cultural model. The cultural model at stake in Japanese political conflicts is still the collectivist model of Japanism.

III

In order to look more closely for signs of right ultraliberalism or the 'market agenda' in modern Japan, we have to first sketch in the general pattern of Japanese political development. The disappearance of politics, which some see as a symptom of the contemporary postmodern political condition, occurred earlier in Japan than in the West. Indeed, it is arguable that politics ever really made more than a faint appearance. The Meiji Restoration was an example of 'modernisation without democratisation' as the ideology of *kokutai* elevated the emperor into an alternative form of political legitimacy vastly different from either the forms of constitutional monarchy or popular sovereignty typical of the West. Japanese modernisation involved the re-emergence of imperial legitimacy and its synchronisation with the fused strands of forms of feudal and bureaucratic legitimation. What it legitimated was a revolution from above that saw the self-transformation of the dominant aristocratic stratum into a dominant bureaucratic stratum under the imperial aegis. This stratum identified democratisation with Westernisation and, hence, while the modernisation programme did entail the modernisation of the political system, it did not entail anything more than timid democratisation. The adoption of a German constitutional model by the oligarchies of the Meiji Restoration permitted a kind of elite control, which was designed not so much to keep the bourgeoisie from political power as to forcibly create the conditions for capitalist industrialisation. Although the Showa Restoration demonstrated the pitfalls of such an anti-Western logic of 'modernisation without democratisation', there is no reason why such a system could not stabilise itself short of all-out war. The imposed process of self-transformation that underlay the modernisation programme led to open hostility from the left against those powers that had imposed it in the first place; and against all those elements within the political system that showed signs of Western democratic influence from the right. The victory of the latter forces during 'the dark valley' was not a revolution from below, but an ultranationalist drift from above. The self-transformation of the bureaucratic ruling stratum that then occurred entailed both the rise to greater power of the military bureaucrats, and the turn toward Fascist and Nazi corporatist models by the non-military bureaucrats. Japanism was re-made in the image of the West's own counterrevolutionaries. However, Japanism also gained an anti-imperialist flavour due to the fact that Japan was an oriental power that had largely escaped Western imperial control. The irony is that Japan took on the West with an ideology fashioned out of elements made in the West.

Everything points to the survival of this bureaucracy into the postwar era, even if shorn of its military and internal control components. However, the fact that Japan has been a functioning democracy throughout the postwar period is not without its effect on the way Japan is governed. Furthermore, the strengthening of Japanese capitalism is also not without its effect on the way this bureaucracy can act. This highly complex constellation of factors has given rise to three main ways of interpreting the peculiarity of Japanese postwar politics: the capitalist development state or bureaucratic control thesis, the one-party dominance or political control thesis, and the compensation dynamic or shared power thesis.[23] I will analyse each in turn. The first thesis emphasises the strong continuity between prewar Japan and postwar Japan in terms of the survival of the bureaucratic elite, both due to Western ignorance of how Japan was really run and also because of the necessity of an army of occupation to have expert advice on how to administer occupied territory. The predominance of reform bureaucrats among the postwar political elite and the dominance of Ministry of International Trade and Industry as the bureaucratic engine behind Japan's new modernisation drive are but two of the key pieces of evidence that suggests a bureaucratically-controlled, state-centred pattern of development. The second thesis accepts the conventional hypothesis that the political process should be at the centre of any analysis of the state and explains the rigidities of the Japanese state in terms of such things as electoral systems, funding arrangements for parties, and the like. It is a natural but not necessary corollary of this thesis that Japanese economic development is seen as more independent of state-control. The stability of state structures is not due to the hardness of their bureaucratic spine, but to the immobility of the political process itself. Another variant of this thesis argues that the seventies and eighties have seen society, particularly business interests, emerge from under the shadow of the state. In this variant, the state is seen as weaker than the social forces that infiltrate it. The new constellation is, however, defined somewhat widely as existing precariously between pluralism and corporatism. Hence, what starts out as a pluralist critique of a bureaucratic dominance thesis ends up as a variant of the idea that what has happened is a dilation of the bureaucratic core of the Japanese state.[24] The third thesis argues that the bureaucratic control thesis underestimates the importance of the political process and the way in which the dominant party responds to crises through the buying-off of potential opposition through compensation politics. However, this thesis also stresses the relative immunity of industrial policy to political control and, hence, the important contribution that the bureaucracy makes to economic development. Another variant of this thesis also makes the point that precisely what is turned into a political football in Western politics – that is, industry policy – is immune from political interference in Japan.[25] However, this variant also argues for the importance of market factors in Japanese economic development;

and argues for a conception of the Japanese state as a 'network state' that is able to fashion supple webs of consultative planning.

The first thesis and the third thesis do not appear to me to be incompatible, whereas the second thesis strikes me as an implausible normalisation of Japanese politics within a comparative institutionalist framework that does not deal effectively with different developmental trajectories. The compatibility of the first and third theses can be grasped in one of two ways. The third thesis can be grasped as a necessary corrective to the exaggerations of the first or it can be grasped as a theoretical response to changes in the pattern of bureaucratic control itself, which may involve a relative loosening of bureaucratic control and a concomitant rise of political power, but not necessarily of the power of civil society. These two explanations are not incompatible either, as the emergence of new developments always leads to the revision of former assumptions, but revision does not mean reversal. Hence, the third thesis is an empirical corrective to an overly-drawn picture of bureaucratic control that accords the political process proper more influence than the first thesis, but not as much as the second. However, the important point here is that the continued importance of the bureaucracy does not mean that the 'market agenda' itself has been more crucially driven by bureaucratic forces than in the West. In order to grasp the 'market agenda' in so far as it is evident in Japan we must examine the process of internationalisation.

The first point that needs to be made when dealing with the question of a possible rise of a 'market agenda' is that the 1980s were a period of fiscal retrenchment in Japan. After the social movements of the 1970s and the passing of the progressive experiments at the local level that came out of them, the reconsolidation of liberal-democratic rule enabled the state to wind back expenditures on social consumption. In short, the compensation dynamic of fiscal expenditure to curb social instability was not as necessary as it had been. However, this means that the winding back of the state in Japan was rather different to what occurred in the West. In particular, what strikes one as being absent is the shrill ideological tones that 'the new right agenda' brought with it in the West. In Japan, the 'winding back of the state' was more of a pragmatic readjustment. The reason would seem to lie in the fact that fiscal retrenchment was not due to any perceived overexpansion of the welfare state as the result of the expansion of citizenship rights. Indeed, this central dynamic of Western political systems seems to be remarkably absent in Japan. The second point is that the 'privatisation programme' that was pursued in Japan was also markedly different from what was meant by that term in the West. Above all else, privatisation did not mean either the wide-scale entry of foreign corporations into domestic markets or the uninhibited opening up of domestic markets to internal competition. Although examples can be cited that contradict this statement, these are the exceptions rather than the rule. The closed, oligopolistic character of Japanese capitalism is oriented not to the consumer, but to the producer and the need of the producer for a stable platform from which to conquer international markets. The third point concerns the emergence of the Japanese multinational in the 1980s which, once again, seems to have some prima facie similarities to processes of economic globalisation in the West. The internationalisation of Japanese capitalism has been a response both to rising domestic costs, a higher exchange rate and the need for a presence within major trading blocs in order to remain politically immune from protectionist measures. What has been missing from this approach is a genuinely economic multinationalism, as head office still retains control while branch offices act as relays. What has also been missing from this process is a genuinely political dimension of increased integration such as has happened in Europe and the Americas. These deficits can only be partly corrected by companies developing more explicitly global strategies or adhering more closely to multilateral agreements. The logic of Japan's internationalisation permits a greater element of foreign manufacture of second-generation mass-produced items, while retaining the creation and production of high value-added, first-generation items in Japan. Pocket calculators will be made abroad, while supercomputers and supersonic transport will remain at home. Hence, internationalisation simultaneously allows Japanese firms to continue to compete on the world market by going offshore, while retaining onshore the process of fitting out new Japanese products for the world market.[26]

All this points toward a more thorough-going internationalisation of the Japanese economy; however, the social forces that drive it forward are different from those in the West. Once again, it is the state bureaucracy and corporate conglomerates, rather than social forces, which are of decisive importance. Privatisation in Japan is not the result of the state's fiscal embarrassments as is so often the case in the West, nor is internationalisation a way of simply abandoning whole sectors of the population to a life-time of unemployment. Privatisation and internationalisation are neither market nor consumer driven in Japan even at an ideo-logical level, but are driven by the need for Japan to keep inter-national markets open now that it is becoming the world's leading economy through financial domination, technological interlink-ages and offshore production. Internationalisation is, above all else, a bureaucratic strategy.[27] As the MITI report for the 1980s made clear, Japan's effort to internationalise was, first of all, part of an effort to obtain resource security after the oil shocks of the 1970s. The report also makes it clear that the Meiji era was finally over in so far as Japan's modernisation had now both caught up with and surpassed that of the West. The new problem was that, in the vital area of the exploitation of knowledge-intensive commodities, Japan could no longer rely on Western research and development, but had to become a leader in these fields. Japan is now the pioneer economy of the world. It is where techno-scientific fantasy becomes reality. Hence, the internationalisation strategy had four prongs. Firstly, Japan's educational system had to emphasise creativity over rote-learning in order to develop the type of thinking that is conducive to scientific discovery.[28] Sec-ondly, Japan's multinationals went on a buying spree for small knowledge-intensive companies with good ideas or entered into partnerships with foreign multinationals to develop new techno-logies. Thirdly, assembly-type work was either transferred off-shore or sold to third parties in fields where the technology potentially transferred was no longer 'state-of-the-art'. Fourthly, Japanese financial institutions moved offshore in order to make Japan a financial power. This kind of internationalisation strategy required reciprocal concessions: the opening up of Japanese financial markets and the like; but none of the concessions has made too much of a dent in trade balances. This kind of inter-nationalisation strategy also requires a benign international environment; and the MITI report recognised that an increasingly economically and politically multipolar world could prove the undoing of such a strategy. However, the free-market policies of the West of the early and mid-1980s proved a more comfortable environment than was predicted. It may turn out that the 1990s is the decade in which this strategy comes undone.

This kind of internationalisation strategy also requires a benign domestic environment. The domestic environment that counts here is not so much the electorate as elite opinion. The international environment that counts here is America. The dilemma that Japan faces is that, in becoming an economic hegemony with a poorly-developed domestic consumer market and comparatively little military power, it is reliant on America for export markets and military support. The Japanese internationalisation strategy was not contradictory, therefore, when it demanded both the expansion of the Japanese consumer market and the retention of a free trade environment at the international level. The strategy was to open up the domestic market slightly, let private consumption demand grow, and channel some of Japan's economic growth away from being export-led into the area of domestic consumption; and hope, at the same time, that some of this growth in demand would be supplied by American companies. The paradox is that consumerism therfore aids Japanese independence from foreign control. The further paradox is that foreign demands that Japan contribute financially and militarily to world security also contribute to Japanese independence from foreign control. This strategy was articulated in a number of MITI documents and in the Maekawa Commission that was set up in response to the strong revaluation of the yen that occurred in 1985 as a way of reducing global trade imbalances. The strategy worked for a time and trade balances with America improved. However, the turnaround in trade balances that occurred once again under the Bush administration resulted in 1992 in bilateral concessions that specifically favoured American producers. Once again, the logic of such concessions is the necessity for Japan to keep American markets open in the context of a relatively open international economy. What this policy runs up against domestically is the unwillingness of the political system to sacrifice sectors of the economy that are important for political support, such as agriculture, or also less technologically-advanced manufacturing sectors. The former are more important than the latter, as the competitive nature of the Japanese economy has resulted in no 'hollowing out' of its industrial sector, as has happened in Western economies.[29] The former are also easier to protect, in so far as agriculture, as the main example, has not really been an integral part of GATT negotiations until the current round. The dynamism of the Japanese manufacturing sector and the immunisation of its agricultural sector does not make internationalisation a political problem, as it is in many Western economies, where the increasing international exposure of the domestic manufacturing economy usually results in its destruction. In the case of efficient primary product exporters, internationalisation means the extinction of the domestic manufacturing base with no compensating access for competitive agricultural exports.

There is no doubt that the state bureaucracy could not effect this shift by itself, and that Japanese industrial policy requires both competition as well as co-ordination. Yet, the point I want to emphasise here is the connection between bureaucracy and democracy and the choice of development paths. The 'market agenda' of such Western countries as England and the US can be viewed both as a response to internal domestic pressure against what came to be seen as ineffective policies of state intervention and state redistribution and as a response to an increasingly virulent global competition that squeezed profit margins. The white-collar middle class of the private sector and the business and managerial elites formed the bloc of support behind such governments. The policies chosen bore heavily against the social welfare recipient and the working poor, while the middle class held their own and the business and managerial strata prospered.[30] Where electoral cycles and electoral systems saw these policies introduced by left-of-centre governments such as in France, Australia and New Zealand, these policies were somewhat tempered, with high unemployment being preferred to low wage jobs and with good but increasingly rationed social security as a backup. This form of internationalisation, however, exposed increasing segments of the national economy to competitive forces in order that the already internationally competitive sectors of the national economy could compete better. Instead of an intranational compensation dynamic operating, the international sector became increasingly deterritorialised. Hence, internationalisation came to relatively impoverish national societies as the nomad economy squeezed the sedentary economy. This relative impoverishment was a result of a process that involves some degree of democratic consent to a process whereby business and intellectual elites imposed a no-state-directed industrial policy, and a low wage cost, low investment and low innovation strategy. The irony is that the state-directed industrial policy, high wage cost, high investment, and high innovation strategy chosen by

Japanese elites was not the product of any real popular will, and yet as a strategy it has undoubtedly been of more benefit to their nation, if not to the populace. The fiscal retrenchment that the Japanese state did undertake during the more benign political climate of the 1980s was one that undoubtedly affected the populace, but it did not affect the state-directed policy of national development. Internationalisation has made Japan a stronger nation, but it has done so because of state intervention. Internationalisation has left many Western nations weaker, and it has done so both because of social forces and weak elites. In the West, the weakness of elites and social forces have complemented one another. In Japan, the absence of social forces has been made up for by strong, intelligent elites that constitute a 'social network' (Okimoto) sui generis in which both consensually-oriented communication and competitively-driven economic action can, contrary to the Western model, precariously coexist.

IV

The difference agenda and the market agenda have come together in quite a perverse way to mutually reinforce the inability of nation-states in some countries of the West to enhance their international position. The national conservatism of Japan has meant that the emergence of a difference agenda is implausible, and the re-interpretation of the market agenda merely serves to meet new national goals. In the competition between the cosmopolitan liberal project of internationalisation, it is now quite clear which one is winning. Japanese internationalisation is creating a missionary economy as whole sectors of foreign economies are made over according to Japanese production practices, and in a way that brings benefits to the domestic economy. Western internationalisation is creating a normal economy where the knowledge-based and service-based sectors sell their skills into the global economy in ways that tend to diminish the domestic economy, which the postindustrial ideologues declare for the large part passé. Japanese trade with the West has a pronounced asymmetrical character.[31] Japan imports primary goods and exports elaborately transformed manufactures. For countries like Australia, that means that around 70–80 per cent of our exports are primary products, with only countries like America, with 40 per cent (due mainly to computers and aerospace), and those of East

Asia, with 30–40 per cent (due mainly to the export of old-technology manufactured goods), exporting significantly less primary products. Where Japan invests directly abroad it does so either to avoid protectionism or to invest in industries that are essential to the import of the primary goods that are required. Furthermore, it is clear also that direct investment in foreign tourist and retail industries is a way of tapping value out of the temporary export of its own citizens. Where Japanese internal markets open, Japanese companies simply buy up the foreign suppliers. The main new trend in Japanese direct investment abroad, and the largest arena for direct investment in the financial sector, went from 7 per cent to 31 per cent between 1982 and 1985. Hence, Japan is now in greater control of the capital that it exports around the world due to its trade balance. Japanese internationalisation has worked, therefore, for the national benefit by increasing, rather than decreasing, trade asymmetries. This new economic order has been brought about, not by comparative advantage, but by political will. There was no contradiction between the MITI report's desire to allow more room for the private sector and its championing of global free trade, and its equal insistence on the government's role in promoting new technologies through industry policy and on a strategic trade policy that was integrated into, rather than at odds with, its industry policy. The success of the Japanese economy in the 1980s was not simply due to good bureaucratic planning, but the tendency to underestimate it is the greater error. This error stems from the tendency to think of the state and civil society as two separate entities; and to impute inertia to the former and dynamism to the latter. It is this philosophical distinction that usually underlies the neoclassical criticism of those who accord great weight to the role of the bureaucratic state in Japan. The virtue of Johnson's notion of a 'capitalist development state' and of Okimoto's notion of a 'network state' lies in the suspension of the dichotomy between state and civil society that they entail. The latter is a dichotomy whose temporal and geopolitical limits fall far short of modern Japan.

The notion of civil society incorporates, according to Charles Taylor, two differing theoretical traditions.[32] One of these traditions stems from Locke's vision of an arena of private economic activity separate from state control and direction that regulated itself by contracts. The other stems from Montesquieu's vision of an arena of public political activity that struggled to throw off the chains of state control and direction that regulated itself through associations. These two images of civil society are at the heart of the contemporary postmodern political condition, but given that they are a part of this longer tradition, they do not so much come after modernity, but are the exaggerated return of two key elements of the modern Western political tradition. What is striking is the absence of an analysis of the state and state bureaucracy from both theoretical traditions. The state is, for both, either an impediment to free economic activity (as a mercantilist state) or free political activity (as an absolutist state). This aspect of economic and political modernisation is not only a peculiarity of the West, but it is a peculiarity that is unevenly distributed within the West. It is, furthermore, a peculiarity that is not a part of Japanese modernisation. The desacralisation of the monarchy and the transformation of the monarch into a constitutional monarch is not an autochthonous development within Japanese society. Neither is the emergence of new forms of contestatory economic and political power that usurp the prerogative of the sovereign and replace it with private economic power and popular sovereignty. The key moment *par excellence* in modern Japanese history – the Meiji Restoration – sees the re-emergence and re-sacralisation of the sovereign in the context of a revolutionary self-transformation of a ruling warrior aristocracy that had slowly bureaucratised itself in the context of an economy that had already experienced a long period of what is called 'modern economic growth'. It is neither kings nor people that have played the key roles in Japanese history; and, hence, political modernisation does not move from kings to people. The Meiji oligarchies were a variation on an old political pattern and the economic modernisation they undertook was for politico-military reasons. There was room neither for the valorisation of private vices nor for the establishment of genuinely democratic forms in such a state-directed process. Japan's economic and political arrangements are distinctly modern, but they are not Western. Hence, the postmodernity of the contemporary Japanese political condition owes more to the anti-Western nature of Japan's modernisation, with its consequent reinvention and mobilisation of traditional elements, than it does to a conception of postmodernity that is a one-sided projection of Western political modernisation.

Notes

1. Kristeva, 1988.
2. Derrida, 1991.
3. Keane, 1988.
4. For the first formulation, see Cohen-Tanugi, 1989; and for the second see Furet *et al.*, 1988.
5. Featherstone, 1990.
6. For seventeenth-century developments, see Ooms, 1985; and for nineteenth-century developments see Gluck, 1985.
7. This is the assessment of Nolte, 1987.
8. I have in mind here the kind of work that one finds in the collection edited by Ishida and Krauss, 1989.
9. This perspective is derived from the work of Cornelius Castoriadis. There is a recent interview that has some remarks pertinent to Japan. See Castoriadis, 1991: 36–54.
10. This is a reconstruction of Harootunian's account of this symposium that uses the categories developed by J. P. Arnason to analyse the phenomenon of postmodern thought. See Harootunian, 1988; and Arnason, 1989: 323–37.
11. All of these motifs are also clearly present in Heidegger, 1983.
12. Harootunian, 1988: 84. The general information relied on in this paragraph also comes from this work, but I have borrowed the term 'media-steered communication' from the work of Axel Honneth and 'simulacrum' from the work of Jean Baudrillard.
13. This is Sakuma Shozan's phrase as it is quoted in de Bary, 1988: 77.
14. Murakami, 1987.
15. Ishida and Krauss, *op. cit.*
16. Minkenberg and Inglehart, 1989.
17. See Curtis, 1988: 20.
18. See Curtis, *ibid.*: 146–84, and Stockwin, 1982: 177–8, on the failure of the structural reform movement in the JSP.
19. See Calder, 1988 for this concept.
20. The expression is from Pempel and Tsunekawa, 1979.
21. See Curtis, 1988: 201 for this observation.
22. Kajiti, 1990.
23. See for the first thesis Johnson, 1982; the second Ishida and Krauss, *op. cit.*; and the third Calder, 1988.
24. See Allison and Sone, 1993.
25. See Okimoto, 1989.
26. See Valéry, 1990. For the consequences of the strategies of Japanese multinationals for America see Holstein, 1990; and for East Asia see Bello and Rosenfeld, 1992.
27. See the Ministry of International Trade and Industry's 'The Vision of MITI Policies in the 1980's' published in Menzel, 1989.

28. This has led to the valorisation of what was formerly construed as a problem: namely, the case of school children who have been educated overseas. The fact that their difference is now seen as an asset, rather than a problem, has been put down, in large part, to the current 'internationalisation' drive. See Goodman, 1990. Goodman's analysis makes the now familiar point that such a shift indicates that there is no inherent tendencies of the Japanese psyche or culture that predisposes them to either xenophobia or xenophilia. However, the more interesting conclusion that can be drawn from his data is one that points toward the immense capacity of Japanese elites to affect rapid and far-reaching transformations of public opinion; or, rather, their capacity to present to themselves the image of public opinion that they desire.

29. See Higashi and Lauter, 1987: 106 and 204 in particular.

30. See Harrison and Bluestone, 1988; and Reich, 1992.

31. See Röpke, 1989; and, especially, Menzel, 'Von der industriellen zur finanziellen Supermacht', in Menzel, 1989.

32. See Taylor, 1990.

12 JAPANESE STUDIES
Nihonjinron *at the End of the Twentieth Century: A Multicultural Perspective*

Ross Mouer and Yoshio Sugimoto

Japanese Studies in a Changing World

As the world moves through the 1990s, two sets of forces seem to pull it in opposing directions. One set consists of the push for globalisation and for universalistic criteria. With the emphasis on higher levels of economic rationalisation, international economic competition seems to have heightened. Such competition, however, appears to have shifted attention away from national boundaries, as technologies, capital, information and the techno-professional elites tend to move increasingly freely from one nation to another. The other set of forces revolves around a kind of fundamentalist interest in preserving ethnic and racial purity. The tragedies in Bosnia, Cambodia, Rwanda and many other trouble spots around the world indicate that a global society still has a way to go before emerging as the dominant reality, and that ethnic loyalties are still a powerful element in maintaining particularistic concerns.

Social science and the humanities have not been unaffected by these developments. On the one hand there is the growing literature on world systems,[1] global culture,[2] and world production systems.[3] On the other is the ongoing interest in ethnic minorities, ethnicity, multiculturalism and cultural disintegration.

Following the collapse of the bubble economy of the 1980s, which was characterised by new levels of national pride and confidence, the Japanese have faced a new kind of uncertainty. The end of the Cold War has been accompanied by heightened competition among the capitalist nations as the ideology of confrontation with the socialist block has lost its poignancy. Given these developments, one might well ask about the extent to which *nihonjinron* has adapted to changes in Japan's international context.

One additional concern rising over the past decade has considerable methodological implications for how national entities

237

are conceived. This is the articulation of the poststructuralist perspective.[4] This perspective has come to be influential across the social sciences, and, as indicated by a number of recent works on Japanese society,[5] needs increasingly to be considered in debates about *nihonjinron*. While such perspectives require changes to our definition of Japan, the first step is to deconstruct Japan. At the same time, this thrust underlines the interplay between the cultural domain and the social domain. Culture and discourse have social contexts.

Over a decade ago we began to publish a number of articles and books which examined critically that body of literature which became codified in the 1970s as *nihonjinron*. We asserted that *nihonjinron* served as a dominant paradigm, and argued not only that its cultural determinism was methodologically flawed but that it had outlived its usefulness and had become a considerable barrier to the efforts of many Japanese to 'internationalise'. By the time our last volume[6] on *nihonjinron* appeared, we found that most reviewers accepted the limitations of *nihonjinron* as we described it, but some claimed that we had exaggerated the extent to which serious academics ascribed to such holistic schemes which relied so heavily on national character stereotypes.

In this paper we wish (i) to argue that such stereotypes continue to colour a good deal that is written about Japan by academics both inside and outside Japan, (ii) to explore further the difficulties faced by the *nihonjinron* theorists when we problematise the concept of Japan and the Japanese, and then (iii) to consider the implications of having a definitive concept of Japan and the Japanese for Japanese studies in view of the global changes mentioned above.

The Continuation of a Tradition

It is highly unlikely that the *nihonjinron* theorists could remain unaffected by the master trends mentioned above. For many Japanese, Japan's economic successes in the 1980s brought with it a new awareness of Japan's destiny. And with that came the need for a new identity as Japanese came to be increasingly prominent on the international stage. In the concern with identity we can see a certain continuity with the past – a need to work out a place for Japan in the new order. Although one would have thought the question of identity would have been resolved once and for all with the flood of publications on the subject in the late 1960s and 1970s, we find many Japanese intellectuals continuing to grapple with the problem. Umehara, Umesao, Sakaiya, Hamaguchi, Watanabe, Kusayanagi[7] and others continue to publish works with titles such as '*Nihonjin to wa nani ka*' (What are the Japanese?) and '*Nihon to wa nanika*' (What is Japan?), or works with references to '*Nihonrashisa*' (the essence of being Japanese). Many of these authors were writing in the 1970s, and have continued to issue revised editions, changing only the vocabulary. To be sure, there have been changes as new key words have been coined to capture the essence of the Japanese experience. For example, many have shifted from writing about 'Japanese culture' to writing about 'Japanese civilisation', with the emphasis perhaps changing from something to be appreciated to something which is seen as an advanced form of social organisation in global terms (for example, in terms of the superior organisation of the Japanese business firm). These features can also been seen in the English-language literature.[8]

This reorganisation and elevation of *nihonjinron* can be understood in the context of two kinds of cultural nationalism overseas which may have been inspired by the Japanese experience and the perception that the Japanese are 'uniquely unique'. The first emerges from the ongoing trade friction which has characterised a good deal of American-Japanese economic relations over the past decade or so. Here we are referring to the new theories asserting Japanese difference – a claim largely from North America and Europe that the Japanese continue to both organise themselves unfairly and to reinforce a culture which promotes social dumping in economic relations.

On the surface, much of the writing in this vein claims to shift attention from Japanese culture to Japanese structure (in line with the above-mentioned shift from culture to civilisation). In doing so, it appears to stand in opposition to the earlier cultural theories, which tended to present Japanese ways of doing things in a positive light and which only too often relied on assumptions and assertions about cultural relativism to legitimate such moral judgments. However, a closer look at this literature suggests that the distinction between structure and culture is not so clearly articulated. As Vogel[9] demonstrated much earlier, the emphasis on structural uniqueness tends inherently to reveal assumptions about cultural uniqueness. What has shifted is not so much the assumptions about cultural uniqueness and cultural homogeneity as the values attached to them. While appearing to present objective analyses of the situation in Japan, much of this literature cloaks a good deal of American and European national interest. Not surprisingly, a view which results in conclusions consistently at odds with the interests of the Japanese nation-state would come to be labelled as 'Japan bashing'.

The other development is seen in the emergence of a literature in Asia which emphasises pecularly Asian modes of thought in explaining the viability of an alternative approach to economic development and rationalisation. This view is most conspicuous in Lee Kuan Yew's suggestion[10] that there is a peculiarly Asian mode of democracy which downplays the importance of individual rights while highlighting the importance of social stability in the pursuit of collectivist goals of the state. It also constitutes the thinking behind the 'Look East' policy promoted throughout the 1980s by another prime minister in Southeast Asia, Mahathir Mohamad. Between the lines of much that is written in this vein lies an allusion to the West as a kind of enemy attempting to impose its will and values on Asia in what is a form of ethical imperialism.[11] In this formulation of an Asian mode of work and governance is a parochial siege mentality which seeks to coalesce the national populations of Asia into supporting yet another bootstraps operation – a kind of forced postindustrialisation designed to keep themselves one step ahead of the encroaching economic imperialism of the West and its multinational enterprises.

Some time ago we indicated ways in which *nihonjinron* had been used or could function to achieve similar ends.[12] Just as *nihonjinron* tended to build psychological walls around Japan by positing that foreigners could never understand what happened inside, so too does the Look East policy eschew the 'Look Inside' policy when it comes to human rights issues and other matters relating to national mobilisation.[13] In short, in line with the notion of a Japanese model this policy tends to impose on all Asians the goals and values relatively small technoprofessional middle class elites that populate the urban areas and run the national bureaucracies in many of the countries of Asia. While the task may have appeared to be easier in Japan, if one concedes that there is a certain racial and ethnic homogeneity in this country which is less common in other parts of Asia, the ideological thrust is nevertheless one of unification, homogenisation, and assimilation.

Reflecting back on the literature of the 1960s on nation building and nationalism, one can see how the issue of identity is resolved in periods of rapid economic and social change by constructing such national self-images and contrasting those self-images against counterimages of imaginary enemy societies (for example, competitor societies in the international pecking order of nation-states). In these attempts to develop a sense of national unity of purpose and direction, one can see the new '*Ajia-teki kachi ron* (Asian values literature) following from (and thereby vindicating) the major thrust of the *nihonjinron* theorists, who function to serve the Japanese state in a similar manner.[14] This major thrust is an extrapolation of the 'Japan model': the arguments are that the society in question is stable and united, that it is unambiguouslydifferentiated from Western norms and approaches, and that it is beyond the ability of ethnocentric Westerners to comprehend this society.

Both these views of Japan (that of the bashers and that of the adorers) share the same methodological predilections of the earlier *nihonjinron*: (i) a tendency to downplay or even ignore important variations within each society, and various conflicts of interest between organised groups within Japanese society, (ii) an insistence on the use of *emic* concepts as the only viable means of describing Japanese society, (iii) a readiness to assume that cultural tendencies are biologically fixed and inherited like genes, and (iv) a reliance on sweeping statements contrasting with a conglomeration of Western societies as if the latter formed one homogeneous cultural block.

The notions of '*ie shakai*'[15], '*kanjinshugi*'[16], '*bokashi*'[17] and '*ganbari*'[18] provide examples of key words used to encapsulate the entire mentality or at least a major culturally defined thought pattern of the Japanese. The linguistic reductionism characteristic of a reliance on these kinds of *emic* concepts as representing core phenomena is similar to that found in the explanations for *amae* and *haji* in the *nihonjinron* of the 1960s and 1970s. For example, the equivalence of vocabulary to thought is a basic assumption in Nagara.[19] Although the vocabulary changes, the new terms continue to preclude analysis with a comparative element. They tend to be used as umbrella concepts to indicate that there exists some kind of special meaning which non-Japanese cannot understand. Basic to this entire approach is the assumption that the term 'the Japanese' means something, that there is a unified concept, 'Japan', which means the same thing to all Japanese. Here we wish to suggest that this very basic building block for these theories of the Japanese is at best a problematic concept.

Deconstructing 'The Japanese'

In much of the *nihonjinron* literature the key terms 'Japan' and 'the Japanese' are always used rather loosely. The field beyond the purely bureaucratic position, which defines 'the Japanese' as those who hold Japanese citizenship, or the field beyond the folk belief in ethnic lineage, are hardly developed at all.

There are two reasons for being sceptical of the validity of 'the Japanese' as a heuristic tool for analysing Japanese society. One concerns the tremendous amount of variation within Japan. 'The Japanese' tends to incorporate too much within a category derived from observations of only a small segment of the Japanese population. The other is that *nihonjinron* tends to assert that there are distinctions between Japanese and non-Japanese in areas where the distinctions are really somewhat blurred. In other words, it fails both on the grounds of excessive claims about inclusiveness and in terms of its excessively exclusivist propensity. We will look at each of these matters in more detail.

Multicultural Japan

Some time ago[20] we put forward the proposition that a variation-conflict model might provide better food for thought than the homogeneity-consensus model when it came to generating insight into the dynamics of Japanese society. At that time we argued that grossly stereotyped images of the 'average Japanese' would neither provide much understanding of Japanese society nor facilitate Japan's integration into international forums.

In teaching about Japanese society and culture, one might pose to students the problem as to how to best serve the needs of someone coming from another planet and who, pressed for time, wished to meet the single most typical Japanese person. Who might that lucky person be? To meet the alien's request, we would first exclude Japanese males, for they are a minority. We would then exclude persons in large firms, since they too are a minority (given that some sixty per cent of the labor force is to be found in firms with less than one hundred employees). The most representative person would be neither a university graduate nor a union member. The most typical Japanese would likely be a female senior high school graduate working in a small firm and unaffiliated with a union. Of course, the obvious thing would be to persuade the alien that it would be more meaningful to meet a variety of Japanese in order to see Japanese society as the mosaic which it is. It has been common, in describing Japanese society, for the *nihonjinron* theorists to focus on Japan's 'first-class citizens' and to ignore the large strata of 'second-class citizens' or 'invisible' Japanese. There is often a pretension that all Japanese are in the same class, defined largely in terms of those persons in the highly visible class who predominate in the official accounts of Japanese society. The invisible are simply left out of those accounts. This process easily gives way to a kind of self-fulfilling prophecy, for many of the second-class citizens are programmed to seek first-class citizenship and to leave behind the mannerisms and consciousness of their earlier invisible existence. There is little that is profound in stating the obvious: that the history of mankind often becomes the history of the ruling elites. Of course, few societies, Japan included, consist simply of only two categories of citizenship in terms of meaningful participation in society.

Even in a formal sense, it would seem that any viable definition of who is and who is not Japanese would involve an interplay between at least five criteria: (i) the holding of citizenship, (ii) native proficiency in the language, (iii) residency in Japan, (iv) biological pedigree and (v) a certain measure of cultural literacy as conceived in terms of the 'officially sanctioned knowledge' imprinted on the minds of most Japanese through the exam-oriented system of education and perhaps also through the mass media. It would seem, in addition, that those who satisfy all five conditions are not as numerous as might appear at first glance. Certainly, many Koreans would qualify as Japanese on all five counts. However, the distinction between those Korean Japanese who differ only in terms of citizenship would in many cases seem to be rather artificial. Should Takamiyama and Konishiki be considered 'Japanese'? What about Japanese-born children growing up abroad, for whom English or some other language might be considered the more familiar language? What about two Japanese working in similar situations overseas and with similar identities as 'Japanese', one however retaining his citizenship while the other taking up citizenship of the country in which he resides? What about Japanese Brazilians who have come to live in Japan? What about Fujimori, the President of Peru, and his wife, who are seen by many Peruvians as 'Japanese'? As these questions suggest, there may be different interpretations as to the rules which delineate 'Japanese' from other peoples.[21] We also

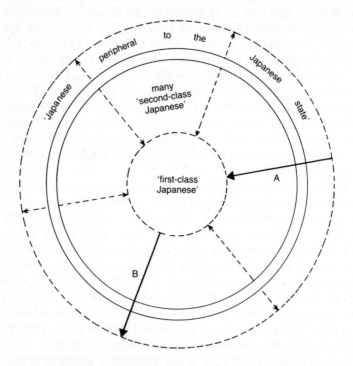

Arrow A: the result of zealously applying all the criteria in Table 12.1 and making each a necessary condition to being a pure 'Japanese'. The population is increased through a process of monocultural assimilation. Demands cultural homogeneity.

Arrow B: the result of eschewing an overly exclusionist definition, and allowing for four or fewer criteria to be viewed as a sufficient condition to being a multi-cultural 'Japanese'. The population is increased through a process of multicultural acceptance. Allows for many sub-cultures to coexist.

Figure 12.1 The expansion and contraction of the definition of 'the Japanese'

have to consider the case of the foreign worker in Japan – a bit short on polite Japanese perhaps, but able to get his or her work done, fairly knowledgeable about the Kamagasaki and Sanya areas and well locked into the economic system, and resident in Japan.

Table 12.1 and Figure 12.1 have been drawn to facilitate our sorting out people according to these types of questions. Each of the questions or five criteria set out here functions in two ways. The first way expands the definition of 'the Japanese'. The second contracts the definition. Table 12-1 reads like a data set; the five criteria across the top are those mentioned above. Down the left-hand column runs a list of types of individuals who might be included or excluded according to the criteria applied. The values in the table indicate scores against four of the five criteria. The column for cultural literacy – a criteria so important to the *nihon-jinron* culturalists – was seen by us as too difficult to complete. That assessment, as well as the further assessments required if we began to list various subtypes of Japanese, is left as a challenge to their ingenuity.

As shown in Figure 12.1, each of the criteria works to separate the heavily articulated circle, which is meant to represent some-thing like the field commonly accepted as being 'Japanese'. The separation results in an inner and an outer circle, the inner circle representing a very tight or exclusivist definition of 'the Japanese' and the outer circle representing an expanded definition of 'the Japanese'. In most cases, the application of any combination of criteria that is less than all five tends to expand the definition. The automatic inclusion of all five criteria results in the exclusion of nearly all the categories of persons listed in Table 12.1. We believe few of the *nihonjinron* theorists would want this.

Especially important here is the ill-defined criterion defined simply as 'Japanese cultural literacy'. The question as to whether there is a coherent Japanese culture is an intriguing one. Certainly, the figures given by the Monbusho suggesting that there is 99.9 percent literacy rate in Japan are at best misleading. The concept to which those figures relate has never been defined. It is highly likely that few Japanese have a 'standard' culture; after all there are Japanese who do not engage in *amae*, who do not read newspapers every day, who are unwilling to devote themselves to their company, who have nothing to do with the so-called examin-ation hell, who know little about tea ceremony or flower arrange-

Table 12.1 Various types of Japanese

Types of Japanese: Some examples	Nationality (citizenship)	Language competence	'Pure Japanese genes'	Current residence in Japan	Certain level of cultural literacy
The so-called *ware ware Nihonjin*	+	+	+	+	?
Korean residents in Japan	-	+	-	+	?
Some returnee students from overseas	+	-	+	+	?
The Ainu; Naturalised citizens	+	+	-	+	?
Japanese businessmen abroad	+	+	+	-	?
First-generation Japanese immigrants overseas who have abandoned their Japanese citizenship	-	+	+	-	?
Most undocumented foreign workers in Japan	-	-	-	+	?
Third-generation overseas Japanese not fluent in Japanese	-	-	+	-	?
Some children of mixed marriage in Japan	+	+	+/-	+	?
Most overseas Japan specialists	-	+	-	-	?

Notes: + denotes the presence of the attribute in question.
– denotes the absence of the attribute in question.

ment, or who fail to understand the full significance of symbols commonly cited as encapsulating the essence of the Japanese outlook. In short, this concept of 'the Japanese' or 'Japanese cultural literacy' suffers from the same shortcomings that have undermined Hirsch's notion of 'cultural literacy for Americans'.[22] In both cases the criticism is that cultural definitions which fit many 'first-class' Japanese and Americans are superimposed on and assumed to be universal for all Japanese and all Americans, and must be rejected for being too 'upper-middle-classish'.

It would seem that a growing number of overseas researchers dealing with Japan are starting to take this more relative position about being Japanese.[23] Perhaps this reflects a generational changing of the guard. Many of these researchers came to Japanese studies after the Vietnam War. They grew up in societies which were rapidly being multiculturalised and which were beginning to recognise the rights of indigenous peoples. At the same time, feminism was maturing and becoming more diffuse as an ideology insisting on gender equality. With ethnicity and gender as two major issues driving the consciousness of informed people in all economically advanced societies, it is reasonable to expect that the paradigm of those studying Japanese society would shift. In this we can see in Japanese studies a connection with postmodernist thinking.

It is our belief that few of the *nihonjinron* theorists have absorbed these postmodernist influences. This is reflected in the continuing references to Japan's monoculturalism and in an inability to incorporate minority cultures into the overall picture. A detailed analysis of much that has been written about Japan in the 1990s will no doubt reveal a basic acceptance of the ruling norms and the middle-classism generally associated with assimilationist views of society.

In this regard, the recent work of Amino[24] is of particular interest. His approach has been to take a fairly well accepted concept such as '*hyakushō*' and show its ambiguity, arguing that '*hyakushō*' encompassed not just peasants, as is commonly thought, but also seagoing folk (*kaimin*), mountain men (*sanmin*), artisans (*shukōgyōsha*), merchants (*shōmin*) and performing artists (*geinōmin*). He demonstrates that the meaning of 'Japan' varies over time and is socially created. His research shows that the masses resident in present-day Hokkaido and Okinawa did not have the notion that they lived in Japan, until the ideology of national unification was pushed by the Meiji government. On this point it should be noted that the considerable regional variation in family or household composition and in the rules for succession in households has for some time been acknowledged by anthropologists and sociologists working on Japan.[25] To the list we can also add the geographical variation in commercial practices recorded in Wigmore's survey[26] of Japanese law in the Tokugawa period. To the extent that *nihonjinron* continues to be produced by and for members of the establishment to legitimate their position as the purveyors of Japanese culture, it is unlikely that the multiplicity of the Japanese pepole will be fully accounted for in their explanations of Japanese society.

Toward a Japan with significant universal components

As we stated at the outset, recent history is the story of the increased flow of technology, goods, people, ideas and information across national and cultural boundaries. One result of these developments is a set of increasingly similar approaches to social organisation and the manipulation of culture. This phenomenon goes far beyond simply the emergence of similar structures. It has come to characterise a portion of consumer culture, urban life style, art, architecture, and aspects of the work and leisure ethics.

Table 12.2 indicates two ways in which Japanese subcultures run parallel to those in many other similarly developed societies. The first is in terms of shared cultural symbols and life styles, which are observable primarily among the technoprofessional elites. The second is in terms of how elites and nonelites occupy similar positions in functional terms, and share different but corresponding symbols related to authority structures and status inequalities. The technoprofessional elites tend to be able to identify with their counterparts elsewhere on both levels. Nonelites as a rule identify with their counterparts primarily in terms of the latter set of feelings about inequality – although they may not be able to share those feelings across national borders in any way that is comparable to the ease with which the elites can (by virtue of their shared culture in respect of the first type).

The situation in terms of international communication reminds one of Bernstein's concepts[27] of elaborated and restricted language codes. Ordinary folk use informal language, whereas elites

Table 12.2 Two dimensions for thinking about similarities and differences between societies

	Extent to which similar symbols are used in communication (cultural overlap)	Extent to which a similar outlook exists in terms of internal power structures (similar structural positioning)
The elites in society (e.g., the techno-professional upper-middle class	HIGH	HIGH
The ordinary masses	LOW	HIGH

Note: This table is compiled from the diagrams appearing in Sugimoto and Mouer, 1982, p. 236, and Mouer and Sugimoto, 1986, pp. 316 and 358.

can use both formal and informal language. Increasingly, symbols associated with the first type of shared culture come to form the elaborated domain for crosscultural exchange. From the perspective of international communication the particularistic or parochial national languages and sublanguages tend to provide restricted codes.

The shared culture of the technoprofessional elites   The first type of shared culture occurs primarily in terms of the emergence and spread of universal cultural symbols, largely among the techno-professional upper-middle class, which is characterised by a number of traits. First, these people enjoy a similar life style in terms of housing, family structure, and leisure-time activities. Second, they are highly educated, often with educational experience overseas. Third, they speak both a local national language and some form of English. Those who are more accomplished may speak several other languages as well. Fourth, they travel internationally fairly frequently and/or feel comfortable about doing so. Fifth, they often serve as interpreters of the outside world for their compatriots. Sixth, they often represent their own country's interests in international negotiations, whether working for the public sector or for the private sector. Some of the symbols with international currency (which members of this class can use) come not only from the spread of the international sports, particularly the professional sports – tennis, golf, boxing, basketball, and maybe football, cricket and baseball – but also from some of the minor sports which come under the spotlight of the Olympics. Some come from exposure to the international news services and a fairly common awareness of warring groups, the starving, music groups, and natural disasters. Some come from the emergence of an international management literature (a product of the ubiquitous MBA?) and the spread of information technologies (the computer culture). Whatever the source of their shared culture, the technoprofessional elites have become particularly conspicuous in the Asian region.

As Figure 12.2 suggests, in much of Asia these elites also have a sense of participating in a Pan-Asian culture as well as a more international culture. Asian publications like *The Far Eastern Economic Review* and *Asiaweek* tend to provide a common experience through Asian English. One might argue that many such elites participate in national, regional and international cultures. One might also argue that the Japanese technoprofessional elite has traditionally been a bit standoffish in terms of their Asian identity – maybe in contrast with their Australian counterparts, many of whom are trying to positively identify themselves with Asia.

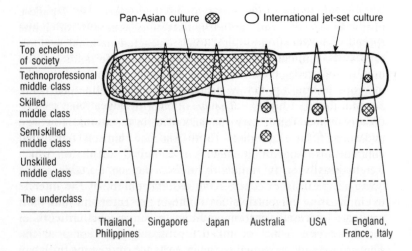

Figure 12.2 The participation of the technoprofessional elites in the national regional and international cultural spheres

Here it is important to note the role of these elites as gatekeepers who regulate the images which the world receives of their own societies and the images which other members of their own societies receive of the world. They are conspicuous in their positions as the cultural spokesmen or translators for their respective societies. As gatekeepers they regulate the flow of ideas, goods, money and people into and out of their country. Because much of the interaction between societies occurs in the media in terms of such images, it is not surprising that many of these gatekeepers have a stake in the production of *nihonjinron* and its counterparts elsewhere.

Tennō capitalists and shōsha capitalists   The technoprofessional gatekeepers in Japan are not a homogenous class. They consist of both the internationalists and the cultural nationalists. In this regard, the illness of the emperor from September 1988 until his death in 1989 revealed an interesting division in Japan's technoprofessional elite.[28] On the one hand there were the 'state capitalists' – the *'tennō* capitalists' who gave priority to policies which revered the ailing emperor. Of course, in so supporting the emperor system one could also say that they were in a sense voting for a system which recognised a traditional form of nationalism. Not only was the emperor central to that system, but so too were views about the ordering of Japanese purity in racial terms, about maintaining a certain discipline through an education system which respected national symbols such as the anthem and the flag, about limiting the rights and the presence of foreign workers, and about protecting 'traditional markets' for 'traditional products' such as rice and whale meat. As Morita and Ishihara's *The Japan That Can Say No*[29] reveals, this genre in concerned with Japan's place in the world. However, as Morita's later attempts to disassociate himself from that volume[30] also suggest, there is a commercial calculation which weighs heavily on the minds of many of Japan's executives. The '*shōsha* capitalists' or commercial traders seem to have an interest in emphasising universal values – both in presenting the way their products look and function and also in staving off criticism of social dumping, which is linked to uniquely Japanese practices. This group tends to recognise the importance of opening up Japan to the outside, of liberalising education and encouraging a system which results in more varied output, of apologising to people in other societies for war-related excesses, of breaking down exclusionist employment practices, and of better integrating Japanese overseas into the networks in Japan. As the number of Japanese technoprofessionals choosing to live overseas permanently has increased, we may have yet another dimension to Japan's elites. Rather than being 'economic migrants', they may be 'social refugees' or 'lifestyle sojourners' seeking another social structure in which to live.[31] Their presence overseas should work to the advantage of the commercial capitalists, and one might predict that their integration into that segment of Japan's techno-professional elite might exacerbate the divisions mentioned above.

If this description has any validity, and if there is a link between the production of *nihonjinron* and the technoprofessional class, we would expect to find that two kinds of *nihonjinron* would come to exist in the 1990s. This is an interesting proposition for those concerned with the sociology of knowledge, and shoud be an added dimension in any future analysis of *nihonjinron*.

Universals arising from similarities in social positioning   As mentioned above, there is another type of similarity which arises out of income and status inequalities within complex industrialised societies. To some extent we can say there is in an objective sense a universal class system based on gender, one based on occupation, and one based on ethnicity (especially from the point of view of indigenous peoples and the smaller ethnic minorities). A fairly simple representation of this kind of crosscultural similarity is shown in Table 12.3. The figure provides contrasting positions for four hypothetical individuals – two Japanese and two Australians. Mr. Smith-Jones and Mr. Toyota, although living in different societies (Australia and Japan), are graduates of elite universities who live in large urban areas and are CEOs for their large firms in the finance sector. Ms. Lee and Ms. Honda are public high school graduates who work as operatives in small food processing plants in rural towns in their respective countries.

If these four persons were suddenly brought together for a nice weekend on an island in the middle of the Pacific, one might suppose that the two Japanese and the two Australians would pair up for conversations, since they speak the same language. However, that might not necessarily be the actual outcome.

Table 12.3 Examples of two pairs of individuals with shared perspectives arising out of similar structural positioning

	Persons living and functioning in Japan	Persons living and functioning in Australia
Male university graduate living and working as president of a large firm located in a large city	Mr. Toyota	Mr. Smith-Jones
Female high school graduate working as an office lady in a small firm in a small rural town	Ms. Suzuki	Ms. Lee

Note: This table is compiled from the diagrams appearing in Sugimoto and Mouer, 1982, p. 236, and Mouer and Sugimoto, 1986, pp. 316 and 358.

Despite having to confront a language barrier, it is likely that the two CEOs would recognise each other as men of responsibility, each noticing that the other read the front page of the morning paper each day, wore a similar type of expensive clothing, worked on a notebook for a few hours in the afternoon, and occasionally took phone calls of some importance and asked to use the hotel fax machine several times a day. In short, they would see each other as belonging to the inner circle in Figure 12.1. Were all four introduced, with their background being made public, and then informed that the hotel offered a free interpreter service, it is likely that the two executives and the two food processors would form natural pairs. Such interactions would represent a recognition of the similarities which emerge from working and living within situations which can be fairly universally recognised and classified in terms of the overall structural inequalities which characterise economic organisation. The argument here is not that the latter type of pairings would occur more frequently, but that they occur at all, and blur somewhat the notion of national identity as a distinguishing category.

'Second-class' Japanese are gradually getting the opportunity to travel abroad. A small number are able to develop enough language competency to communicate with their counterparts abroad. Feminist groups, environmentalist groups, NGOs of various orientations and sizes, groups of indigenous peoples, and labour unions and other groups provide ready examples of this kind of communication. While many sympathetic with those kinds of groupings may not yet share a fully developed basket of cultural concepts, they nevertheless have access to that international culture which is disseminated through the mass media and could be said to be gradually forming a shared subculture which is international in its own right. However, at the present time the degree of opportunity to participate and to imbibe their international subculture does not compare with that available to those in the technoprofessional elites.

The two authors have now spent roughly twenty years each teaching Australian university students about Japan. We have struggled with the challenge of how best to provide students with limited time a basic feeling for contemporary Japan and its people. Should we spend time focusing on the tales of Genji? Should we have them read Doi's book about *amae*? Or essays on women by Kaibara Ekken and Fukuzawa Yukichi? Or films directed by Mizoguchi? Or novels by Nobel prize winners Kawabata and Ōe, by Mishima or Sōseki, which contain a good dose of *emic* concepts having no real English equivalents? Should we given them a lecture about the tattoos that some *yakuza* types sport? Or a video of a *sumō* match? Or a night out at a Japanese restaurant eating *nattō*, *uni*, and *sashimi* and drinking *sake* while also mastering the use of chopsticks? To go beyond a certain level of Japan literacy, these approaches might be useful.

For many coming to the study of Japan for the first time, still other ports of entry call. The English translations of novels by Murakami Haruki or Yoshimoto Banana might provide a more readily accessible Japan. So too might the books available in English by Peter Drucker or Robin Archer. Or a trip downtown in Melbourne to use an automated ticket machine, or a reminder about how to identify a McDonalds? Obviously, there is no simple answer to these kinds of questions. Many of the Japanese that an Australian graduate would interact with have two cultures – the old and the new. While some thoughts and acts can be conceived in only one or the other, many can be conceived in both. Obviously, one's answer would depend on the type of Japanese the Australian would be meeting upon graduation. The point being made here is that there are many types of Japanese and that one can gain some important clues about communicating with a particular person by knowing where they are located in the multi-dimensional social stratification matrix.

Models of contemporary Japanese society which accommodate neither (i) internal variation nor (ii) the shared cultural elements do not facilitate understanding of the society or communication with its members. Approaches which reduce descriptions to specific categories which become labelled as 'the Japanese way' or 'the Japanese people' will not facilitate cross-society communication for the vast majority of our students who are planning to interact with Japanese counterparts upon graduation. As mentioned above, the limits of the monolithic cultural literacy approach are clear from discussions of the concept in North America.

Who Controls the Category Labelled 'Japanese'?

We have argued above that definitions of who the Japanese are must be rethought as a result of globalisation and the advent of multiculturalism. Another factor affecting the definition of Japan (and other countries) is the collapse of the socialist countries and the end of Cold War. While Fukuyama[32] may have been naive in writing about the end of ideology, and it is certain that social justice issues will surface again as prime concerns, it is also true that the end of the Cold War has shifted attention away from the capitalist-socialist divide and focused it much more sharply on each nation's level of international economic competitiveness in terms of its balance of payments figures.

The image of Japan as a rich country

The image of Japan both within Japan and abroad has been affected in a major way by the sharper focus on Japan's economic performance. Despite its overall low standard of living in the ages of many Japanese, the general international perception of Japan is of a rich country with the highest levels of per capita income. On the other hand, as Figure 12.3 suggests, the end of the Cold War has meant a shift in self-perceptions for Australians, who were seen for a long time as members of the wealthy Western coalition of nations during the Cold War, but now as the 'Argentina', the 'banana republic' or the 'poor white trash' of Asia. Although its standard of living has not slipped in any way, its balance of payments has clearly deteriorated and its GNP per

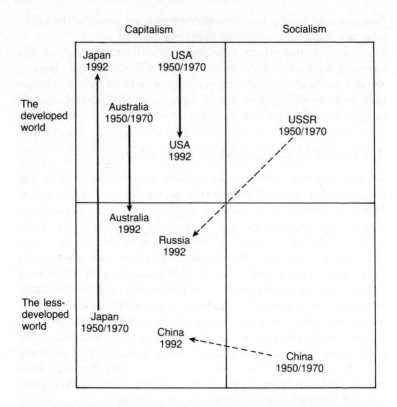

Figure 12.3 Changes in the international perception of nations during and after the Cold War

capita has declined dramatically as a result of changes in exchange rates.

The other side of this coin is the idea that a successful Japan is a model society which is to be emulated. The interest in Japanese-style management is clearly linked to an image of Japan as a successful country with high levels of social consensus and ethnic homogeneity and an exceptionally strong work ethic, the fourth pillar of Japan's industrial relations system according to one OECD report on Japan. Obviously, the interest in Japan as a model among many leaders overseas is linked to a large set of assumptions which define Japan. These assumptions are not accepted as the result of research, but rather because they are promoted by Japan's political and business elites and because they are ideologically convenient to cite by leaders elsewhere who are bent on mobilising their populations for the drive to rationalise further their economies within the context of the evolving international economic system. Obviously, the views of Japan's political and business elites are validated by Japan's success, just as their views would lose legitimacy should Japan's economic performance deteriorate seriously.

The impact on research which defines Japan

As the yen has strengthened against other currencies, it has become more difficult for outside researchers to access Japan. This has resulted in a growing dependence on Japanese foundations and other sources of support in Japan in order to do research. The ramifications of this are seen in terms of a certain proclivity to genuflect toward those controlling such resources in Japan and a kind of self-censorship. It is a climate in which truly independent research comes to be often seen as 'Japan bashing'. It is a climate in which the emphasis in supporting research subtly shifts from '*chinichika*' to '*shinnichika*'.[33] It is a climate in which 'correct understandings of Japan' (*tadashii rikai*) become a discrete category distinguished clearly from the only other category, 'misinformed misunderstandings' (*muchina gokai*). It is a situation in which many become dependent on information supplied overseas by Japan's technoprofessional gatekeepers.

The genuflecting and self-restraint are in many cases subtle. The pressures do not come directly from Japan but work themselves out through intermediate interests abroad. Australia's experience with the Multi-Function Polis[34] and the Very Fast Train projects,[35] which were to be driven with large infusions of Japanese capital, as well as its experience with Japanese investment in tourist developments, revealed a basic tendency for local interests working with the Japanese investors to pressure local media to filter reporting on their activities and to discredit the Japan-related expertise distinguished scholars who held different values for the community. This tended to make the Japanese interests invisible, although it was often reported that jobs would be lost if certain conditions set by the Japanese investors were not met.

In this regard, Japan's economic largess can also be seen as providing a means by which Japan can overcome the language barrier. With English as the international language, Japanese individuals are at a distinct disadvantage in projecting their own definitions of Japan onto the international community. However, in recent years the Japanese bodies mentioned above have been able to buy the translation and editorial services needed to get their message across in English. Japan can now cover the vanity costs of publishing abroad and of making sure that the appropriate gatekeepers are present at international forums to represent Japanese elite interests.

With a surplus in the coffers, the Japanese Government and large firms can now afford to produce glossy public relations information on Japan. For libraries overseas, which are increasingly having to axe subscriptions to Japanese periodicals and cut back on the purchase of Japanese books and other materials for teaching purposes, these abundantly supplied items are welcomed as better than nothing. Of course, it is not only the Japanese establishment which distributes this kind of 'propaganda'. Because most area studies are defined in terms of geopolitical areas which coincide with the sovereign state, these studies are markedly shaped by the competing interests of states and by the relative success which states, their supporting enterprises and other apparatus have in realising a broad range of interests. In this context, it is not surprising that at one point in time we have had an emphasis on the 'welfare state' or the 'codetermination state', and that the emphasis on each model as desirable and as a defining criterion can be associated with particular states at specific junctures in the international flow of events.[36] Were America to recapture people's imagination with a rejuvenated national economy, it is likely that there would be a shift from the assimilationist assumptions of Japan's conservative leadership to the multiculturalist definitions of America's leadership. The role of the Japanese state and establishment groups in defining what Japan is, needs to be seen for what it is *at the present*. Its influence is not a fixed parameter; it has grown over time and could decline in the future. However, in thinking about definitions of what Japan represents and who the Japanese are as they shape Japanese studies, the changing role of the state in that process is an important consideration.

To be sure, not everyone overseas is swallowing the Japanese message or subscribing to the Japanese model. In those societies which are particularly subject to Japan's economic inroads, there is sensitivity to the contradictions. Even accepting that Japanese-style management may be fine in Japan, many workers in

Japanese subsidiaries overseas are aware that none of the locals are given lifetime employment. Many of those who travel to Japan for training also have doubts about how well the model fits their experiences in Japan. They see the wealth, but they also see a standard of living which is not so great, infringements on what they regard as human rights, and a generally high level of regimentation and 'economic animalism'. The problem with much of *nihonjinron* is that it does not recognise the validity of those viewpoints. The tendency to look for monolithic explanations means that the notion of there being a 'number one' economy tends to translate itself into a notion of their being number one in everything else, including self-understanding.

Changing Definition of Japan Within Japanese Studies

Changes in the definition of Japan over time

In participating in the enterprise known as Japanese studies over the past 30 years, it seems to us that the definition of Japan has changed rather dramatically over time. In part the change has reflected a change in paradigm perhaps, but more importantly it has reflected a change in the power relations among the major states in which Japanese studies occur. Perhaps four major periods can be delineated, although as with all attempts at periodisation, it must be remembered that periods are not mutually exclusive or discrete units. Used heuristically to identify relative shifts in terms of ideal types, in reality they overlap to a considerable degree. The periods we have in mind are shown in Figure 12.4, and perhaps reflect the experiences we have had in Japanese studies in the US, Japan and Australia over the past three decades.

The first period would be the first ten to fifteen years after the war. During that time American intellectuals affiliated with the Occupation and with America's cultural and political elite had a dominant influence not only on American definitions of Japan but also on Japanese discourse as well. Australian definitions were largely derived from the American images. In the early 1960s many Japanese intellectuals tended to despair over Japan's failure to adopt [largely American] democratic institutions in all spheres of public and private life. The concern with the Occupation's agenda for Japan's democratisation was dominant, and intellectuals who criticised the agenda risked being associated with

259

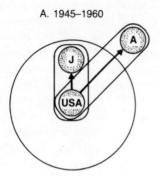

A. 1945–1960

ANZUS > MST > J/A

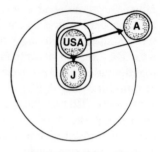

B. 1960–1970

ANZUS = MST > J/A

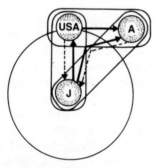

C. 1970–1985

MST > ANZUS > J/A

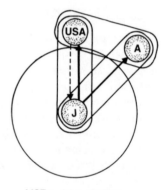

D. 1985–1995

MST > J/A > ANZUS

MST: US-Japan relationship

ANZUS: Australia-US relationship

J/A: Australia-Japan relationship

> indicates strength of relations

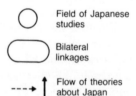

⬭ Field of Japanese studies

⬭ Bilateral linkages

---→ ↑ Flow of theories about Japan

Figure 12.4 Changing international power relations and 'definers' of 'Japan'

prewar fascist tendencies. American researchers were seen as being at the centre of Japanese studies and as asking all the relevant questions about the Japanese experience. Although all such researchers wrote in English, Japanese academics were quick to translate even minor opinions into Japanese and study them with an intensity which surprised even the American student of Japan. The final product of that period might be said to have been the modernisation literature on Japan.

The second period, from 1960 to 1970, was characterised by Japan's emergence as an economic force. It was a period when Japanese scholars could reassert their views and give legitimacy to other trajectories. In questioning the modernisation schema, they were able to argue that Japan was defined differently and could follow other paths to industrialisation and further economic development. In Figure 12.4 we try to show this change by placing Japan at the centre of Japanese studies but also recognising the continuing (though waning) influence of American theory.

In the third period, from the early 1970s to the mid-1980s, Japan's economic prowess came to be more fully felt, in several ways. Most important was the renewed economic confidence within Japan, which gave way to the final ousting of left-wing scholarship and criticism from the public arena, consequences of along the emasculation of left-wing unionism and the ascendancy of chauvinistic *nihonjinron*. The emphasis on everything in Japan being so uniquely unique put the definition of Japan beyond the realm of defining concepts in most of the Western-generated theory. This was coupled with the generation of huge amounts of information in Japan about the Japanese and which only a small number of non-Japanese researchers could really tap. In the United States as well, these changes were recognised by a willingness to defer to those Japanese scholars and spokespersons who were associated with the Japanese establishment. It was the period in which the Japan Foundation was established and both the government and large business further took the initiative with a huge campaign to export *nihonjinron*. Also, American influence in defining Japan declined, although much of the *nihonjinron* of writers such as Vogel and Reischauer remained couched in American terms for American audiences. Interestingly, however, it is also a period in which a number of Australian scholars maintained contact with dissident Japanese and began to contribute directly to debate in Japan, a contribution couched largely in Japanese terms for Japanese audiences. A look through *The Bulletin of Concerned Asian Scholars* might suggest that this was a more widespread phenomenon, although few of the contributors to that journal were geared up specifically to debate directly in Japan.

In the final period, from the mid-1980s to the present, Japan's technoprofessional elites have taken full control of debate about Japan. They tend to push back the 'Japan bashers' with a superior control of 'the objective facts' verifiable with Japanese data. Their investment in the US and particularly in Australia tends to invite self-censorship. The left has become very quiet in Japan, and their counterparts overseas are not getting much data on contemporary Japan from that quarter.[37] In Australia critical definitions tend to be dismissed as racist Japan bashing, as was very obvious in the MFP debate.[38] Japan came increasingly during the 1980s to be presented as post-Fordist and postmodernist. During this period, the emphasis on Japan's uniqueness did not wane, but it was recast as being unique in the universal sense that it was out in front leading the pack, that its traditional approaches and values had leapfrogged to the front, and that it was now the other advanced societies which would converge with Japan. It was also a period in which the Japanese establishment came to invest considerable amounts of money into promoting the teaching of the Japanese language abroad.

In short, the above periodisation suggests that the definition of Japan changes as the research agenda for Japan and the uses of Japan-specific understandings change. However, it further suggests that changes in the definition of Japan may reflect changes occurring in power relations between first- and second-class citizens in Japanese society and changes occurring in the international balance of power among the major states and regional groupings.

The coming tug of war over the definition of Japan

As we move toward the end of this century, it is likely that two conflicting forces will pull the definition of Japan in different directions. On the one hand, as Japan's economic influence increases even further, there is further incentive for Japan's elites to manufacture definitions of Japan which portray them (and therefore Japan itself) in as favourable a light as possible. Given the generally accepted view that elites are able to generate a fair degree of tacit agreement among themselves about what they do, this would, it seems to us, tend to promote an official definition of Japan, perhaps with a narrow range of variations.

At the same time, Japan's images will change in a different direction owing to its expanded presence in an increasing number of other countries. As non-Japanese working in Japanese enterprises overseas come to form their own images of Japan, they will see Japan not only from a different and more critical perspective in terms of the major agents of stratification and status inequality (and that will be an especially important perspective for many of the disenfranchised foreign workers in Japan), but also in terms of their own country's unique positioning vis-a-vis Japan. These tendencies will, it seems to us, tend to promote a proliferation of definitions as to what Japan is all about.

To some extent these phenomena can be seen in how the past emperor has come to be defined. Even before his death, competing definitions of Hirohito existed in Japan. However, the government took the lead in promoting a huge state funeral, inviting dignitaries from around the world to make it the most internationally attended funeral in the history of mankind. With that went all the symbols of the emperor as the father of the nation. However, as the above reference suggests, overseas the emperor was not 'the emperor' but simply Hirohito, often 'Hirohito the war criminal'. Important to note is the fact that editorials around the world painted the deceased in various ways, and this was somehow communicated to many Japanese through the media. The Japanese State could get official representatives of high social standing from every major country around the world to attend the funeral and genuflect before the officials attending to the guest books, but with the funeral the emperor became such a centre of world-wide attention that the ironic result was that the Japanese State lost control of its ability to define its most important symbol.

Another facet of this tension between the corporatist forces and the centrifugal forces in Japanese studies is the notion of having a world organisation to coordinate or to facilitate Japanese studies. It is not surprising that this approach would be generated by those in Japanese studies who are affiliated with the American and Japanese cultural elites. In that context one should not be surprised to learn of an idea to merge two leading English-language publications on either side of the Pacific – perhaps journals such as the scholarly American *Journal of Japanese Stud-*

ies and the Japanese Government backed *Japan Echo* – to create the supreme journal of Japanese studies. Not only is there the assumption here that bigger is better when it comes to area studies and perhaps social science research in general. One is also reminded of Low's recent work on Japan's colonial science and the Japanese attempts to objectify the construction of Manchuria.[39] Turned in on itself, officially sponsored scientism in Japanese studies may also be characterised by the tendency to objectify the invisible Japanese underclass for its own purposes.

The other tendency, however, is to see ways in which small is beautiful. Given the likelihood that members of different societies will be positioned to view and to define the Japanese experience differently, the other option is to promote a diffuse, even anarchical approach to Japanese studies. The idea is to go beyond letting one hundred ideas compete, by letting them coexist. In pushing for this approach, one would have to grapple with the difficulty Japanese gatekeepers have with such an approach and with a Japanese studies which is truly independent of the Japanese establishment. To be sure, there are many interests, and care would need to be taken to keep such an enterprise independent of other governments as well. The agenda of those interested in truly independent Japanese studies must allow for a careful consideration of the effect of bureaucratising and corporatising Japanese studies.

Toward 'Japan' and 'the Japanese' as Indefinite Equations

As Japan's position in the world has become more noticeable as a result of its tremendous economic growth, so too has the number of persons with an interest in Japan increased. Of course, at the grass roots level one sign of this is the increase in the number of persons studying the Japanese language. At the academic level another sign is the increase in the number of books and articles being written about Japan. Yet another indicator of this change is the growing number of scholars in Southeast Asia who are working on Japan. At the same time, the number of observers adopting the conflict and variation model for conceptualising Japan has also increased.

As a result, it is necessary to update the earlier tables we have used for considering the distribution of the consensus-homogeneity model and the conflict-variation model. Compared with our

Table 12.4 The distribution of the consensus-homogeneity and the conflict-variation paradigms in global perspective

A. In the early 1990s

Country in which writings about Japan appear	The consensus-homogeneity paradigm	The conflict-variation paradigm
Japan	Monopolistic position	Almost nonexistent
Western Europe and North America	Dominant position	Fairly conspicuous
Australia	Dominant (among the developmentalists – those for MFP/VFT, etc.)	Dominant (among those concerned with human rights, environment, etc.)
Asia	Fairly conspicuous (among those friendly to Japan)	Fairly conspicuous (among those suspicious of Japanese interests)

B. In the late 1990s

Country in which writings about Japan appear	The consensus-homogeneity paradigm	The conflict-variation paradigm
Japan	Monopolistic position	Almost nonexistent
Western Europe and North America	Dominant position	Fairly conspicuous
Australia	Dominant (among the developmentalists – those for MFP/VFT, etc.)	Dominant (among those concerned with human rights, environment, etc.)
Asia	Dominant (among the developmentalists those for MFP/VFT, etc.)	Fairly conspicuous (among those suspicious of Japanese interests)
Latin America	?	?
Africa	?	?
Middle East	?	?

earlier portrait of the distribution of those two models in the mid-1970s,[40] it is clear that the number of geopolitical and geocultural areas with an interest in how Japan is defined has increased dramatically over time. One might better characterise the current situation by reference to all of the countries shown in Table 12.4. A comparison of the earlier and later distributions suggests that the conflict and variation model has declined in Japan, but may have gained a stronger following in North America and Europe. This would mean that full assessment of *nihonjinron* in the contemporary world has become a much larger task involving a much larger range of authors.

It is likely that these changes will couple with Japan's internationalisation and multifaceted interface with the world to blur further key concepts in the Japanese studies enterprise – concepts such as 'Japan' and 'the Japanese'. By talking about relative degrees of 'Japaneseness' we will be more sensitive to the context in which we use such concepts. We will also be more sensitive to the ends to which Japanese studies are used. It seems to us that *nihonjinron* which seek definitive definitions of 'the Japanese' will lead to increasingly structured and irrelevant Japanese studies.

Two considerations or tasks remain in the back of our minds when theorising about *nihonjinron*. Both are necessary to building a reflexive perspective into Japanese studies as a discipline in its own right.

The first task is to define more precisely what we mean by the term 'culture'. There has been confusion in past discussions of *nihonjinron* as to whether such descriptions are about (i) culture as a mental construct existing independently of how the Japanese actually behave, or about (ii) a set of practices commonly found in Japan. Those who appear to write along the first vein tend to treat ideas as the dominant ideology, although they tend also to use arbitrary examples to illustrate and to 'prove' that those ideas are dominant and that they are located primarily in Japan and are thereby 'Japanese'. Those who focus on behaviour have been less interested in developing an overall cognitive model; they have tended to award behaviour significance not as a system of ideas but in terms of the people who display such behaviour. Those taking the first approach often promote these ideas in the form of a functional model which highlights particular sets of structures as engines for change. To maximise the outcomes from adopting such models, assimilation is advanced as a means of consolidating agreement about the goals of the state and of society. Rather than the goals being questioned, they come to be taken for granted. Those taking the second approach problematise the extent to which there is consensus about the goals. They are interested in those who become the engineers who drive the locomotive forward. Whereas those of the first orientation are integrationist, those of the second are multiculturalist. Whereas the first approach is concerned with quantifying the extent to which goals are achieved, the second approach focuses more on the issues of social justice.

The notion of the developmental state and the image of a peculiarly Japanese approach to work relations show this dichotomy. To a large extent, the concern abroad with learning from Japan has been an interest in developing a new model, a new ideology to get things organised in a different way. Whether Japanese actually behave according to the ideology has not been treated as a matter for empirical investigation. Rather, the major proposition is simply that Japan is a plausible location where it can be said that the model is successfully being implemented.

The notion of social classes connects with the organisational requisites of mobilising a society to move in given directions. However, many who focus on class 'realities' tend to reify structural abstracts such as 'class'. Class cultures are often presented as being self-sufficient cultures. The interactions and interdependencies between class cultures are given relatively less attention. By focusing on conflict and other structurally promoted differences in behaviour, the 'dominant culture' comes to be seen simply as the 'ruling ideology' and the role of an overall culture which glues together persons from various subcultures tends to get downplayed.

The second set of concerns is with the origins of culture. The significance attached to a set of ideas is at least partially determined by the size of the populations which embrace it and by the number of persons who reject it. Labels such as 'Japanese', 'Australian', 'American', 'Western' and 'Eastern' come to be meaningful because they give a culture a location and a meaningful population or following. Alternative life styles seem much less viable when a practising population cannot be found. Here we are talking about the relative importance of state-led attempts to maintain or promote certain ideologies as culture. Culture also emerges from market-sensitive responses to the collective orientations of a general populace. Such responses come to be codified within the marketplace when suppliers seek to gratify consumers of ideas by giving them what they want.[41] To some extent, these two sources of culture can be seen in what we have referred to above as '*tennō* capitalism' and '*shōsha* capitalism'.

Putting aside arguments about Japan's past and the relative amount of variation and conflict which characterised that history, it is clear today that a process of differentiation has occurred and that many subcultures are flourishing in contemporary Japan. What is needed is a framework which not only recognises those subcultures but also accounts for the political, economic and social relations between the subgroupings which produce the subcultures. It must also be a framework which can, in an increasingly globalised setting, recognise the points at which international linkages produce and reinforce universal tendencies, and also highlight ways in which international structures dovetail with national structures in what many years ago Kunihiro[42] – referred to as the 'inter-domestic age'. In our earlier writings we have argued that the multidimensional model of stratification provides the best framework for incorporating these kinds of elements. It remains, we believe, not only the best model for analysing social relations in the political and economic spheres, but also a heuristic tool for developing a metatheory of Japanese studies. In the end, these are the two tasks facing those who would move down the road from deconstruction to reconstruction.

Notes

1. Wallerstein, 1974–89; 1979; 1984; 1991.
2. Featherstone, 1990; Robertson 1992; Waters forthcoming.
3. Womack *et al.*, 1990; Harvey 1982.
4. Cf. Feyerabend, 1993.
5. For example Kondo, 1990.
6. Mouer and Sugimoto, 1986.
7. Umehara, 1990; Umesao, 1986; Sakaiya, 1991 and 1993; Hamaguchi, 1977 and 1988 reprint; Watanabe, 1989, and Kusayanagi, 1990.
8. For example Hendry, 1993; March, 1993; Matsumoto, 1988; Ballon, 1992; Pharr, 1985; Rosenberger, 1992; and Singer, 1993.
9. Vogel, 1979.
10. Lee Kuan Yew, 1993.
11. Cf. Mahathir and Ishihara, 1994.
12. Sugimoto and Mouer, 1982; Mouer and Sugimoto, 1986.
13. Girling, 1991; Hsiung, 1985.
14. Mahathir and Ishihara, 1994.
15. Murakami, 1984.

16. Hamaguchi, 1993; Masuda, 1992.
17. Nakayama, 1982.
18. Amanuma, 1987.
19. Nagara, 1991.
20. For example, Sugimoto and Mouer, 1982, and Mouer and Sugimoto, 1986.
21. Fukuoka, 1993: 2–20; Mori, 1993.
22. Hirsch, 1988.
23. Maher and Macdonald, 1995; Kondo, 1990; Sugimoto, forthcoming; Brinton, 1992.
24. Amino, 1990, 1991, 1994.
25. Fukutake, 1982; Shufu to Seikatsusha, 1992.
26. Wigmore, 1967–86.
27. Bernstein, 1966: 126–33.
28. Sugimoto, 1988.
29. Morita and Ishihara, 1989.
30. Cf. Ishihara, 1991.
31. Sato, 1993.
32. Fukuyama, 1992.
33. Mouer, 1987b.
34. Mouer and Sugimoto, 1990; Hamilton, 1991.
35. See James, 1990.
36. Kassalow, 1982.
37. The data of Steven (1983) are now outdated.
38. Mouer and Sugimoto, 1990.
39. Low, 1994.
40. Mouer and Sugimoto, 1986: 87.
41. On this issue, see Yoshino, 1992.
42. Kunihiro, 1979.

Bibliography

Abegglen, James, 1958, *The Japanese Factory: Aspects of Its Social Organisation*. Illinois: The Free Press.

Adam, Ian and Tiffin, Helen (eds), 1991, *Past the Last Post: Theorizing Post-Colonialism and Post-Modernism*. London: Harvester Wheatsheaf.

Akamatsu, Ryōko, 1990, *Danjo Koyō Kikai Kintōhō Oyobi Rōdō Kijunitō Hō (Joshi Kankei)* [The Equal Opportunity Law and the Labour Standards Law (Items related to women)]. Revised edition. Tokyo: Josei Shokugyō Zaidan.

Akita, Yuri, 1984, 'Seishinteki dokushinsha no sugata' [The appearance of spiritual singles]. *Bijutsu Techō* June.

Alexander, Jeffrey, 1982, *Theoretical Logic in Sociology, Volume 1*. Berkeley: University of California Press.

Allison, Gary D. and Sone, Yasunori, 1993, *Political Dynamics in Contemporary Japan*. Ithaca and London: Cornell University Press.

Amanuma, Kaoru, 1987, *'Ganbari' no kōzō: Nihonjin no kōdō genri* [Structure of 'endurance': Principles of Japanese behaviour]. Tokyo: Yoshikawa Kōbundō.

Amino, Yoshihiko, 1990, *Nihonron no shiza* [Perspective on theories of Japan]. Tokyo: Shōgakkan.

——, 1991, *Nihon no rekishi o yominaosu* [Re-reading Japanese history]. Tokyo: Chikuma Shobō.

——, 1994, *Nihon shakai saikō* [Reconsidering Japanese society]. Tokyo: Shōgakkan.

Anderson, Nancy, 1984, *Work With Passion: How To Do What You Love for a Living*. New York: Carroll and Graf Publishers.

Aoki Masahiko, 1988, *Information, Incentives, and Bargaining in the Japanese Economy*. Cambridge: Cambridge University Press.

——, 1990, 'Frontiers in corporate globalization.' *Japan Echo* Vol. 17 (special issue).

Aoki, Tamotsu, 1986, 'Rokūjunendai ni koshitsu suru Murakami Haruki ga naze hachijūnendai no wakamonotachi ni shiji sareru no darō' [Why do youngsters in the 1980s support Haruki Murakami who clings to the 1960s?], in Rei Hisahara (ed.), *Murakami Haruki*. Tokyo: Seidōsha.

Aoki, Yayoi (ed.), 1986, *Bosei to wa nani ka?* [What is motherhood?]. Tokyo: Kaneko Shobō.

Arai, Mitsuru, 1986, 'Kankyō shōsetsu no tanjō' [The birth of environmental novels], in Rei Hisahara (ed.), *Murakami Haruki*. Tokyo: Seidōsha.

Arnason, J. P., 1989, 'The imaginary constitution of modernity.' *Revue Européenne de Sciences Sociales* No. XX: 323–37.

Arzeni, Flavia, 1987, *L'immagine e il segno: Il giapponismo nella cultura europea tra Ottocento e Novocento*. Bologna: Mulino.

Asada, Akira, 1983, 'Fukō na dōke toshite no kindaijin no shōzō' [The profile of the modern man as an unhappy clown]. *Gendai Shisō*. Vol. 11 No. 2.

——, 1985, 'Japan-Postmoderne des Kapitalismus.' *Kagami-Japanischer Zeitschriftenspiegel* No. 1.

——, 1990, 'Posto-modaan kara Posto-modaan e' [From postmodern to postmodern], in H. Kobayashi (ed.), *The Eighties*. Tokyo: Gallery Kobayashi.

Atsumi, Reiko, 1979, '*Tsukiai* – obligatory personal relationships of Japanese white-collar company employees.' *Human Organization* Vol. 38 No. 1 (Spring): 63–70.

Bacchi, Carol, 1990, *Same Difference: Feminism and Sexual Difference*. Sydney: Allen and Unwin.

Bachelard, Gaston, 1984, *The New Scientific Spirit*. Boston: Beacon Press.

Ballon, Robert J., 1992, *Foreign Competition in Japan: Human Resource Strategies*. London: Routledge.

Bauman, Zygmunt, 1989, 'Sociological responses to postmodernity.' *Thesis Eleven* No. 23: 35–63.

——, 1991, 'A sociological theory of postmodernity.' *Thesis Eleven* No. 29: 33–46.

Beaud, Michel, 1990, *Le Système Nationale Mondial Hiérarchisé*. Paris: La Découverte.

Beechey, Veronica, 1987, *Unequal Work*. London: Verse.

Beechey, Veronica and Perkins, Tessa, 1987, *A Matter of Hours: Women, Part-time Work and the Labor Market*. Cambridge: Polity Press.

Befu, Harumi, 1990, *Ideorogii to shite no Nihon bunkaron* [Japanese culture theories as an ideology]. Tokyo: Shisō no Kagakusha.

Bellah, Robert, 1962, 'Values and social change in modern Japan.' *Asian Cultural Studies* No. 3. Tokyo: International Christian University.

——, 1976, *Beyond Belief: Essays on Religion in a Post-traditional World*. New York: Harper and Row.

——, 1983a, *Tokugawa Religion: The Cultural Roots of Modern Japan*. New York: The Free Press.

——, 1983b, 'Cultural identity and Asian modernization.' Kokugakuin University (ed.), *Cultural Identity and Modernization in Asian Countries*. Tokyo: Kokugakuin University.

Bello, W. and Rosenfeld, S., 1992, *Dragons in Distress: Asia's Miracle Economies in Crisis*. Harmondsworth: Penguin.

Benedict, Ruth, 1946, *The Chrysanthemum and the Sword: Patterns of Japanese Culture*. Boston: Houghton Mifflin Co.

Berger, Peter L. and Hsiao, Hsing-huang (eds), 1988, *In Search of an East Asian Development Model*. New Brunswick and Oxford: Transaction Books.

Berger, Suzanne, 1980, 'The traditional sector in France and Italy', in S. Berger and M. Piore (eds), *Dualism and Discontinuity in Industrial Societies*. Cambridge: Cambridge University Press.

Berggren, Christian, 1992, *Alternatives to Lean Production*. Ithaca: ILR Press, Cornell University.

Bernstein, Basil, 1966, 'Elaborated and restricted codes: An outline', S. Lieberson (ed.), *Explorations in Sociolinguistics*. Bloomington: Indiana University Press.

Berque, Augustin, 1992, 'French Japanology as an objective contribution to a post-modern paradigm', in H. Befu and J. Kreiner (eds), *Othernesses of Japan*. Munchen: Judicium Verlag.

Bestor, Theodore, 1985a, 'Tradition and Japanese social organization.' *Ethnology* Vol. 24.

——, 1985b, 'Suburbanization in Tokyo, 1920–1940.' Paper presented to annual meeting of American Anthropological Association.

——, 1989, *Neighbourhood Tokyo*. Stanford: Stanford University Press.

Blau, Peter M. and Duncan, Otis D., 1967, *The American Occupational Structure*. New York and Sydney: J. Wiley.

Bottomley, Gill *et al.* (eds), 1991, *Intersexions: Gender/Class/Culture/Ethnicity*. Sydney: Allen and Unwin.

Boudon, Raymond, 1982, *The Unintended Consequences of Social Action*. New York: St Martins Press.

Bourdieu, Pierre, 1979, *La distinction: Critique sociale du jugement*. Paris: Les Éditions de Minuit.

——, 1989, *Distinction: A Social Critique of the Judgement of Taste*. London: Routledge.

Bower, Lisa C., 1991, ' "Mother" in law: conceptions of mother and the maternal in feminism and feminist legal theory.' *Differences: A Journal of Feminist Cultural Studies* Vol. 3 No. 1.

Bowles, Gilbert (compiler), 1915, *Japanese Law of Nationality*. Tokyo: Shūeisha.

Boxer, Charles R., 1967, *The Christian Century in Japan: 1549–1650*. Berkeley: University of California Press.

Brinton, Mary C., 1992, *Women and the Economic Miracle: Gender and Work in Postwar Japan*. Berkeley: University of California Press.

Broadbent, Kaye, 1991, 'Flexibility and work: conceptualizing the feminization of part-time work in Japanese supermarkets.' Paper presented at 7th Biennial Conference of the Japanese Studies Association of Australia, Australian National University, Canberra.

Buckley, Sandra, 1988, 'Body politics: abortion law reform', in G. McCormack and Y. Sugimoto (eds), *The Japanese Trajectory: Modernization and Beyond*. Cambridge: Cambridge University Press.

Bunkachō [Agency for Cultural Affairs], 1988, *Waga kuni no bunka to bunka gyōsei* [Japanese culture and cultural policies]. Tokyo: Gyōsei.

Bunka Seisaku Kenkyūkai [The Research Society on Cultural Policies] (ed.), 1990, *Gendai bunka seisaku deeta fuairu* [Data files on contemporary cultural policies]. Tokyo: Dai Ippōki.

Calder, Kent E., 1988, *Crisis and Compensation: Public Policy and Political Stability in Japan*. Princeton: Princeton University Press.

Capra, Fritjof, 1975, *The Tao of Physics: An Exploration of the Parallels between Modern Physics and Eastern Mysticism*. Boulder: Shambhala.

——, 1982, *The Turning Point*. New York: Simon and Shuster.

Carroll, Lewis, 1946, *Alice's Adventures in Wonderland*. New York: Puffin Books.

Castoriadis, Cornelius, 1991, 'Le délabrement de l'Occident: Entretien avec Cornelius Castoriadis.' *Esprit* No. 177 (Dec.): 36–54.

Chakrabarty, Dipesh, 1991, 'Subaltern studies and the critique of history.' *Arena* No. 96.

Chapman, Christine, 1990, 'Power and patronage.' *Art News* March.

Chiba, Shigeo, 1986, *Gendai Bijutsu Idatsushi*. Tokyo: Shōbunsha.

Chow, Rey, 1992, 'Postmodern Automatons', in Judith Butler and Joan W. Scott (eds), *Feminists Theorize the Political*. New York: Routledge.

Chung, Daekyun, 1992, *Nik-Kan no pararerizumu (Atarashii nagameai wa kanō ka)* [Japan-ROK parallelism (Are new views of one another possible?)]. Tokyo: Sankosha.

Chūshō Kigyōchō [Small and Medium Enterprise Agency], 1989, *Chūshō kigyō hakusho 1989* [The 1989 white paper on small and medium enterprises]. Tokyo: Ōkurashō Insatsu-kyoku.

Clammer, John, 1991, 'Knowledge and society: The role of self, belief and social order in Japanese social thought.' *Transactions of the International Conference of Orientalists in Japan* No. XXXVI.

Clark, John, 1991, 'Postmodernism and expressionist tendencies in recent Chinese oil painting.' *Asian Studies Reviews* Vol. 15 No. 2 (Nov.).

Clark, John (ed.), 1993, *Modernism in Asian Art*. Sydney: Wild Peony Press.

Cohen-Tanugi, Laurent, 1989, *La Metamorphose de la Démocratie*. Paris: Odile Jacob.

Cole, Robert E., 1971, *Japanese Blue Collar: The Changing Tradition*. Berkeley: University of California Press.

——, 1979, *Work, Mobility and Participation: A Comparative Study of American and Japanese Industry*. Berkeley: University of California Press.

273

Collins, Randall, 1979, *The Credential Society*. New York: Academic Press.

Community Union Kenkyū Kai [Research society of community union] (eds), 1988, *Community union sengen* [Community union declaration]. Tokyo: Daiichi Shorin.

Coulmas, F., 1988, 'The surge of Japanese.' *International Journal of the Sociology of Language* No. 80.

Curtis, Gerald L., 1988, *The Japanese Way of Politics*. New York: Columbia University Press.

David, Abe and Wheelwright, Ted, 1989, *The Third Wave: Australia and Asian Capitalism*. Sutherland: Left Book Club.

De Bary, Theodore, 1988, *East Asian Civilizations: A Dialogue in Five Stages*. Cambridge Mass.: Harvard University Press.

Derrida, Jacques, 1991, *L'autre cap*. Paris: Minuit.

Deutsch, Morton, 1985, *Distributive Justice*. New Haven: Yale University Press.

Dohse, Knuth, Jurgens, Ulrich and Malsch, Thomas, 1985, 'From "Fordism" to "Toyotism"? The social organization of the labor process in the Japanese automobile industry.' *Politics and Society* Vol. 14 No. 2.

Dore, Ronald, 1958, *City Life in Japan: A Study of Tokyo Ward*. Berkeley: University of California Press.

——, 1974, *British Factory – Japanese Factory: The Origins of National Diversity in Industrial Relations*. Berkeley: University of California Press.

Dower, John, 1975, 'E. H. Norman, Japan and the uses of history', in J. Dower, (ed.), *Origins of the Modern Japanese State: Selected Writings of E.H. Norman*. New York: Pantheon Books.

Eccleston, Bernard, 1989, *State and Society in Postwar Japan*. Cambridge: Polity Press.

Eysteinsson, Astradur, 1990, *The Concept of Modernism*. Ithaca and London: Cornell University Press.

Featherstone, Mike, 1988, 'In pursuit of the postmodern: An introduction.' *Theory, Culture and Society* Vol. 5.

Featherstone, Mike (ed.), 1990, *Global Culture: Nationalism, Globalization and Modernity*. London: Sage Publications.

Feyerabend, Paul K., 1993, *Against Method*. London: Verso.

Field, N., 1989, 'Somehow: The post-modern as atmosphere', in M. Miyoshi and H. D. Harootunian (eds), *Postmodernism and Japan*. London: Duke University Press.

Ford, Bill, 1991, 'Integrating technology, work organization and skill formation: lessons from manufacturing for ports', in Michael Costa and Michael Easson (eds), *Australian Industry: What Policy?* Leichhardt, NSW: Pluto Press Australia.

Foster, Hal (ed.), 1983, *The Anti-Aesthetic*. Port Townsend: Bay Press.

——, 1985, *Postmodern Culture*. London and Sydney: Pluto Press.

Frank, Andre G., 1971, *Capitalism and Underdevelopment in Latin America*. Harmondsworth: Penguin.

Fraser, Nancy, 1987, 'What's critical about critical theory? The case of Habermas and gender', in S. Benhabib and D. Cornell (eds), *Feminism as Critique*. Cambridge: Polity Press.

——, 1989, 'Women, welfare and the politics of need interpretation', in Nancy Fraser, *Unruly Practices: Power, Discourse and Gender in Contemporary Social Theory*. Cambridge: Polity Press.

Friedman, Jonathan, 1988, 'Cultural logics of the global system: a sketch.' *Theory Culture and Society* Vol. 5.

Fukuoka, Yasunori, 1993, *Zainichi Kankoku Chōsenjin* [Resident Koreans]. Tokyo: Chūō Kōronsha.

Fukutake, Tadashi, 1982, *The Japanese Social Structure*. Tokyo: University of Tokyo Press.

Fukuyama, Francis, 1992, *The End of History and the Last Man*. New York: Free Press.

Furet, François *et al.* (eds), 1988, *La Republique du Centre: La Fin de L'exception Française*. Paris: Calmann-Lévy.

Fussel, Anne, 1990, 'Rewriting a ritual art.' *The Weekend Australian* Oct. 27–8.

Gershuny, Jonathon, 1978, *After Industrial Society? The Emerging Self Service Economy*. London: Macmillan.

Giedeon, Siegfried, 1948, *Mechanisation Takes Command: A Contribution to Anonymous History*. New York: Oxford University Press.

Girling, John (ed.), 1991, 'Human rights in the Asia-Pacific region', *Canberra Studies in World Affairs* No. 29. Canberra: Department of International Relations, Research School of Pacific Studies, Australian National University.

Gluck, Carol, 1985, *Japan's Modern Myths: Ideology in the Late Meiji Period*. Princeton: Princeton University Press.

Glyphis, Sue, 1989, *Leisure and Unemployment*. Philadelphia: Open University Press.

Goldstein, Ann and Jacob, Mary Ann, 1989, *A Forest of Signs: Art in the Crisis of Representation*. Cambridge Mass.: The MIT Press.

Goodman, Roger, 1990, *Japan's 'International Youth': The Emergence of a New Class of Schoolchildren*. Oxford: Oxford University Press.

Goonatilake, Susantha, 1984, *Aborted Discovery: Science and Creativity in the Third World*. London: Zed Books.

Gumpertz, Lyn, 1990, 'A distant mirror.' *Art News* March.

Habermas, Jürgen, 1981, 'Modernity versus postmodernity.' *New German Critique* No. 22 (Winter).

Halbreich, Cathy, Sokolowski, Tom, Kōmoto, Shinji and Nanjō, Fumio,

1989, *Against Nature: Japanese Art in the Eighties*. New York: Grey Art Gallery and Study Center, New York University.

Hall, John W., 1965, 'Changing conceptions of the modernization of Japan', in M. B. Jansen (ed.), *Changing Japanese Attitudes Towards Modernisation*. Princeton: Princeton University Press.

Hall, Stuart, 1988, 'Brave new world.' *Marxism Today* October.

Hamada, Tomoko, 1992, 'Under the silk banner: The Japanese company and its overseas managers', in Takie Sugiyama Lebra (ed.), *Japanese Social Organization*. Honolulu: University of Hawaii Press.

Hamaguchi, Eshun (ed.), 1993, *Nihongata moderu to wa nanika: Kokusai jidai ni okeru meritto to demeritto* [What is the Japanese model? The merits and demerits of the Japanese approach in the era of internationalization]. Tokyo: Shinyōsha.

Hamaguchi, Eshun, 1977, *'Nihon-rashisa' no Saihakken* [A discovery of 'Japaneseness']. Tokyo: Nihon Keizai Shinbunsha (republished in 1988 by Kōdansha).

——, 1982, *Kanjinshugi no shakai: Nihon* [The contextual society: Japan]. Tokyo: Tōyō Keizai Shinpōsha.

——, 1985, 'A contextual model of the Japanese: Toward a methodological innovation in Japanese studies', *Journal of Japanese Studies* Vol. 11 No. 2 (Summer): 289–321.

Hamilton, Gary, 1989, 'Patterns of East Asian capitalism.' Paper presented at the 1989 conference of the American Sociological Association, San Francisco.

Hamilton, Walter, 1991, *Serendipity City: Australia, Japan and the Multifunction Polis*. Crows Nest: Australian Broadcasting Corporation.

Hara, Junsuke (ed.), 1990, *Kaisō–ishiki no dōtai* [Dynamics of class consciousness]. Tokyo: Tokyo Daigaku Shuppan-kai.

Hara, Toshio and Fox, Howard T., 1990, *A Primal Spirit*. Tokyo: Hara Museum of Contemporary Art. Also, Los Angeles: Los Angeles County Museum of Art.

Haraway, Donna, 1987, 'A manifesto for cyborgs: science, technology and socialist feminism in the 1980s.' *Australian Feminist Studies* No. 4 (Autumn).

Harding, Sandra, 1986, *The Science Question in Feminism*. Milton Keynes: Open University Press.

Harootunian, H.D., 1988, 'Visible discourses/invisible ideologies.' *The South Atlantic Quarterly* Vol. 87 No. 3 (Summer).

Harris, Marvin, 1981, *Why Nothing Works: The Anthropology of Daily Life*. Touchstone Edition. New York: Simon and Schuster.

Harrison, Bennett and Bluestone, Barry, 1988, *The Great U-Turn: Corporate Restructuring and the Polarizing of America*. New York: Basic Books.

Harvey, David, 1982, *The Limits to Capital*. Oxford: Basil Blackwell.

——, 1989, *The Condition of Postmodernity*. Oxford: Blackwell.

Hasegawa, Yūko and Terakado, Toshiaki, 1990, *Dassō suru shashin* [Escaping photographs]. Mito: Mito Geijutsukan.

Heidegger, Martin, 1983, *Die Selbstbehauptung der Deutschen Universität, das Rektorat 1933/34*. Frankfurt: Vittorio Klostermann.

Hendry, Joy, 1993, *Wrapping Culture: Politeness Presentation and Power in Japan and Other Societies*. Oxford: Clarendon Press.

Henny, Sue and Lehmann, Jean-Piérre, 1988, *Themes and Theories in Modern Japanese History*. London: Atlantic Highlands.

Higashi, C. and Lauter, G. Peter, 1987, *The Internationalization of the Japanese Economy*. Boston: Kluwer.

Hiromatsu, Wataru, 1989, *'Kindai no chōkoku' ron* [On 'transcending the modern']. Tokyo: Kōdansha.

Hirsch, E.D. Jr., 1988, *Cultural Literacy: What Every American Needs to Know*. New York: Vintage Books.

Holloway, John, 1987, 'The red nose of Nissan.' *Capital and Class* No. 32 (Summer).

Holstein, William J., 1990, *The Japanese Power Game: What It Means for America*. New York: Scribner.

Hook, Glenn D. and Weiner, Michael I. (eds), 1992, *The Internationalization of Japan*. London: Routledge.

Hoshino, Yoshirō, 1956, *Gendai Nihon gijutsushi gaisetu* [An outline of the history of modern Japanese technology]. Tokyo: Dai-Nihon Tosho.

Hsiung, James C. (ed.), 1985, *Human Rights in East Asia*. New York: Paragon House.

Hutcheon, Linda, 1989, *The Politics of Postmodernism*. London: Routledge.

Huyssen, A., 1984, 'Mapping the postmodern.' *New German Critique* No. 33 (Fall).

Hymes, D.H., 1962, 'The ethnography of speaking', in T. Gladwin and W. C. Sturtevant (eds), *Anthropology and Human Behavior*. Washington: Anthropological Society of Washington.

Ijima, Yoichi, 1986, 'Hi no suijaku' [Weakening fire]. *Bijutsu Techō* November.

Imada, Takatoshi, 1987, *Modan no datsukōchiku* [Deconstruction of the modern]. Tokyo: Chūō Kōronsha.

——, 1989, *Shakai-kaisō to seiji* [Social stratification and politics]. Tokyo: Tokyo Daigaku Shuppan-kai.

——, 1991, 'Modernity and its deconstruction: Metamorphosis of civilization.' *International Review of Sociology* New Series No. 3: 197–211.

Imai, Ken'ichi, 1984, *Jōhō nettowaaku shakai* [Information network society]. Tokyo: Iwanami Shoten.

Inoue, Tadashi and Itō, Shuntarō, 1984, 'Taidan: Nyū saiensu no paradaimu' [The paradigm of new science: A round table discussion]. *Gendai Shisō* January.

Ishida, Takeshi and Krauss, Ellis S., 1989, *Democracy in Japan*. Pittsburgh: University of Pittsburgh Press.

Ishihara, Shintaro, 1991, *The Japan That Can Say No*. Trans. Frank Baldwin. New York: Simon and Schuster.

Ishii, Takemochi, 1983, *Tekunorando Nihon no gijutsu wa saikō niomoshiroi* [The technology of Japan as techno-land is most interesting]. Tokyo: Purejidento-sha.

Ishiko, Junzō, 1987, *Imeejiron, Chosakushū Dainikan* [On images, Volume Two of the collection of Junzō Ishiko's works]. Tokyo: Ramasha.

Isozaki, Arata and Tagi, Kōji, 1984, 'Kosumikku Janpu no shōdō de saemo' [Even the impulse of the cosmic jump]. *Bijutsu Techō* June.

Isozaki, Arata and Yoshimoto, Takaaki, 1985, 'Taidan: "Ima" to iu mui-shiki no hōtō' [The unconscious method of the 'contemporary': A tête-a-tête]. *Bijutsu Techō* January.

Iverson, Margaret, 1989, 'The positions of postmodernism.' *Oxford Art Journal* Vol. 12 No. 1.

James, Paul (ed.), 1990, *Technocratic Dreaming: Very Fast Trains and Japanese Designed Cities*. Sutherland: Left Book Club.

Jameson, Frederic, 1983, 'Postmodernism and consumer society', in Hal Forster (ed.), *The Anti-Aesthetic*. Port Townsend: Bay Press.

——, 1984, 'Postmodernism, or the cultural logic of late capitalism.' *New Left Review* No. 146 (July-Aug.).

——, 1985, 'Postmodernity and consumer society', in Hal Foster (ed.), *Postmodern Culture*. London: Pluto Press.

——, 1989, 'Marxism and postmodernism'. *New Left Review* No. 176 (July-Aug.).

——, 1991a, *Postmodernism*. Durham: Duke University Press.

——, 1991b, *Postmodernism: Or the Cultural Logic of Late Capitalism*. New York: Verso.

Jansen, Marius B., 1962, 'On studying the modernization of Japan.' *Asian Cultural Studies* No. 3: 1–11.

——, 1965, *Changing Japanese Attitudes Towards Modernization*. Princeton: Princeton University Press.

Japan Foundation, 1990, *Overview of Programs for Fiscal 1989, Annual Report for Fiscal 1988*. Tokyo: Japan Foundation.

Jernudd, B. and J. V. Neustupný, 1987, 'Language planning: for whom?', in L. Laforge (ed.), *Proceedings of the International Symposium on Language Planning*. Ottowa: Les presses de l'Universite Laval.

Johnson, Chalmers, 1982, *MITI and the Japanese Miracle*. Stanford: Stanford University Press.

——, 1988, 'Studies of Japanese political economy: a crisis in theory.' *The Japan Foundation Newsletter* Vol. XVI No. 3.

Junkerman, John, 1987, 'Nissan, Tennessee: It ain't what it's cracked up to be.' *The Progressive* June.

Kadowaki, Atsushi, 1978, *Gendai no shussekan* [The contemporary idea of rising in the world]. Tokyo: Nihon Keizai Shinbunsha.

Kagaku Gijutsu-chō [Science and Technology Agency], 1990, *Kagaku gijutsu hakusho* [White paper on science and technology]. Tokyo: Kagaku Gijutsusha.

Kajita, Takamichi, 1988, *Esunishiti to shakai-hendō* [Ethnicity and social change]. Tokyo: Yūshindō.

——, 1990, 'Les mouvements sociaux dans le japon contemporain: leurs rapports à l'"État dirigiste", *L'État et l'individu au japon*, s.l.d. de Yōichi Higuchi and Christian Sautter. Paris: Écoles des hautes études en sciences sociales.

Kamata, Satoshi, 1982, *Japan in the Passing Lane*. New York: Pantheon Books.

——, 1984, *Kyōiku kōjō no kodomotachi* [Children of Japan's education factory]. Tokyo: Iwanami Shoten.

Kanai, Yoshiko and Kanō, Mikiyo (eds), 1990, *Onnatachi no shisen* [Women's perspectives]. Tokyo: Shakai Hyōronsha.

Kanatani, Chieko, 1983, 'Josei no hataraku kenri to rōdō hōki' [Women's rights of work and labour laws] in Emiko Takenaka (ed.), *Joshi rōdō-ron: Kikai no byōdō kara kekka no byōdō* [On female labour: from equality of opportunities to equality of outcomes]. Tokyo: Yūhikaku Sensho.

——, 1984, 'Rōdōsha Hogohō Henkōshi ni Miru Bosei Hogo: "Kintōhō" Jōtei o Ki ni Rōdō Kijunhō o Futatabi Kangaeru' ['Motherhood protection' in the history of protective labour legislation: Rethinking the Labour Standards Law on the occasion of the enactment of the Equal Opportunity Act]. *Agora* 'Tokushō-Kintō, Byōdō, Hogo' [Special issue on equality and protection] No. 89 (Aug.).

Kanō, Mikiyo, 1990, *Jiga no kanata e: Kindai o koeru feminizumu* [Beyond the self: Feminism that transcends the modern]. Tokyo: Shakai Hyōronsha.

Karabel, J. and Halsey, A. H. (eds), 1977, *Power and Ideology in Education*. New York: Oxford University Press.

Karatani, Kōjin, 1988, *Nihon kindai bungaku no kigen* [Origins of Modern Japanese Literature]. Tokyo: Kōdansha.

——, 1989a, 'One spirit, two nineteenth centuries', in M. Miyoshi and Harootunian, H. D. (eds), *Postmodernism and Japan*. Durham: Duke University Press.

——, 1989b, *Inyu toshite no kenchiku* [Architecture as a metaphor]. Tokyo: Kōdansha.

——, 1990, *Shūen o megutte* [Concerning the eschatological ending]. Tokyo: Fukutake Shoten.

Kassalow, Everett M., 1983, 'Japan as an industrial relations model', *Journal of Industrial Relations* Vol. 25 No. 2 (June): 201–19.

Katase, K. and Tomoeda, T., 1990, 'Kachi-ishiki' [Value consciousness], in J. Hara (ed.), *Kaisō-ishiki no dōtai* [Dynamics of class consciousness]. Tokyo: Tokyo Daigaku Shuppan-kai.

Katayama, Osamu, 1993, *Nihongata keiei no shinsenryoku: Kigyō wa ima nani o mezasubekika* [New strategies for Japanese-style management: Today's urgent tasks for Japan's business firm]. Tokyo: PHP.

Kato, Shuichi, 1979, *A History of Japanese Literature: The First Thousand Years*. Tokyo: Kodansha International.

Kato, Tetsuro, 1984, 'A preliminary note on the State in contemporary Japan.' *Hitotsubashi Journal of Social Studies* Vol. 16 No. 1.

——, 1987a, *Kore kara no Nihon o yomu* [Reading the future of Japan]. Tokyo: Rōdō Junpōsha.

——, 1987b, 'Der Neo-etatismus im heutigen Japan.' *Prokla* No. 66 (West Berlin).

——, 1988, *Japamerika no jindai ni* [At the age of Japamerica]. Tokyo: Kadensha.

——, 1989a, *Sengo ishiki no henbō* [Changes of popular consciousness in postwar Japan]. Tokyo: Iwanami Shoten.

——, 1989b, 'The age of "Japamerica" – Taking Japanese development seriously.' *Hitotsubashi Journal of Social Studies* Vol. 21 No. 1.

Kato, Tetsuro and Steven, Rob, 1991, *Is Japanese Capitalism Post-Fordist?* Papers of the Japanese Studies Centre No. 16. Melbourne: Japanese Studies Centre.

——, 1993, *Is Japanese Management Post-Fordist?* Tokyo: Madosha.

Kawamoto, Saburō, 1986, 'Murami Haruki o meguru kaidoku' [Deciphering the work of Haruki Murakami], in Rei Hisahara (ed.) *Murakami Haruki*. Tokyo: Seidōsha.

Kawamura, Minato, 1989, 'A survey of literature in 1988.' *Japanese Literature Today*, Japan PEN Club, No. 14 (Mar.).

Kawanishi, Hirosuke, 1992, *Enterprise Unionism in Japan*. Trans. Ross Mouer. London: Kegan Paul International.

Keane, John, 1988, *Democracy and Civil Society*. London: Verso.

Keizai Kikakuchō [Economic Planning Agency], 1989, *1989 Keizai haku-sho* [1989 white paper on the economy]. Tokyo: Ōkurashō Insatsukyoku.

Keizai Kikakuchō Sōgō Tōkeikyoku [General Statistical Bureau of the Economic Planning Agency], 1988, *Shitsugyō (Sono kōzō to shinkokudo)* [Unemployment: Its structure and gravity]. Tokyo: Ōkurashō Insatsukyoku.

Kenney, Martin and Florida, Richard, 1988, 'Beyond mass production:

Production and the labour process in Japan.' *Politics and Society* Vol. 16 No. 1.

Kenrick, Douglas Moore, 1991, *Where Communism Works*. Basingstoke: Macmillan. (Originally published in 1988 as *The Success of Competitive Communism in Japan*.)

Kishida, Toshiko, 1988, 'Is Japan a postmodern society?', *Japanese Studies Association of Australia Newsletter* Vol. 8 No. 4.

Kitaya, Yukio, 1985, *Horonikku kanpanii* [Holonic company]. Tokyo: TBS Books.

Kobayashi, Kōichi, 1991, 'Dōjidai hihyō ni muketa atsui giron' [Debate contributing to a contemporary critique]. Book review of *Murakami Haruki o meguru bōken*. (Adventures concerning Haruki Murakami). *Shūkan Dokushojin* No. 1897 (Aug. 26).

Kobayashi, Yasuo and Matsuura, Toshio, 1984, 'Taidan: Geijutsu no postomodaan jōkyō' [The postmodern situation in art: A talk]. *Geijutsu Hyōron* No. 3 (Summer).

Kodama, Fumio, 1991, *Analyzing Japanese High Technologies: The Techno-Paradigm Shift*. London and New York: Pinter Publisher.

Koestler, Arthur, 1978, *Janus: A Summing Up*. New York: Random House.

Kogawa, Tetsuo, 1988, 'New trends in Japanese popular culture', in G. McCormack and Y. Sugimoto (eds), *The Japanese Trajectory: Modernization and Beyond*. Cambridge: Cambridge University Press.

Koike, Kazuo, 1988, *Understanding Industrial Relations in Modern Japan*. Trans. Mary Saso. London: Macmillan.

Kondo, Dorinne K., 1990, *Crafting Selves: Power, Gender and Discourses of Identity in a Japanese Workplace*. Chicago: University of Chicago Press.

Koo, Hagen, 1987, 'Industrialization and labor politics in the East Asian NICS: A comparison of South Korea and Taiwan.' Paper presented to the American Sociological Association, Chicago.

Koplos, Janet, 1989, 'Through the looking glass.' *Art in America* July.

Kosaka, Kenji (ed.), 1994, *Social Stratification in Contemporary Japan*. London: Kegan Paul International.

Kōuchi, Nobuko (ed.), 1984, *Bosei hogo ronsō* [Debate on the protection of maternity]. Tokyo: Domesu Shuppan.

Koyama, Hirotake, 1953, *Nihon shihonshugi ronsō shi* [A history of the debate on Japanese capitalism]. Tokyo: Aoki Shoten.

Kozai, Yoshishege, 1984, *Wakon-yōkon nōto* [Notes on the Japanese spirit]. Tokyo: Iwanami Shoten.

Kristeva, Julia, 1988, *Étrangers a nous-mêmes*. Paris: Fayard.

Kruger, B. and Mariani, P. (eds), 1989, *Remaking History*. Seattle: Bay Press/Dia Art Foundation.

Kuba, Yoshiko, 1984, 'Jisshitsu-teki byōdō to rōdō shijō no sabetsu teki kōzō' [Substantive equality and the discriminatory structure of the labour market]. *Agora*. 'Tokushū: Kintō, Byōdō, Hogo' [Special issue of *Agora* on equality of opportunities, equality of outcomes and protection] No. 89 (Aug.).

Kuhn, Thomas, 1977, *The Structure of Scientific Revolutions*. Chicago: University of Chicago Press.

Kumazawa, Makoto, 1988, 'Sangyō shakai to shokugyō seikatsu' [Industrial society and working life], in Rokurō Hidaka (ed.), *Asu no Nihon o kangaeru* [Thinking about tomorrow's Japan]. Tokyo: Chikuma Shobō.

Kunihiro, Masao, 1979, 'Interdomestic age', *PHP* Vol. 10 No. 6 (June): 6–16, 77–8.

Kurabashi, Yasushi, 1986, ' "Posto Modaan" aruiwa imeeji no ana kizumu ni tsuite' [On the 'postmodern' or the anarchism of images], *Bijutsu Techō* July.

——, 1989, 'Kyōshin suru jikan wa sekai no henyō o kijutsu suru' [The resonant time records the transformation of the world], *Bijutsu Techō* April.

Kusayanagi, Daizō, 1990, *'Nihon-rashisa' no shin-dankai* [The new phase of 'Japaneseness']. Tokyo: Rikuruto Shūppan.

Kyogoku, Jun'ichi, 1985, 'Modernization and Japan', in N. Hagihara et al. (eds), *Experiencing the Twentieth Century*. Tokyo: University of Tokyo Press.

Lacoste, Yves, 1989, 'Perestroïka et géopolitiques.' *Hérodote* No. 54–5: 3–25.

Lam, Alice, 1993, 'Equal employment opportunities for Japanese women: Changing company practice', in Janet Hunter (ed.), *Japanese Women Working*. London: Routledge.

Latouche, Serge, 1989, *L'occidentalisation du Monde*. Paris: La Découverte.

Leadbeater, Charlie, 1988, 'Power to the person.' *Marxism Today* October.

Lee, Keun, 1993, *New East Asian Economic Development: Interacting Capitalism and Socialism*. Armonk: M. E. Sharpe.

Lee Kuan Yew, 1993, 'Is democracy necessary?' *The Weekend Australian* (24–25 Apr.): 20.

Lee, U-fan, 1971, *Deai o motomete* [In search of encounters]. Tokyo: Tabata Shoten.

——, 1986, *Lee U-fan*. Tokyo: Bijutsu Shuppansha.

Leopold, W.F., 1968, 'The decline of German dialects', in J. A. Fishman (ed.), *Readings in the Sociology of Language*. The Hague: Mouton.

Leung, James, 1991, 'Interpersonal relations in a medium-sized printing firm in Japan: A comparison with its Hong Kong counterpart.' Honours thesis submitted to the Department of Japanese, Monash University, Melbourne.

Levering, Robert, 1988, *A Great Place to Work*. New York: Avon Books.

Lipietz, Alain, 1986, *Mirages and Miracles*. London: NLB.

Low, Morris F., 1994, 'Making space in Shanghai and Manchuria: Japanese colonial science and the mapping of China'. Paper presented at the conference 'Making Space: Territorial Themes in the History of Science'. Canterbury: University of Kent at Canterbury, 28–30 March.

Lufty, Carol, 1990, 'Gaining face.' *Art News* March.

Lummis, Douglas C., 1982, *A New Look at the Chrysanthemum and the Sword*. Tokyo: Shokakusha.

Lyotard, J.F., 1984, *The Postmodern Condition*. Minneapolis: University of Minnesota Press.

McCaughey, Jean, 1987, *A Bit of a Struggle: Coping with Family Life in Australia*. Ringwood: Penguin Books Australia.

McClelland, David, 1961, *The Achieving Society*. Princeton: Van Nostrand.

McCormack, Gavan, 1991, 'The price of affluence: The political economy of Japanese leisure.' *New Left Review* No. 188.

McCormack, Gavan and Sugimoto, Yoshio (eds), 1986, *Democracy in Contemporary Japan*. Sydney: Hale and Iremonger.

——, 1988, *The Japanese Trajectory: Modernization and Beyond*. Cambridge: Cambridge University Press.

McCullough, William H., 1967, 'Japanese marriage institutions in the Heian period.' *Harvard Journal of Asiatic Studies* Vol. 27: 103–67.

McGowan, John, 1991, *Postmodernism and Its Critics*. Ithaca and London: Cornell University Press.

Mackie, Vera, 1988a, 'Feminist politics in Japan.' *New Left Review* No. 167.

——, 1988b, 'The motherhood protection debate revisited.' Paper presented at the ASAA Biennial Conference, Australian National University, February.

——, 1989, 'Equal opportunity in an unequal labour market: the Japanese situation.' *Australian Feminist Studies* No. 9 (Autumn).

Mackie, Vera and Taylor, Veronica, 1994, 'Ethnicity on trial: Foreign workers in Japan.' Unpublished paper presented at the Conference on Identities, Ethnicities, Nationalities; La Trobe University, Melbourne, July.

Maharey, Steve, 1989, 'New times, privatisation and the democratic alternative.' Paper presented to the Public Service Association's Conference on Privatisation, May.

Mahathir, Mohamad and Ishihara, Shintarō, 1994, *'Nō' to ieru Ajia* [The Asia that can say 'No']. Tokyo: Kōbunsha.

Maher, John and Macdonald, Gaynor (eds), 1995, *Diversity in Japanese Culture and Language*. London: Kegan Paul International.

Maraini, Fosco, 1988, 'Japan the essential moderniser', in S. Henry and

J. P. Lehmann (eds), *Themes and Theories in Modern Japanese History*. London: Athlone Press.

March, Robert, 1993, *The Japanese Business Mind*. Belrose, Australia: IMDC Australia.

Maruyama, Masao, 1963, *Thought and Behaviour in Modern Japanese Politics*. Ed. Ivan Morris. London: Oxford University Press.

——, 1965, 'Patterns of individuation and the case of Japan: A conceptual scheme', in M. B. Jansen (ed.), *Changing Japanese Attitudes Toward Modernization*. Princeton: Princeton University Press.

——, 1988a, 'The structure of matsurigoto', in Sue Henry and Jean-Pierre Lehmann (eds), *Themes and Theories in Modern Japanese History*. London: Athlone Press.

——, 1988b, *Denken in Japan*. Trans. W. Schamoni and W. Seifert. Frankfurt: Suhrkamp.

Masuda Kokusai Kōryū Kyōiku Zaidan Nihongata Shisutemu Kenkyūkai (Masuda Foundation's Research Project Team for Japanese Systems), Hamaguchi, Eshun (Convenor/Editor), 1992, *Japanese Systems: An Alternative Civilization?* Yokohama: Sekotakku. Also in Japanese in the same volume as *Nihongata shisutemu: Jinrui bunmei no hitotsu no kata*.

Matsumoto, Michihiro, 1988, *The Unspoken Way Haragei: Silence in Japanese Business and Society*. Tokyo: Kodansha International.

Mead, George H., 1936, *Movements of Thought in the Nineteenth Century*. Ed. M. H. Moore. Chicago: University of Chicago Press.

——, 1938, *The Philosophy of the Act*. Ed. Charles Morris. Chicago: University of Chicago Press.

——, 1982, '1927 class lecture in social psychology', in D. L. Miller (ed.), *The Individual and the Social Self*. Chicago: University of Chicago Press.

Meakin, David, 1976, *Man and Work: Literature and Culture in Industrial Society*. London: Methuen.

Melville, Stephen, 1989, 'Picturing Japan: Reflections on the workshop', in M. Miyoshi and H. D. Harootunian (eds), *Postmodernism and Japan*. Durham: Duke University Press.

Menzel, V. (ed.), 1989, *Im Schatten des Siegers: Japan, Band 3, Okonomie und Politik*. Frankfurt: Suhrkamp.

Miller, Richard J., 1974, *Ancient Japanese Nobility: The Kabane Ranking System*. Berkeley: University of California Press.

Milner, Andrew and Worth, Chris (eds), 1988, *Postmodern Conditions*. Melbourne: Centre for General and Comparative Literature.

Minemura, Toshiaki, 1987, *Monoha to postomonoha no tenkai* [The development of the mono school and the post-mono school]. Tokyo: Tama Bijutsu Daigaku and Seibu Bijutsukan.

——, 1990, *Kaiga/Nihon: Dansō kara no shutsugen* [Art/Japan: Its emergence from a dislocation]. Tokyo: Tōkō Museum of Contemporary Art.

Minkenberg, Michael and Inglehart, Robert, 1989, 'Neoconservatism and value change in the USA: Tendencies in the mass public of a postindustrial society', in John Gibbins (ed.), *Contemporary Political Culture*. London: Sage.

Miyajima, Takashi, 1983, *Gendai shakai-ishiki-ron* [Theories on contemporary social consciousness]. Tokyo: Nihon Hyōronsha.

Miyakawa, Hirayuki, 1954–5, 'An outline of the Naito hypothesis and its effects on Japanese studies of China'. *The Far Eastern Quarterly* Vol. 4: 533–57.

Miyoshi, Masao, 1987, 'Ōinaru bunkatsusen saikō: noberu no mondai' [The great divide revisited: The question of novels]. Trans. Hidetoshi Tomiyama. *Gendai Shisō, sōtokushū: Nihon posutomodan rinji zōkan* [A special comprehensive number on contemporary thought: An extra issue on the Japanese postmodern] Vol. 15 No. 15.

Miyoshi, Masao and Harootunian, H.D. (eds), 1988, Special issue on postmodernism and Japan. *South Atlantic Quarterly* Vol. 87 No. 3 (Summer).

——, 1989, *Postmodernism and Japan*. Durham: Duke University Press.

Mogi, Kazuyuki, 1984, 'Kigyō no naka ni ikiru kagaku seishin' [The scientific spirit alive in enterprises]. *Chūō Kōron* June.

Mori, Atsushi, 1993, 'Comments', in Yoshio Sugimoto, *Nihonjin o yameru hōhō* [Deconstructing Japaneseness]. Tokyo: Chikuma Shobō.

Morishima, Michio, 1983, *Why Has Japan 'Succeeded'? Western Technology and the Japanese Ethos*. Cambridge: Cambridge University Press.

Morita, Akira and Ishihara, Shintarō, 1989, *Nō to ieru Nihon* [The Japan that can say 'No']. Tokyo: Kōbunsha.

Morris, Meaghan, 1988, *The Pirate's Fiancée: Feminism, Reading, Postmodernism*. London: Verso.

Morris-Suzuki, Tessa, 1991, 'Concepts of nature and technology in pre-industrial Japan.' *East Asian History* No. 1.

Mouer, Ross, 1987a, 'Kokusaika jidai ni okeru kinbensei' [The work ethic in the era of internationalization]. *Kyoto Rōdō Keizai* No. 90.

——, 1987b, 'Ōsutoraria ni okeru Nihon kenkyū: Sono genjō to tenbō' [Japanese studies in Australia: The present and the future]. *Fukuoka UNESCO* Vol. 22 (Jan.): 36–46.

——, 1989, 'Japanese model of industrial relations: Warnings or opportunities?' *Hitotsubashi Journal of Social Studies* Vol. 21.

Mouer, Ross, and Sugimoto, Yoshio, 1986, *Images of Japanese Society: A Study in the Social Construction of Reality*. London: Kegan Paul International.

——, 1989, 'A multi-dimensional view of stratification: A framework for comparative analysis', in Yoshio Sugimoto and Ross Mouer (eds), *Constructs for Understanding Japan*. London: Kegan Paul International.

——, 1993, 'Democracy: The Japanese problematique'. *Asian Studies Review* Vol. 17 No. 1 (July): 58–64.

Mouer, Ross and Sugimoto, Yoshio (eds), 1990, *The MFP Debate: A Background Reader*. Melbourne: La Trobe University Press.

Murakami, Haruki, 1989, *A Wild Sheep Chase*. Trans. Alfred Birnbaum. Tokyo: Kodansha International.

Murakami, Yasusuke, 1984, '*Ie* society as a pattern of civilization'. *Journal of Japanese Studies* Vol. 10 No. 2 (Summer): 281–367.

——, 1986, 'Technology in transition: Two perspectives on industrial policy', in H. Patrick and L. Meissner (eds), *Japan's High Technology Industries: Lessons and Limitations of Industrial Policy*. Seattle and London: University of Washington Press.

——, 1987, 'Modernization in terms of integration: The case of Japan', in S. Eisenstadt (ed.), *Patterns of Modernity, Volume 2: Beyond the West*. London: Cornell University Press.

——, 1990, 'Two types of civilization, transcendental and hermeneutic.' *Nichibunken Japan Review* No. 1: 1–34.

Murata, Keinosuke; Fujieda, Teru and Tatehata, Akira, 1990, *Miminaru Aato* [Buzzing art]. Osaka: Kokuritsu Kokusai Bijutsukan.

Murray, Oswyn and Price, S. (eds), 1990, *The Greek City: From Homer to Alexander*. Oxford: Clarendon Press.

Murray, Robin, 1988, 'Life after Henry Ford.' *Marxism Today* October.

Nagara, Susumu (ed.), 1991, *Nihon kyōiku nōryoku kentei: Shiken keikō to taisaku* [The Japanese language teaching proficiency test: A strategy for responding to recent trends]. Tokyo: Baberu Shuppan.

Nagoya Shiritsu Daigaku Kyōju Gurūpu (The group of professors from Nagoya City University), 1993, *Yasashii Nihon keizai no hanashi* [An introduction to the Japanese economy]. Tokyo: Yūhikaku.

Naitō, Kanji, 1941, 'Shūkyō to keizai rinri' [Religion and the economic ethic]. *Shakaigaku* Vol. 8: 243–86.

——, 1973, *Basshi sōzoku no kenkyū* [Studies on ultimogeniture]. Tokyo: Kōbundō.

Nakahara, Yūsuke and Yamaguchi, Katsuhiro, 1982, 'Kūchū to chijō, media sōkan no ningenzō' [Up in the air and down on the ground: A grand media sight of people's profiles]. *Bijutsu Techō* January.

Nakahara, Yūsuke *et al.*, 1989, *Japan '89, Europalia '89*. Gent: Museum van Heidendaagse Kunst.

Nakahara, Yūsuke; Yaguchi, Kunio and Sakai, Tadayasu, 1990, 'Kokusaiten no shikumi' [The framework of international exhibitions]. *Bijutsu Techō* July.

Nakajima, Tokuhiro and Ozaki, Shinichirō, 1990, *Aato nau, Kansai no*

80 nendai [Art now: The Kansai region in the 1980s]. Kōbe: Hyōgo Kenritsu Kindai Bijutsukan.

Nakaoka, Tetsurō, 1986, 'Gijutsushi no shiten kara mita Nihon no keiken' [The Japanese experience seen from the perspective of the history of technology], in *Kindai Nihon no gijutsu to gijutsu seisaku* [Technology and technological life in modern Japan]. Tokyo: Kokuren Daigaku.

——, 1990, 'Nihon no kindaika to gijutsu kakushin' [Japan's modernization and technological innovation]. Paper presented to the International Symposium 'Sekai no naka no Nihon' [Japan in the world], International Research Centre for Japanese Studies, Kyoto.

Nakayama, Ichiro, 1975, *Industrialization and Labor-Management Relations in Japan*. Trans. Ross Mouer. Tokyo: The Japan Institute of Labour.

Nakayama, Osamu, 1982, *'Bokashi' no Nihon bunka* [Japanese culture of 'ambiguity']. Tokyo: Arufaa Shuppan.

Nakazawa, Shin'ichi, 1984, 'Kagaku no Taoisuto wa Yōsuko o oyogikiru ka' [Can the scientific Taoist swim across the Yangtze River?]. *Chūō Kōron* June.

Nanjō, Fumio and Weiermair, Peter, 1990, *Japanische Kunst der Achtziger Jahre*. Frankfurt am Main: Edition Stemmle.

Neustupný, J. V., 1965, 'First steps towards the conception of "oriental languages".' *Archiv Orientln* No. 33: 83–92.

——, 1978, *Post-Structural Approaches to Language*. Tokyo: University of Tokyo Press.

——, 1980, 'On paradigms in the study of Japan.' *Social Analysis* Nos 5/6: 20–28.

——, 1982, *Gaikokujin to no komyunikeeshon* [Communicating with foreigners]. Tokyo: Iwanami Shoten.

——, 1984, 'Literacy and minorities: divergent perceptions', in F. Coulmas (ed.), *Linguistic Minorities and Literacy*. Berlin and New York: Mouton Publishers.

——, 1987, *Communicating with the Japanese*. Tokyo: The Japan Times.

——, 1989a, 'The role of typologies in understanding Japanese culture and society: from linguistics to social science', in Y. Sugimoto and R. Mouer (eds), *Constructs for Understanding Japan*. London: Kegan Paul International.

——, 1989b, 'Nihon kenkyū no paradaimu – sono tayōsei o rikai suru tame ni' [Paradigms in Japanese studies – towards the understanding of their diversity]. *Sekai no naka no Nihon I* [Japan in the world], International Research Centre for Japanese Studies (ed.). Kyoto: International Research Centre for Japanese Studies.

——, 1990, 'The follow-up interview'. *JSAA Newsletter* Vol. 10 No. 2.

——, 1991, *On Romanizing Japanese*. Melbourne: Japanese Studies Centre.

NHK Yoron Chōsabu [Bureau of public opinion survey of NHK] (ed.), 1985, *Gendai Nihonjin no ishiki kōzō* [Consciousness structure of contemporary Japanese]. 2nd edition. Tokyo: Nihon Hōsō Shuppan Kyōkai.

Nicholson, Linda J. (ed.), 1990, *Feminism/Postmodernism*. New York: Routledge.

Nohara, H. and Fujita, E., 1989, *Jidōsha sangyō to rōdōsha* [Workers and the car industry]. Tokyo: Hōritsu Bunkasha.

Nolte, Sharon H., 1987, *Liberalism in Modern Japan: Ishibashi Tanzan and His Teachers 1905–1960*. Berkeley: University of California Press.

Oe, Kenzaburo, 1989, 'Japan's dual identity: A writer's dilemma', in M. Miyoshi and H. D. Harootunian (eds), *Postmodernism in Japan*. Durham: Duke University Press.

Ogura, Masashi (ed.), 1990, *Konnichi no sakka ten, 1964–1989* [Exhibition of contemporary artists, 1964–1989]. Yokohama: Yokohama Shimin Gyararii.

Ōhinata, Masami, 1988, *Bosei no kenkyū* [A study of maternity]. Tokyo: Kawashima Shoten.

Okada, Takahiko and Namba, Hideo, 1990, *Japanese Art Today*. Tokyo: Sezon Museum of Art.

Okimoto, D.I., 1989, *Between MITI and the Market: Japanese Industrial Policy for High Technology*. Stanford: Stanford University Press.

Ōmura, Eishō *et al.*, 1990, *Posto modan no Shinran* [The postmodern and Shinran]. Tokyo: Dōhōsha.

Ong, Aihwa, 1987, *Spirits of Resistance and Capitalist Discipline: Factory Women in Malaysia*. Albany: State University of New York.

——, 1991, 'The gender and labour politics of postmodernity'. *Annual Review of Anthropology* Vol. 20.

Ooka, M., 1992, 'Antidote for anomie: Poetry for the computer age.' *The Japan Foundation Newsletter* Vol. 20 No. 1.

Ooms, Herman, 1985, *Tokugawa Ideology: 1570–1680*. Princeton: Princeton University Press.

Ormonde, Tom, 1990, 'Large, lucky and lazy.' *The Age*. Saturday Extra 18 August.

Oyama, Shigeo, 1989, 'Semiconductors and the Japanese mind.' *Japan Quarterly* Vol. 36 No. 1.

Parmar, P., 1982, 'Gender, race and class: Asian women in resistance', in Centre for Contemporary Cultural Studies (eds), *The Empire Strikes Back*. London: Hutchinson.

Parsons, Talcott, 1951, *The Social System*. New York: The Free Press.

Pathak, Zakia and Rajan, Rajweswari Sunder, 1992, 'Shahbano', in Judith Butler and Joan W. Scott (eds), *Feminists Theorize the Political*. London: Routledge.

Pempel, T.J. and Tsunekawa, Keiichi, 1979, 'Corporatism without labor?

The Japanese anomaly', in G. Lehmbruch and P. Schmitter (eds), *Trends Towards Corporatist Intermediation*. Beverley Hills: Sage Publications.

Pharr, Susan J. (chief consultant), 1985, *Japan*, a volume in the series 'Library of Nations'. Amsterdam: Time-Life Books.

Phelan, Shane, 1991, 'Specificity: Beyond equality and difference.' *Differences: A Journal of Feminist Cultural Studies* Vol. 3 No. 1.

Piore, Michael and Charles Sabel, 1984, *The Second Industrial Divide*. New York: Basic Books.

Pollack, David, 1989, 'Modernism minceur, or is Japan postmodern?' *Monumenta Nipponica* Vol. 44 No. 1 (Spring).

Prigogine, I. and Stengers, I., 1984, *Order Out of Chaos: Man's New Dialogue with Nature*. London: Fontana.

Pringle, Rosemary, 1988, *Secretaries Talk: Sexuality, Power and Work*. Sydney: Allen and Unwin.

Reich, Robert B., 1992, *The Work of Nations: Preparing Ourselves for 21st Century Capitalism*. New York: Vintage Books.

Roberts, Glenda, 1994, *Staying on the Line: Blue Collar Women in Contemporary Japan*. Honolulu: University of Hawaii Press.

Robertson, Roland, 1992, *Globalization: Social Theory and Global Culture*. London: Sage.

Rōdōshō Fujin Fukushika (ed.), 1992, *Wakari yasui ikuji kyūgyō hō* [An introduction to maternity leave law]. Tokyo: Yūhikaku.

——, 1994, *Wakari yasui paato taimu Rōdō hō* [An introductio, to part-time labor law]. Tokyo: Yūhikaku.

Röpke, Jochen, 1989, 'Von Nachzügler zum Pioneer. Industriepolitische Anmerkungen zum Erwerb innovativer Fähigkeit in Prozeß der nachholenden Entwicklung', in M. Menzel (ed.), *Im Schattendes Siegers, Band 3, Ökonomie und Politik*. Frankfurt: Suhrkamp.

Rose, Margaret, 1991, *The Post-modern and the Post-industrial: A Critical Analysis*. Cambridge: Cambridge University Press.

Rosenberger, Nancy R. (ed.), 1992, *Japanese Sense of Self*. Cambridge: Cambridge University Press.

Ryan, Michael, 1987, 'Posuto modan no seijigaku' [Postmodern politics], trans. Kazuko Takemura. *Gendai Shisō*, 'Sōtokushū: Nihon no posuto-modan, Rinji zōkan' [Special issue on Japanese Postmodernism]. Vol. 15 No. 15.

Sacks, Karen, 1989, 'Towards a unified theory of class, race and gender.' *American Ethnologist* Vol. 16 No. 3.

Sakai, Naoki, 1988, 'Modernity and its critique: The problem of universalism and particularism,' *The South Atlantic Quarterly* Vol. 87 No. 3.

Sakaiya, Taichi, 1991, *Nihon to wa nanika* [What is Japan?]. Tokyo: Kōdansha.

———, 1993, *What Is Japan?* Tokyo: Kodansha International.

Sakakibara, Eisuke, 1993, *Bunmei toshite no Nihon-gata shihonshugi: 'Tomi' to 'kenryoku' no kōzu* [Japanese capitalism as a civilization: The structure of wealth and power in contemporary Japan]. Tokyo: Tōyō Keizai Shinpōsha.

Sanwa Sōgō Kenkyūjo, 1992, *1993–nen Nihon wa kō naru* [What Japan will be in 1993]. Tokyo: Kōdansha.

Sato, Ikuya, 1991, *Kamikaze Biker: Parody and Anomie in Affluent Japan*. Chicago: University of Chicago Press.

Satō, Machiko, 1993, *Shin kaigai teijū jidai* [A new age of Japanese settlement overseas]. Tokyo: Shinchōsha.

Satō, Yoshiyuki, 1991, 'Kyōsei shakai no ronri to soshiki' [Logic and organisation in cooperative society]. *Shoshiki Kagaku* Vol. 24 No. 4.

Schodt, Frederik L., 1988, *Inside the Robot Kingdom: Japan, Mechatronics and the Coming Robotopia*. Tokyo and New York: Kodanasha International.

Schwartz, B.I., 1964, *In Search of Wealth and Power: Yen Fu and the West*. Cambridge Mass.: Harvard University Press.

Scott, Joan, 1988a, 'Deconstructing equality versus difference; Or, the uses of post-structuralist theory for feminism.' *Feminist Studies* Vol. 14 No. 1 (Spring).

———, 1988b, *Gender and the Politics of History*. New York: Columbia University Press.

Seto, Bernadette, 1991, 'No longer good wives and wise mothers.' Unpublished honours thesis, Griffith University, Brisbane.

Sharpe, Sue, 1984, *Double Identity: The Lives of Working Mothers*. Ringwood: Penguin Books.

Shimada, Haruo, 1984, *Furii ranchi wa mō kuenai* [No more free lunches]. Tokyo: Nihon Hyōronsha.

Shimizu, Hiroshi, 1987, 'Seimei no jiritsusei to atarashii gijutsu' [The autonomy of life and new technology], in Waturu Mori *et al.* (eds), *Baiotekunorojii to shakai* [Biotechnology and society]. Tokyo: Tokyo Daigaku Shuppankai.

Shufu to Seikatsusha, 1992, *Todōfuken-betsu kankon sōsai daijiten* [Dictionary of prefectural variations in the ceremonies of coming of age, marriage, funerals and ancestral worship]. Tokyo: Shufu to Seikatsusha.

Silverman, Sydel, 1979, 'On the uses of history in anthropology.' *American Ethnologist* Vol. 6: 413–36.

Singer, Peter, 1993, *How Are We to Live? Ethics in an Age of Self-Interest*. Melbourne: The Text Publishing Company.

Smith, Robert J., 1983, *Japanese Society: Tradition, Self and the Social Order*. Cambridge: Cambridge University Press.

Smuts, J.C., 1936, *Holism and Evolution* (3rd edition). London: Macmillan.

Sokoloff, Natalie, 1980, *Between Money and Love: The Dialectics of Women's Home and Market Work*. New York: Praeger Publishers.

Sourgnes, Michel and Homma, Masayoshi, 1989, *Japanese Ways, Western Means, Art of the 1980s in Japan*. Brisbane: Queensland Art Gallery.

Spector, Dave, 1991, 'An interview with Miyazawa Kiichi.' *Shūkan Bunshun* 20 October.

Spivak, Gayatri Chakravorty, 1988, *In Other Worlds: Essays in Cultural Politics*. New York: Routledge.

Stauth, Georg and Turner, Bryan S., 1988, 'Nostalgia, postmodernism and the critique of mass culture.' *Theory, Culture and Society* Vol. 5.

Steenstrup, Carl, 1976, 'Did political rationalism develop along parallel lines in premodern Japan and in the premodern west? Prolegomena to a comparative study.' *Journal of Intercultural Studies* No. 3.

Steven, Rob, 1983, *Classes in Contemporary Japan*. Cambridge: Cambridge University Press.

——, 1988, 'The high yen crisis in Japan.' *Capital and Class* No. 34.

——, 1990, *Japan's New Imperialism*. London: Macmillan.

Stiehm, Judith Hicks (ed.), 1983, *Women and Men's Wars*. New York: Pergamon Press.

Stockwin, J. A. A., 1982, *Japan: Divided Politics in a Growth Economy*. London: Weidenfeld and Nicholson.

Sugawara, Mariko, 1987a, *Shin kazoku no jidai* [The new family age]. Tokyo: Chūō Kōronsha.

——, 1987b, *Paasoaru aidentitii no susume* [An invitation to personal identity formation]. Osaka: Sōgensha.

Sugeno, Kazuo, 1992, *Japanese Labor Law*. Trans. Leo Kanowitz. Seattle and London: University of Washington Press.

Sugii, Shizuko, 1990, *Sexual harassment shohōsen* [Prescriptions for sexual harassment]. Tokyo: Adoa Shuppan.

Sugimoto, Yoshio, 1986, 'The manipulative bases of "consensus" in Japan', in Gavan McCormack and Yoshio Sugimoto (eds), *Democracy in Contemporary Japan*. Sydney: Hale and Iremonger.

——, 1988, ' "Keizai Nippon" to "jishuku Nippon" ' [The 'economic Japan' and the 'self-controlling Japan'], *Sekai* December: 37–40. Reprinted in Shunsuke Tsurumi and Rokuhei Nakagawa (eds), *Tennō hyakuwa* [One hundred stories on Hirohito], Vol. 2. Tokyo: Chikuma Shobō, 1989.

——, 1990, 'A postmodern Japan?' *Arena* No. 91: 56–9.

——, Forthcoming, *An Introduction to Contemporary Japan: A Multicultural Perspective*. Cambridge: Cambridge University Press.

Sugimoto, Yoshio and Mouer, Ross, 1982, *Nihonjin wa 'Nihonteki' ka: Tokushuron o koete tagenteki bunseki e* [How 'Japanese' are the

Japanese? Going beyond theories emphasising Japan's uniqueness to a multi-dimensional analysis]. Tokyo: Tōyō Keizai Shinpōsha.

——, 1989, 'Cross-currents in the study of Japanese society', in Yoshio Sugimoto and Ross Mouer (eds), *Constructs for Understanding Japan*. London: Kegan Paul International.

Suzuki, Takao, 1990, *Nihongo to gaikokugo* [Japanese and foreign languages]. Tokyo: Iwanami Shoten.

Suzuki, Yūko, 1989, *Joseishi o hiraku 1: Haha to onna* [Towards women's history 1: Mother and Woman]. Tokyo: Miraisha.

Tahara, Soichiro, 1986, 'Pioneers of the new bioscience.' *Japan Echo* Vol. 3 No. 3.

Takagi, Ikuo, 1988, 'Community union sengen' in Community Union Kenkyū Kai (eds), *Community union sengen* [Community union declaration]. Tokyo: Daiichi Shorin.

Takeoka, Yaeko, 1988, '2000 men in muketa rōdō undō to Pātō Taimā [The labour movement and part-timers towards 2000]. *Rōdō Sentā Nuusu* No. 65 (May).

Takeuchi, Yō, 1991, *Risshi, kugaku, shusse* [Achievement orientation, academic study under adversity, and success in life]. Tokyo: Kōdansha.

Tani, Arata, Hayami, Shō and Mangi, Yasuhiro, 1983, 'Kakusansuru ko no amarugamu ni mukete' [Towards amalgamation of the diversifying self]. *Bijutsu Techō* March.

Tatsuno, Sheridan M., 1990, *Created in Japan: From Imitators to First Class Innovators*. New York: Ballinger Publishing Company.

Taylor, Charles, 1990, 'Modes of a civil society.' *Public Culture* Vol. 3 No. 1: 95–118.

Toby, Ronald Paul, 1977, 'The early Tokugawa bakufu and seventeenth century Japanese relations with East Asia.' Doctoral dissertation, Columbia University.

Toffler, Alvin, 1980, *The Third Wave*. New York: Morrow.

Tokugawa, Munemasa, 1990, 'Nihongo no chiikisa to sono shōchō' [Regional variation in Japanese language and its representations], in T. Umesao and R. Ogawa (eds), *Kotoba no hikaku bunmeigaku* [Comparative civilisational analysis of language]. Tokyo: Iwanami Shoten.

Tominaga, Ken'ichi, 1989, 'Hoshuka to posuto-modan no aida' [Between conservatisation and the postmodern]. *Sekai* March.

——, 1990, *Nihon no kindaika to shakai hendō* [Modernisation in Japan and social change]. Tokyo: Kōdansha.

Trinh, T. Minh-ha, 1990, *Woman, Native, Other: Writing Postcoloniality and Gender*. Bloomington: Indiana University Press.

Tsunoda, Yukiko, 1991, *Sei no hōritsugaku* [Legal studies of gender]. Tokyo: Yūhikaku.

——, 1993, 'Sexual harassment in Japan: Recent legal decisions.' *US-Japan Women's Journal* (English supplement) No. 5: 52–69.

Turnbull, Colin M., 1966, *Tradition and Change in African Tribal Life*. New York: The World Publishing Company.

Ueno, Chizuko, 1991, 'Josei-shi to kindai' [History of women and modernity], in T. Yoshida (ed.), *Gendai no Shikumi* [Contemporary social structure]. Tokyo: Shin'yōsha.

Umehara, Takeshi, 1976, *Nihon Bunka ron* [On Japanese culture]. Tokyo: Kōdansha.

Umehara, Takeshi (ed.), 1990, *Nihon to wa nan-nanoka* [What is Japan?]. Tokyo: Kōdansha.

Umesao, Tadao, 1982, 'Tsuma muyō-ron' [Why wives are unnecessary], in Chizuko Ueno (ed.), *Shufu ronsō o yomu* (Readings on the domestic labor debate). Tokyo: Keisō Shobō. Originally published in the July 1959 issue of *Fujin Kōron* (191–206).

——, 1986, *Nihon to wa nani-ka* [What is Japan?]. Tokyo: Nippon Hōsō Shuppan Kyōkai.

Usami, Keiji, 1985, 'Keitaigakuteki kaiga no yokan' [Anticipating morphological art], in Keiji Usami, *Kigō kara keitai e* [From semiotics to morphology]. Tokyo: Chikuma Shobō.

Valéry, Nicholas, 1990, 'Japanese companies go multinational'. *The World in 1991*. London: The Economist Publications.

Veblen, Thorstein, 1934, 'The opportunity of Japan', in L. Adzrooni (ed.), *Essays in Our Changing Order*. New York: The Viking Press.

Vogel, Ezra F., 1979, *Japan as Number One*. Cambridge: Harvard University Press.

——, 1979, 'Yōkon wasai no jidai' [The age of *yōkon wasai*]. *Chūō Kōron* September: 136–45.

Von Laue, Theodore, 1987, *The World Revolution of Westernization*. New York: Oxford University Press.

Wakita, Haruko (ed.), 1985, *Bosei o tou: Rekishiteki henkō* [Questioning motherhood: Historical transformations]. Vol. 2. Kyōto: Jinbun Shoin.

Wallerstein, Immanuel, 1974–89, *The Modern World-System*. 3 Vol. New York: Academic Press.

——, 1979, *The Capitalist World-Economy: Essays*. Cambridge: Cambridge University Press.

——, 1984, *The Politics of the World-Economy: Essays*. Cambridge: Cambridge University Press.

——, 1991, *Geopolitics and Geoculture: Essays on the Changing World-System*. Cambridge: Cambridge University Press.

Watanabe, Masao, 1976, *Nihonjin to kindai kagaku* [The Japanese and modern science]. Tokyo: Iwanami Shoten.

Watanabe, Naomi, 1991, 'Hyōshō e no amae o haisu' [Rejecting the dependence upon representations]. Discussion with Tokio Iguchi. *Tosho Shinbun* No. 2064 (August 3).

Watanabe, Shōichi, 1989, *Nihonshi kara mita Nihonjin, kodai-hen: Nihon-*

rashisano gensen [The Japanese in Japanese history, the ancient period: The origins of 'Japaneseness']. Tokyo: Shōdensha.

Waters, Malcolm (forthcoming), *Globalization*. London: Routledge.

Watts, Alan, 1962, *The Way of Zen*. London: Penguin Books.

Waugh, Patricia, 1989, *Feminine Fictions: Revisiting the Postmodern*. New York: Routledge.

Weber, Max, 1968, *The Protestant Ethic and the Spirit of Capitalism*. London: Unwin University Books.

Wigmore, John, 1967–86, *Law and Justice in Tokugawa Japan*. Tokyo: University of Tokyo Press.

Womack, James P. *et al.*, 1990, *The Machine That Changed The World*. New York: Rawson Associates.

Woolf, Janet, 1981, *The Social Production of Art*. London: Macmillan.

Woronoff, Jon, 1980, *Japan: The Coming Social Crisis*. Tokyo: Lotus Press.

Yamada, Ryoichi and Tuchiya, Fumiaki, 1985, *An Easy Guide to the New Nationality Law*. Tokyo: The Japan Times.

Yamaguchi, Katsuhiro and Murakami, Yōichirō, 1981, 'Fuirutaa Eiji no bunmyaku' [A context for the 'filter age']. *Bijutsu Techō* May.

Yanagida, Kunio, 1949, 'Tamashil no yukue' [The abode of the departed soul]. *Yanagida Kunio Shū* Vol. 15. Tokyo: Chikuma Shobō.

Yanai, Kenji and Numata, Jirō (eds), 1976, *Kaigai kōshō shi no shiten* [Perspectives on the history of overseas relations] Vol. 2. Tokyo: Nihon Shoseki.

Yoshimoto, Takaaki, 1984, *Masu Imeejiron* [On mass images]. Tokyo: Fukutake Shoten.

Yoshino, Kosaku, 1992, *Cultural Nationalism in Contemporary Japan*. London: Routledge.

Yoshioka, Hitoshi, 1986, *Kagaku shakai no kōzō: Haisaiensu hihan* [Structure of scientific society: A critique of high science]. Tokyo: Libra.

Yukawa, Hideki, 1967, 'Modern trend of western civilization and cultural particularities of Japan', in C. Moore (ed.), *The Japanese Mind: Essentials of Japanese Philosophy and Culture*. Honolulu: University of Hawaii Press.

——, 1973, *Creativity and Intuition*. Tokyo: Kōdansha International.

Zukav, Gary, 1979, *The Dancing Wu Li Masters: An Overview of the New Physics*. New York: William and Morrow.

Index

Index

Ishiko, Junzō 175n
Islamic fundamentalism 13–14
Isozaki, Arata 173n, 175n
Itō, Shuntarō 118, 130n
Iversen, Margaret 173n
Iwamoto-Sakurai, Tokiko 85

Jacob, Mary Ann 173n, 174n
James, Paul 269n
Jameson, Frederic 146, 151n, 173n, 179
Japan Echo 264
Japan Foundation 165, 261
Japanese Socialist Party (JSP) 222
Japanese studies 237–68
Japanism 224, 225
Jernudd, B. 192n
Johnson, Chalmers 16, 30n, 32–3, 64n, 233
Journal of Japanese Studies 263–4
Junkerman, John 89
just-in-case systems 32, 33
just-in-time system 32, 33, 82–7, 89

Kadowaki, Atsushi 203
Kagaku Gijutsu-chō 130n
Kaibara, Ekken 254
Kaitō, Kon 158
Kajita, Takamichi 212n, 223–4
Kamata, Satoshi 93n
Kamiyama, Akira 158
Kanatani, Chieko 99
kanban system *see* just-in-time
Kaneko, Mitsuharu 186
Kanō, Mikiyo 112n
Karabel, J. 207
Karatani, Kōjin 31n, 140, 148, 173n, 175n
Kasahara, Emiko 158
Kashihara, Etsutomu 157
Kassalow, Everett M. 269n
Katase, K. 203
Katayama, Masahito 156
Katō, Ichirō 121–2
Katō, Shūichi 27, 31n
Katō, Tetsurō 6, 64n, 92n, 93n, 94n
Katsura, Yūki 158
Kawabata, Yasunari 254
Kawamata, Tadashi 157

Kawamoto, Saburō 145
Kawamura, Katsuhiko 158
Kawamura, Minato 152n
Kawanishi, Hirosuke 64n
Kawashima, Keijū 158
Keane, John 235n
Keizai Kikakuchō 93n
Kenmochi, Kazuo 157
Kenney, Martin 65, 66–71, 73–5, 77–85, 88–9
Kenrick, Douglas Moore 11n
Kentucky Fried Chicken 64n
Keynesianism 87, 91–2
Kishida, Toshiko 192n
Kitaya, Yukio 124, 132n
Kitayama, Yoshio 157
Kiyomizu, Kyūbei 156
Kobayashi, Kōichi 152n
Kobayashi, Yasuo 173n
Kodama, Fumio 132n
Koestler, Arthur 120
Kōmoto, Shinji 173n
Kon, Michiko 158
Kondo, Dorinne K. 108, 268n, 269n
Konishiki 243
Koo, Hagen 132n
Koplos, Janet 173n
Korea: economy 18; unification prospect 9
Koreans in Japan 187, 243
Kosaka, Kenji 2–3, 211n, 212n
Koshimizu, Susumu 156
Kōuchi 112
Koyama, H. 212n
Krauss, Ellis S. 221
Kristeva, Julia 235n
Kruger, B. 173n
Kuba, Yoshiko 110n
Kuhn, Thomas 127–8
Kumaoka, Shun'ichi 119
Kunihiro, Masao 268
Kuniyasu, Takamasa 157
Kurabayashi, Yasushi 170, 174n
Kusama, Yayoi 158
Kusayanagi, Daizō 239
Kyōgoku, Jun'ichi 130n

labour, division of 35, 98–9

Index

Index